IMAGES of America

Warwick Township Lancaster County

On the Cover: On July 5, 1892, this large group of people posed to have their picture taken. With its beautiful creek and country pastures, Millway made a wonderful setting for this gathering on a warm summer day. Pitchers that might have held lemonade can be seen. Several men are holding rifles, giving a sense that small game hunting or target practice took place that day. (Courtesy of the Robert "Sketch" Mearig collection.)

IMAGES
of America

WARWICK TOWNSHIP
LANCASTER COUNTY

Cory Van Brookhoven

ARCADIA
PUBLISHING

ISBN 978-0-7385-7429-5

Published by Arcadia Publishing
Charleston, South Carolina

Printed in the United States of America

Library of Congress Control Number: 2010935097

For all general information, please contact Arcadia Publishing:
Telephone 843-853-2070
Fax 843-853-0044
E-mail sales@arcadiapublishing.com
For customer service and orders:
Toll-Free 1-888-313-2665

Visit us on the Internet at www.arcadiapublishing.com

This book is dedicated to my late grandfather Robert "Sketch" Mearig, who was a lifetime collector of photographs, postcards, and antiques relating to Lititz and Warwick Township. A large number of items in this volume came directly from his collection, and it was through him that I was bitten with the history bug at an early age.

Contents

ACKNOWLEDGMENTS

It is my feeling that books of this type are not written by one person alone. Rather, it is more of a collaborative effort between many historians, genealogists, and members of the community who share in the author's love and passion for the local area. During this book's production, I was very blessed to have a gifted and knowledgeable group of people who assisted me in gathering pictures, obtaining facts and dates, and helping me to unearth many lost nuggets of information. Truly, they were both inspirational and helpful. Although space restraints prevent me from thanking every person who submitted a picture or story for this volume, please know your generosity was very much appreciated.

Tom Hackman served as my expert on Brunnerville. His knowledge and true passion for that village really shone through. Clair Amand and Polly Garner were my authorities on Kissel Hill, and I really cherish every moment I got to spend with them. Rick Reitz and John David Wissler were my Millway experts. Their generosity in sharing their knowledge of Millway with me was never failing. Sharyn Deater served as my guide regarding all things Rothsville, and she is a very loving and caring soul who was always there to offer encouragement and new information. Warren Becker shared some facts and photographs on the Becker property and distillery, and I look forward to visiting with him on his porch again soon. Donna Heisey, John Kline, and the Wenger family at Forgotten Seasons Bed and Breakfast were also very helpful, supplying various pictures and information for this project. Ron Reedy is a true expert on all things related to Lititz, railroads, and trolleys. His willingness in providing help will not be forgotten. Finally, I wanted to especially recognize Martee Xakellis, who served as my extra set of eyes during this venture. Her expertise in fact-checking dates, locations, and background information time and time again to ensure that this finished publication was the best and most accurate it can be was second to none. She has really gone the extra mile, and I could not have done it without her.

INTRODUCTION

Located within Pennsylvania's gorgeous farmland is Warwick Township, one of the first townships laid out during the formation of Lancaster County. The original boundaries included the modern townships of Warwick, Elizabeth, Clay, Penn, and the borough of Lititz. Richard Carter, who arrived from Warwickshire, England, was the area's first inhabitant. He settled close to the mouth of the Conestoga River in 1716 and renamed the place in honor of his homeland. Christian Bomberger was another early settler, arriving in 1722. By 1734, Bomberger was granted a patent of about 548 acres of land. As time passed, small villages formed, each one having their own unique characteristics and charm.

An area of the township was originally settled in the early 1820s and eventually called White Hall. However, when a post office was created in that town in 1861, the name of Brunnerville was adopted to honor the Brunner family of that hamlet. The town had various businesses throughout the years, including a wagon and iron foundry, blacksmith shops, furniture manufacturers, dairies, and several general stores. Other businesses and schools grew within Brunnerville, and the township certainly benefitted from its hardworking residents, many of whom were granted copyright patents for their various inventions.

In 1733, George Eby took up land in what is now Millway, where he constructed a gristmill. Soon this area grew and years later served as an important oil distribution center and railroad town. It had many thriving farms and general businesses, and the Cocalico Creek flowed through part of the town. The creek served as a beautiful setting where religious camp meetings were held. Many Christians arrived to Millway every year from both near and far to listen to the preaching.

Rothsville, originally known as Rabbit Hill, got its start in 1790, when Phillip Roth decided to establish a hotel at the busy intersection of two roads where many teamsters passed. Although this particular crossroads was known early on for often being muddy, the tavern proved to be a very successful venture. Originally known as Roth's Tavern, the name has changed over the years, but the White Swan Hotel still stands today at the same location. It is the oldest still-functioning tavern in the township. Another popular meetinghouse, the Keystone Hotel, was also a place for local residents to get a room for the night, join in on a celebration, or catch up on local gossip. Rothsville also flourished as a cigar-manufacturing town, with many residents (including women and children) working in the industry. The Reading and Columbia Rail Road system passed through, picking up and delivering goods for transport throughout all of Lancaster County.

Lexington was first known as Dundee as early as 1805. It is a quaint area within the township. Over the years, it housed many cigar factories, stores, a hotel, a blacksmith shop, an undertaker, various carpenters, an undergarment factory, a candy-making operation, three generations of butchers, two schools, and many other businesses and places of worship. Lexington is also known as one of the highest points of altitude in the county. The Lexington Rod and Gun Club also holds meetings here and serves as an organization that promotes safe hunting and conservation within the neighborhood.

Millport was laid out into lots in 1813 by Christian Kauffman. In the beginning, there was a milling operation, which for several years provided products to the residents of the township. Today the area is a very peaceful and picturesque village, containing more than a few homes. The Lititz Run passes through this area, with wildlife often spotted along the stream.

In a deed dated October 5, 1734, Thomas and Richard Penn transferred 165 acres of land to Hans George Kiesel for the sum of 25 pounds, 11 shillings, and 5 pence. Early on, this area was known as "Kissel-berg" (the hill belonging to Kissel), eventually changing its name to New Haven. When a post office was established, the name was permanently changed to what it is known as today—Kissel Hill. It was here in 1823 that a cornerstone for a church was laid, and the area served as a needed place of worship. Additionally, Kissel Hill was a convenient trolley stop for passengers traveling between Lancaster and Lititz. The area also boasted a hotel, blacksmith shop, numerous early schools, and a family roadside produce stand that grew into a multimillion-dollar supermarket entity. Other thriving businesses throughout the years helped Kissel Hill fast become a popular place to live and to do business in.

Pine Hill is a small hamlet located east of Brunnerville. At one time it had a hotel, a one-room schoolhouse called the Lookout School, and a distillery. Although containing only a small number of houses, this unique and beautiful area is a perfect setting and safe place to raise a family or enjoy the countryside.

Rome is situated just east of Lititz in the township and had its humble beginnings in the 1730s, when a hotel was established there. For numerous years it operated as a stopping place for travelers who were passing through the area. Rome also contained the earliest school in the area, which was erected in 1746 and was known as the Warwick Gemeinhaus and School, also part of the Moravian settlement in Lititz. This town also contained a distillery, which was founded in 1815 by Peter Fielis. The distillery proved to be very successful and continued through the years having many different owners and operators until Prohibition ended its whiskey production. An early compass mill was also situated in Rome. It still stands to this day.

Thumbtown is a very small grouping of houses located between Brunnerville and Pine Hill, and Seminole is a quaint area just past Rothsville. Although both are part of Warwick Township, they will not be covered in this publication.

Throughout its long existence, the rich heritage of Warwick Township has certainly proven to be so unique that it holds an important place in the history of Lancaster County. From its beautiful countryside settings to its modern-day growth, the township is a very special place not only to longtime residents and newcomers, but also to out-of-town visitors.

One

Around the Neighborhood

Well-maintained and prosperous farms with crops of grain, hay, and tobacco are located around Warwick Township. Additionally, produce is grown that is then sold from roadside stands. Fresh-picked corn, tomatoes, beans, lettuce, cabbage, broccoli, cauliflower, squash, cucumbers, and delicious apples are just some of the wide variety of fruits and vegetables that can be purchased. These vegetables are perfect for a summertime meal or are prepared in mass quantities for canning. Black and white cows can be seen in pastures on dairy farms where the milk is collected in large tankers and then sold as pasteurized milk, butter, or cheese. There are chicken farms where the end results are eggs by the dozen or chicken perfect for the grill. Many of these farms have been in the same families for generations. Around this large neighborhood are parks and playgrounds where families can enjoy the outdoors or play a quick game of baseball. Numerous hiking and bicycle trails and various other areas off the beaten path are located here. Volunteer fire departments keep residents safe in this township, and it is a place where citizens—both new and old—enjoy a simpler and peaceful quality of life. The photographs in the following chapter paint a scene of everyday life and certainly convey the age-old postcard message "Wish You Were Here."

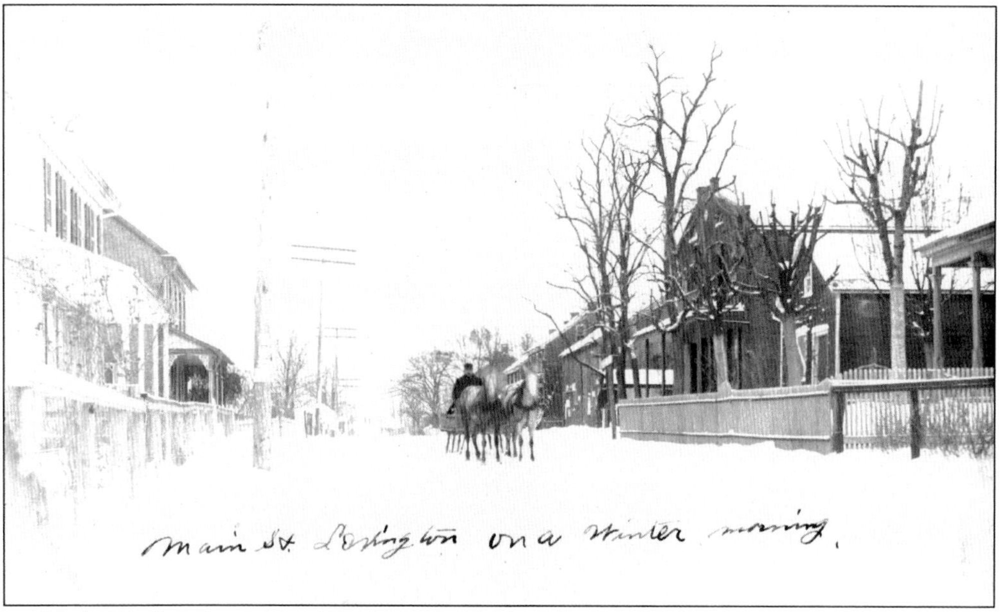

In the days before the automobile, families relied on horse-drawn sleighs, like the one pictured here, as a means to navigate the harsh winters. In this early scene of Lexington looking west, the home of the Markleys, who ran a very popular meat market from 1869 to 1986, can be seen at the left of the picture. To the right, the old Lexington Store can be seen. (Courtesy of the Robert "Sketch" Mearig collection.)

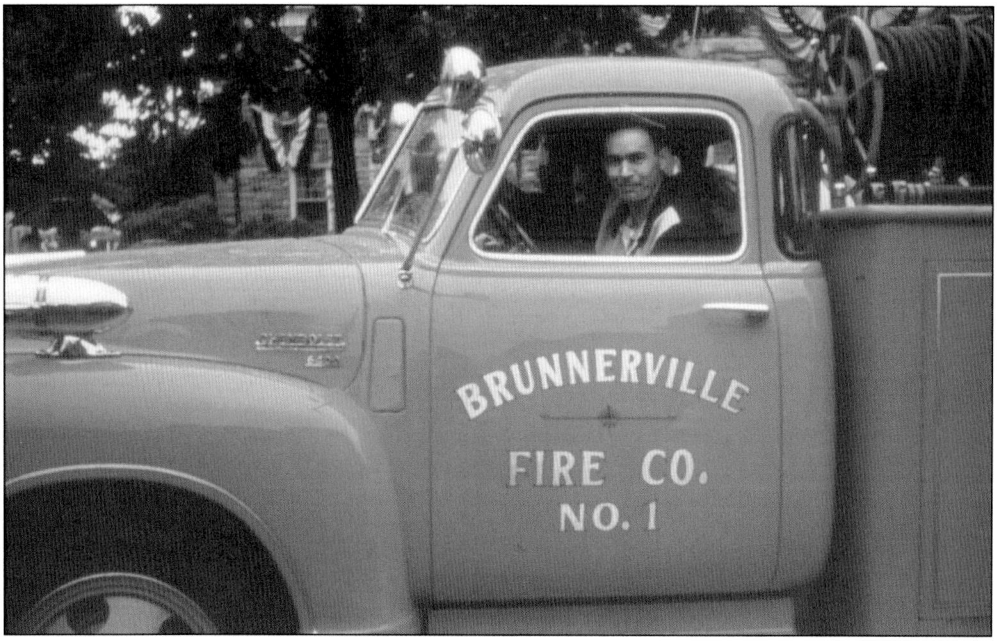

Wayne Grube served on the Brunnerville Fire Company for many years. This picture was taken in downtown Lititz in 1957 at their fireman's parade. Fire trucks from many neighboring towns came to the parade to show off their latest firefighting equipment and also to show the public the antique firefighting equipment they had collected. (Courtesy of the Robert "Sketch" Mearig collection.)

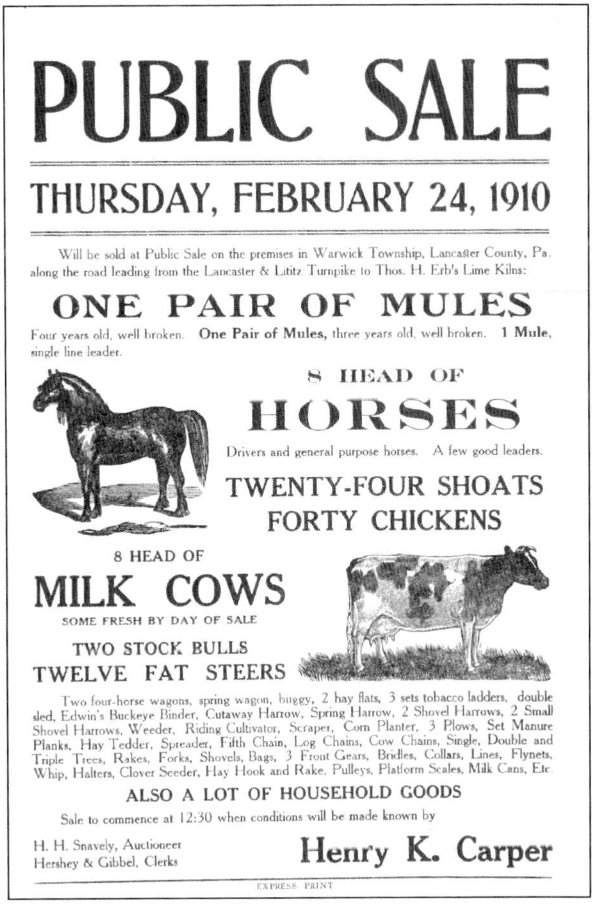

PUBLIC SALE

THURSDAY, FEBRUARY 24, 1910

Will be sold at Public Sale on the premises in Warwick Township, Lancaster County, Pa. along the road leading from the Lancaster & Lititz Turnpike to Thos. H. Erb's Lime Kilns:

ONE PAIR OF MULES

Four years old, well broken. **One Pair of Mules,** three years old, well broken. **1 Mule,** single line leader.

8 HEAD OF

HORSES

Drivers and general purpose horses. A few good leaders.

TWENTY-FOUR SHOATS

FORTY CHICKENS

8 HEAD OF

MILK COWS

SOME FRESH BY DAY OF SALE

TWO STOCK BULLS

TWELVE FAT STEERS

Two four-horse wagons, spring wagon, buggy, 2 hay flats, 3 sets tobacco ladders, double sled, Edwin's Buckeye Binder, Cutaway Harrow, Spring Harrow, 2 Shovel Harrows, 2 Small Shovel Harrows, Weeder, Riding Cultivator, Scraper, Corn Planter, 3 Plows, Set Manure Planks, Hay Tedder, Spreader, Fifth Chain, Log Chains, Cow Chains, Single, Double and Triple Trees, Rakes, Forks, Shovels, Bags, 3 Front Gears, Bridles, Collars, Lines, Flynets, Whip, Halters, Clover Seeder, Hay Hook and Rake, Pulleys, Platform Scales, Milk Cans, Etc.

ALSO A LOT OF HOUSEHOLD GOODS

Sale to commence at 12:30 when conditions will be made known by

H. H. Snavely, Auctioneer
Hershey & Gibbel, Clerks

Henry K. Carper

EXPRESS PRINT

Various public sales around the township are still held to this day. This auction advertised in this sale bill, dated Thursday, February 24, 1910, took place near the location of Thomas Erb's lime kiln on the road leading from Lititz to Petersburg. Some of the goods auctioned off that day were eight horses, one pair of mules, a corn planter, and 40 chickens. H. H. Snavely from Lititz called the sale that day. (Courtesy of the author's collection.)

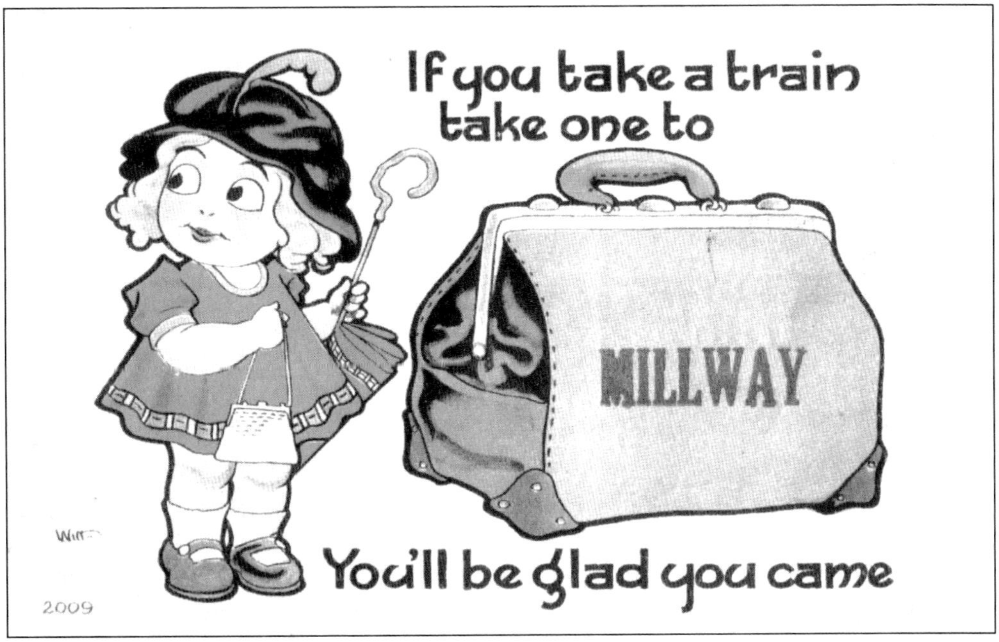

This antique postcard from Millway would certainly catch anyone's attention. Postcards of this nature were mass-produced, and the person or corner store selling the postcard would stamp it with the name of the town in which the business was located. A decoration of glitter and/or paint was used to help display the town's name in an eye-catching manner. (Courtesy of the Robert "Sketch" Mearig collection.)

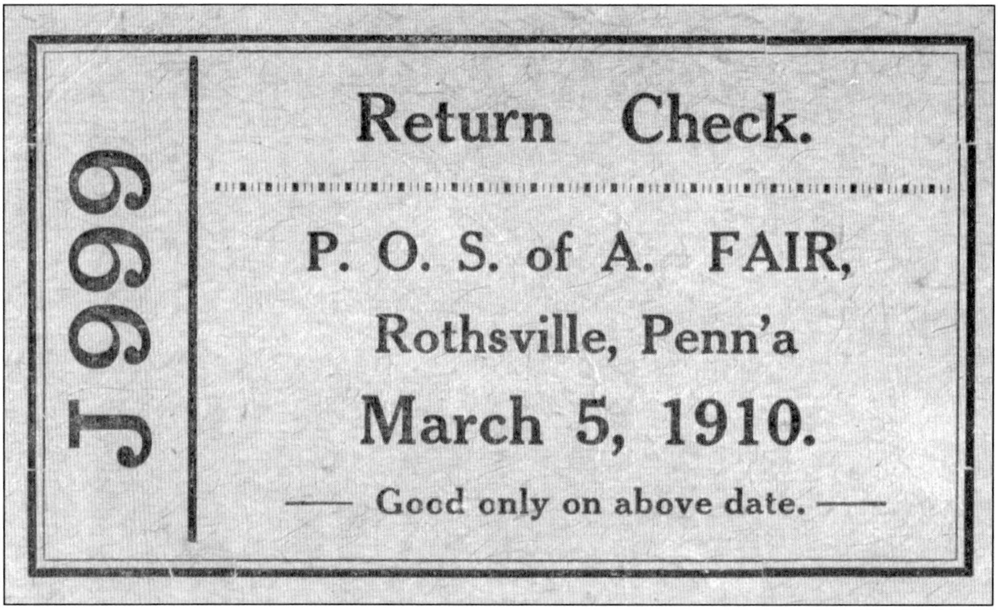
J 999

Return Check.

P. O. S. of A. FAIR,

Rothsville, Penn'a

March 5, 1910.

— Good only on above date. —

The Patriotic Order Sons of America (POSA), founded in 1847, is one of the oldest fraternal and patriotic societies in the United States. Pictured here is a return railway ticket from a meeting that was held by this organization in Rothsville on March 5, 1910. Many veterans would gather at these events to visit and catch up with comrades who fought side by side with them. (Courtesy of the Robert "Sketch" Mearig collection.)

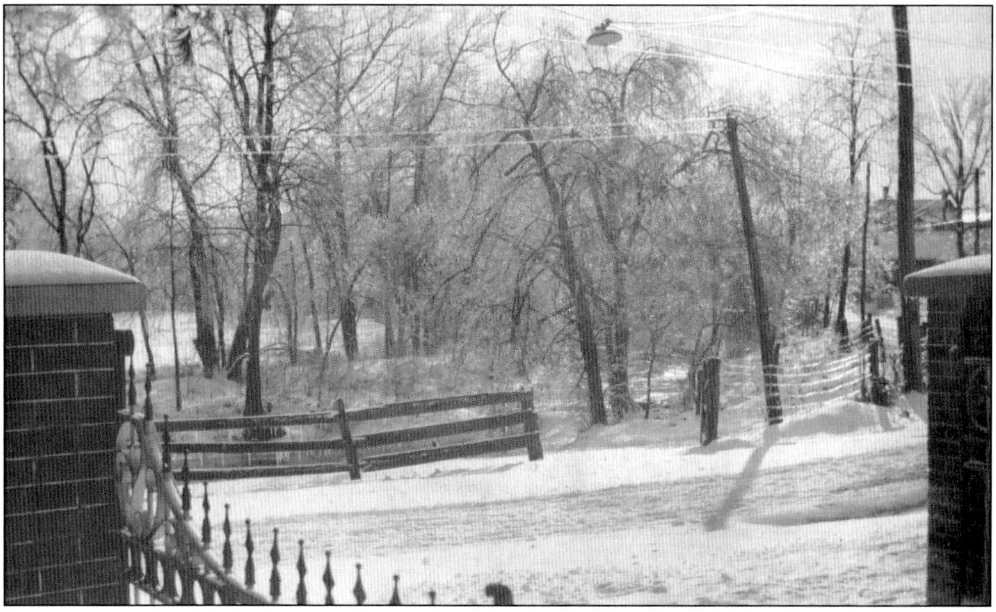

Wissler's porch was a good place from which to take a photograph of a snowy day in Millway. Look closely to see one lonely streetlight dangling from a cable high above the wires in the top of the picture. At the time this photograph was taken, this was the only streetlight in Millway. (Courtesy of John David Wissler.)

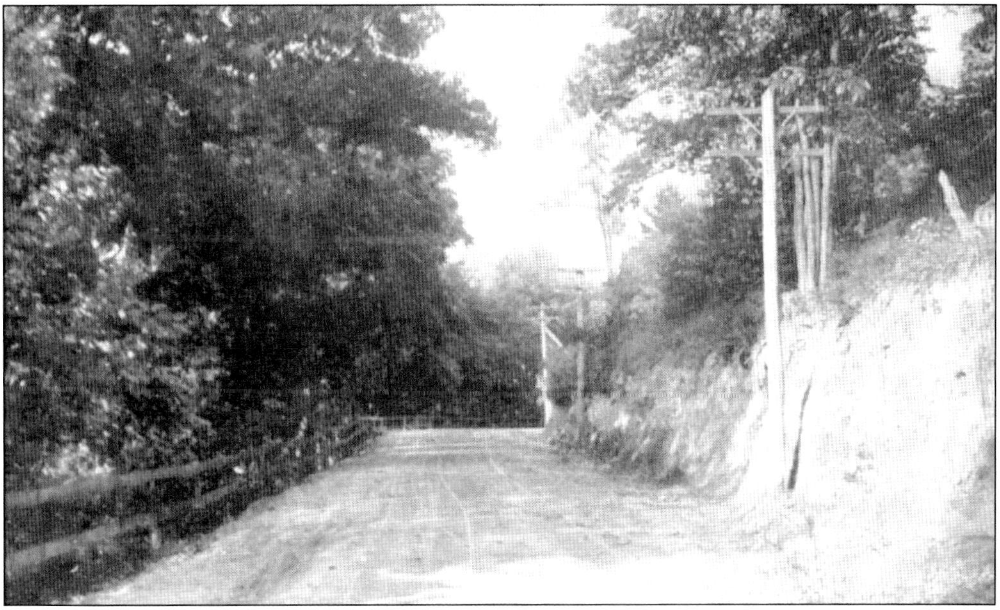

Traveling past Rome heading east toward Rothsville is an area known as Keller Mountain. This gorgeous wooded area was named by the Keller families that lived here many years ago. At one time, this area was known to contain a nickel mine. Below, two well-dressed men and women are out for a walk around this area. This photograph was taken looking west where Heck Road turns off to the left. The water in Lititz Creek that flowed under the bridge where they are standing was utilized by Pfoutz's Mill, located just beyond the house on the right. This mill, constructed of limestone, dates back to 1793 and was used as a flour mill, gristmill, and sawmill. (Both, courtesy of the Robert "Sketch" Mearig collection.)

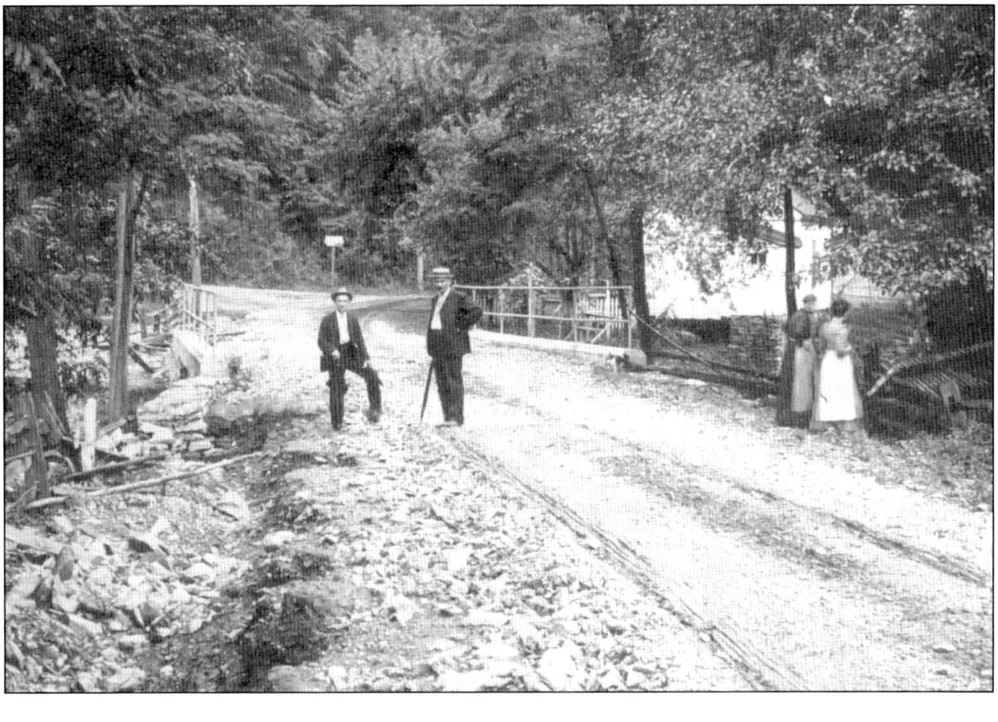

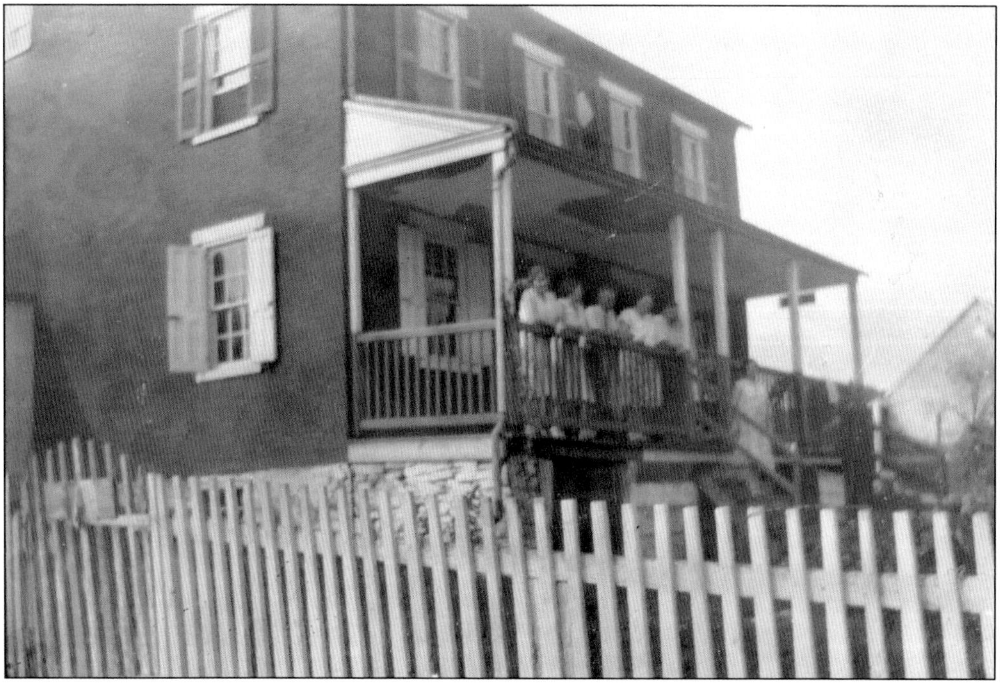

This cottage, located in Millway in the 1930s, was owned by Monroe Widders of Lititz. Widders rented this bungalow to families as a summer cottage at a cost of $10 per month. Renters could go swimming or for a romantic hike along the creek. One of the renters was Sam Hoffman of Lititz and his family. Hoffman is seen standing on the porch at far right. (Courtesy of the Robert "Sketch" Mearig collection.)

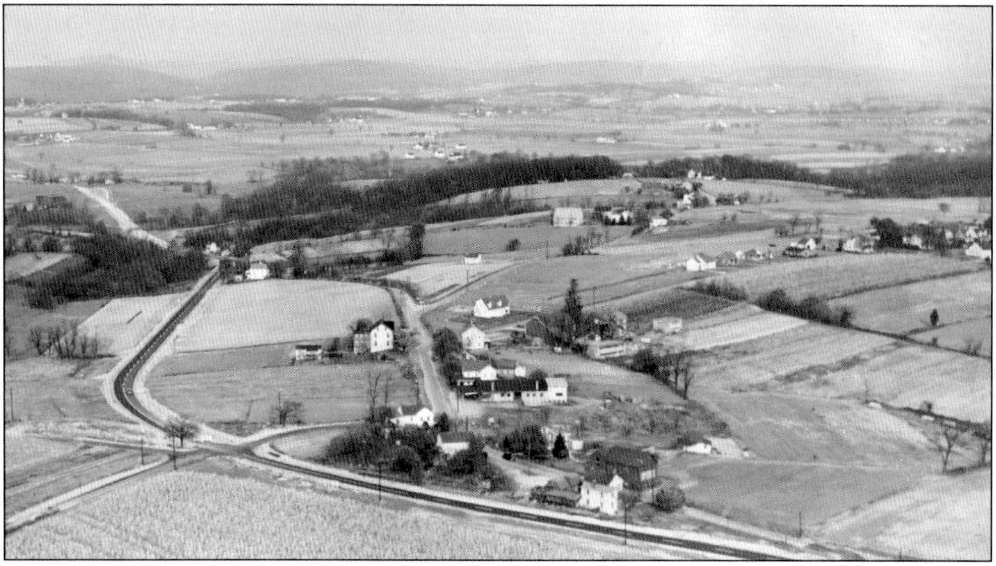

This aerial shot of Lexington looking north shows a road on the left, which is the modern State Route 501. After a post office was established, the town was renamed Lexington. In 1883, the village had 156 residents, and by 1924 this number had grown to 250. The road in the center, now named Loop Road, was the original road north toward Lebanon County. (Courtesy of the Robert "Sketch" Mearig collection.)

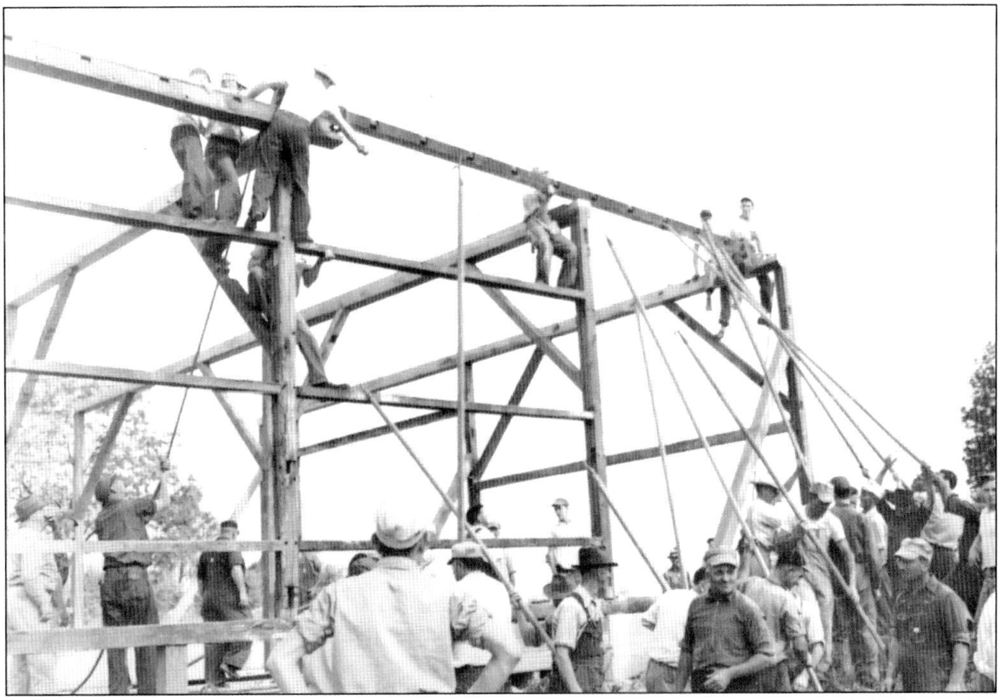

This barn raising, around 1949 or 1950, was necessary due to a fire that destroyed the barn that stood on the property of the Ditzler family in Lexington. Men, young and old, joined together and worked long hours to help build the structure. While the men—sometimes 50 persons or more—worked on building the barn, the women would work at cooking and baking to provide meals for the hardworking men. It could take days to get the framework erected and then close in the building. Seen in the picture below are the women from this barn raising. Violet Noll was 16 years old at the time and is pictured standing third from the left. To her right is her mother, and standing at far left is her aunt. (Both, courtesy of Violet Noll.)

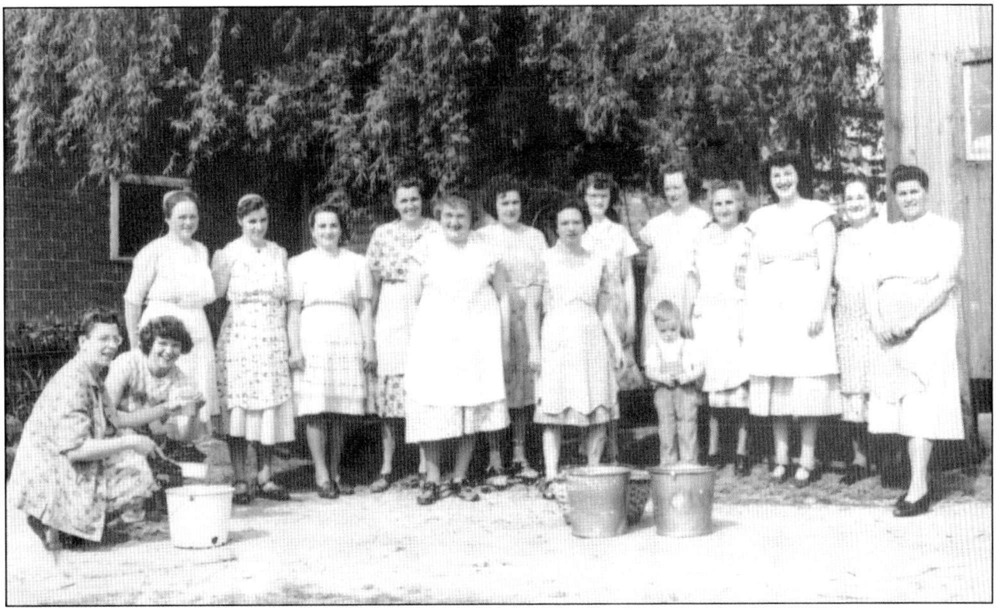

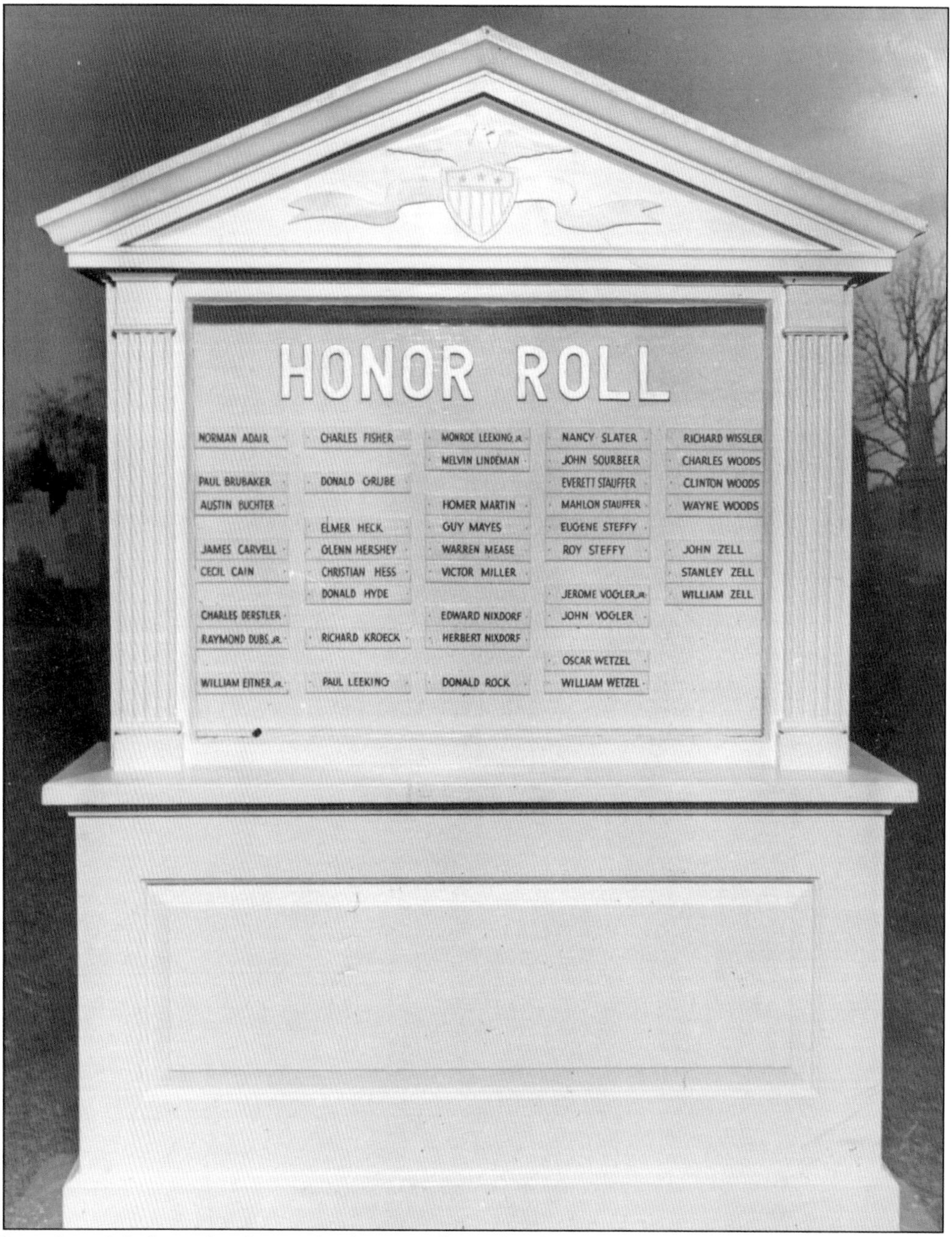

Listed in alphabetical order on this honor roll are all of the men and women who were members of Salem Lutheran Church or residents of Kissel Hill who were fighting the battle of World War II. The honor roll, which at one time sat to the left of the Salem Lutheran Church in Kissel Hill, was dedicated Sunday, December 7, 1944, under the sponsorship of the church's Sunday school. Many towns throughout the United States had these honor rolls in front of their town's post offices, fire stations, or borough halls. If a name listed had a star next to it, that meant that the person who was fighting overseas died while fighting for their country. At the time this photograph was taken, 42 names were listed on this particular honor roll. (Courtesy of the Robert "Sketch" Mearig collection.)

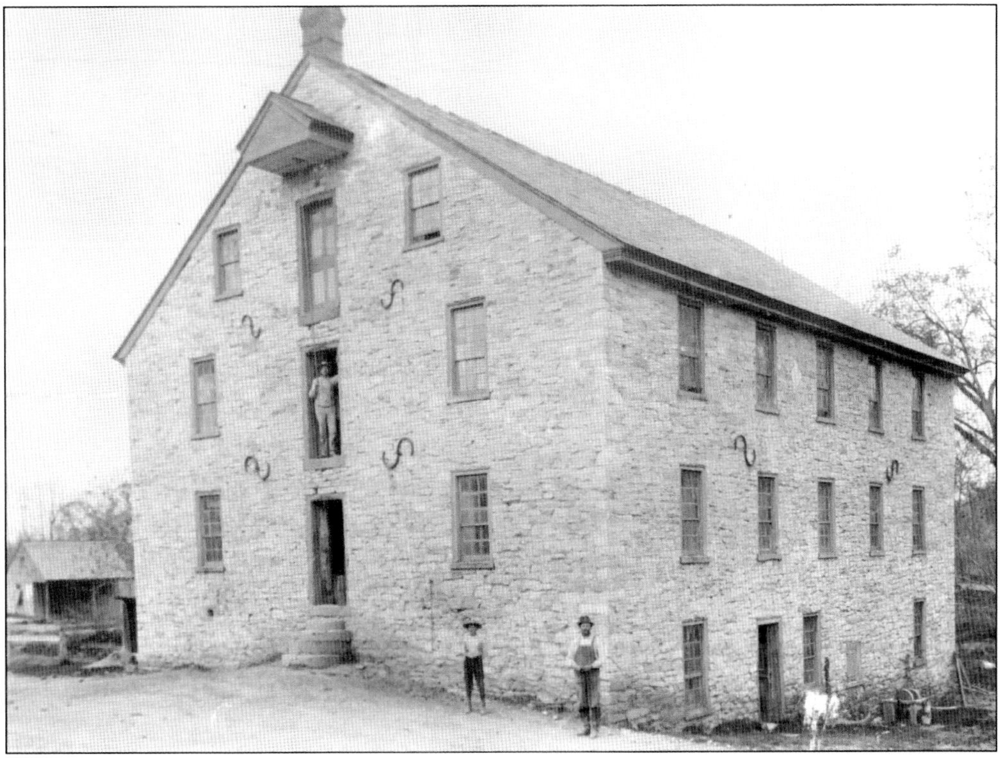

Located in Millway, this three-and-a-half-story gristmill was originally built in 1832 by Jacob Hershey. An earlier mill built of wood in 1760 by George Eby occupied this site before the present mill was constructed. Former owners of the mill at this site included Levi Brubaker, Jonas Nolt, E. H. Shenk, John Reitz, James S. Moore, and H. S. Withers. Withers was the last person to operate it as a functional business, and he can be seen above wearing the top hat and overalls. This photograph dates from sometime in the 1880s to the 1920s. Below is an invoice from this mill, dated October 10, 1902. At this time, the mill was operated by H. S. Withers and Bro. and specialized in flour, feed, and grain. (Above, courtesy of John David Wissler; below, courtesy of the author's collection.)

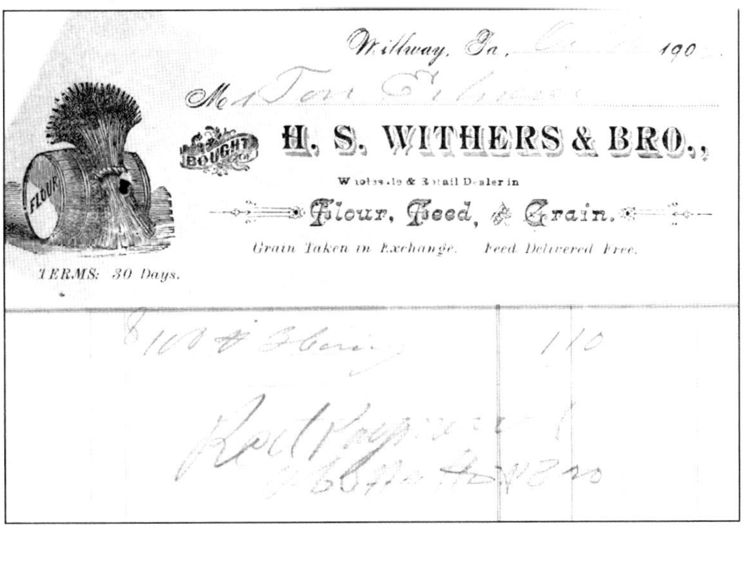

Millway, Pa., 190

Mr

BOUGHT of H. S. WITHERS & BRO.,

Wholesale & Retail Dealer in

Flour, Feed, & Grain.

Grain Taken in Exchange. Feed Delivered Free.

TERMS: 30 Days.

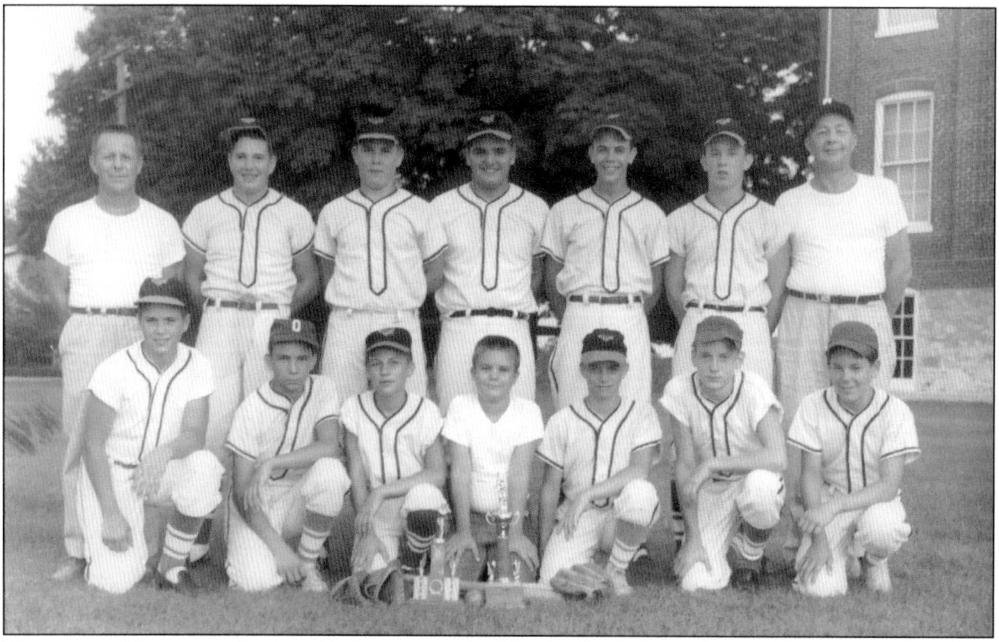

These neighborhood Rothsville boys joined a baseball team in the early 1960s and proudly posed for this picture outside of the Rothsville High School. The members included, from left to right, (first row) Denny Kissinger, Gary Bender, Terry White, an unidentified batboy, Emmett Hannah, Raymond Deater, and Denny Rhoads; (second row) coach Lou White, Claude Young, Gary Young, Doug Gaul, Fred Sample, Larry Donley, and coach Eugene Mellinger. (Courtesy of Sharyn Deater.)

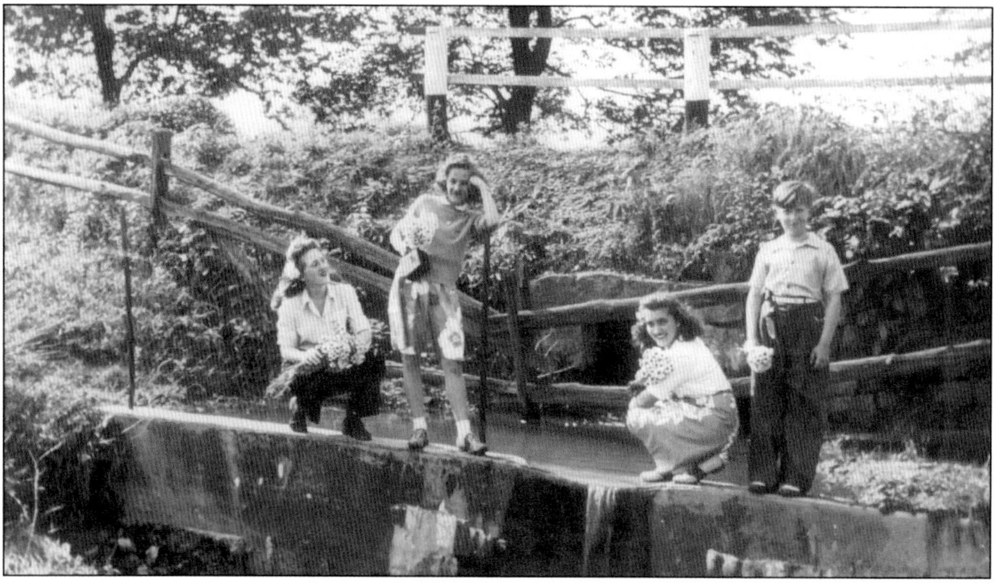

This group of people gathered together for this photograph in the 1940s while picking daisies near what is now Warwick Township's Linear Park. To this day the park provides the public with over 40 acres of recreational area, including athletic fields, a playground, walking trails, and a beautiful stream. Pictured from left to right are Jane Stauffer-Adams, Lois Jane Adams, Dolly Artz-Gockley, and unidentified. (Courtesy of Sharyn Deater.)

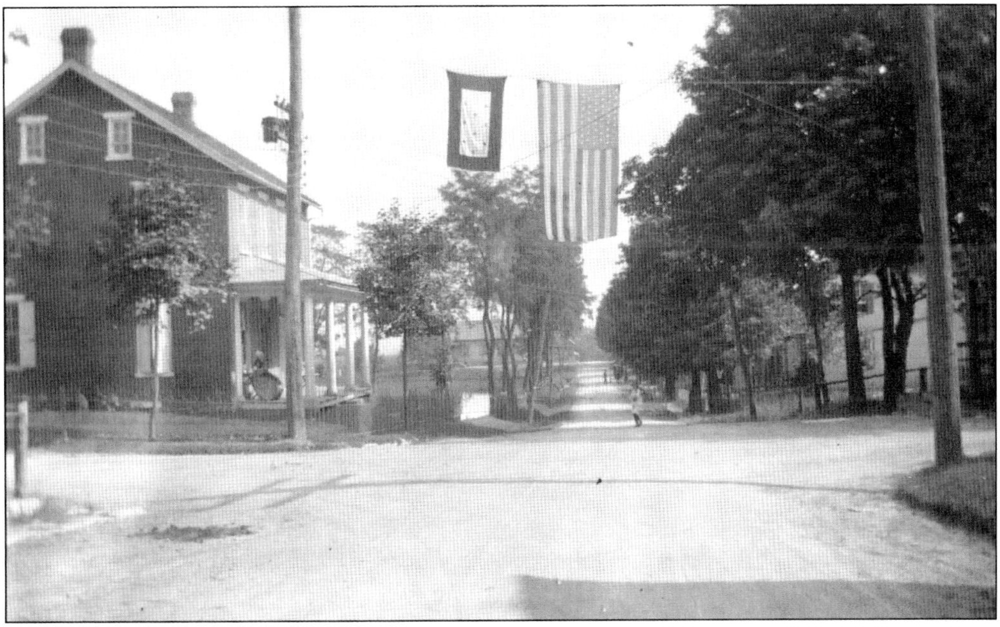

Here is the intersection at Brunnerville in a picture taken around the time of World War I. About 1832, the citizens of the hamlet, led by Abraham Eichler, held a meeting to come up with a name for the area. After a debate, Jacob Erb suggested that the town be known as White Hall, and it was called this until a post office was established in 1861. (Courtesy of the Robert "Sketch" Mearig collection.)

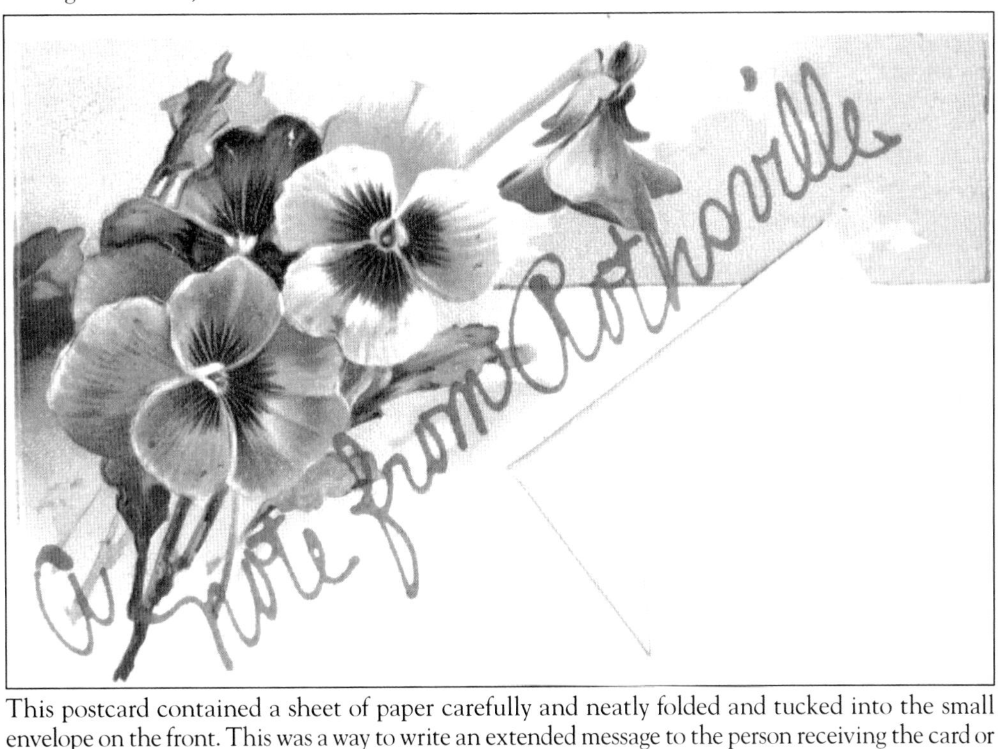

This postcard contained a sheet of paper carefully and neatly folded and tucked into the small envelope on the front. This was a way to write an extended message to the person receiving the card or to send a secret message one's sweetheart. (Courtesy of the Robert "Sketch" Mearig collection.)

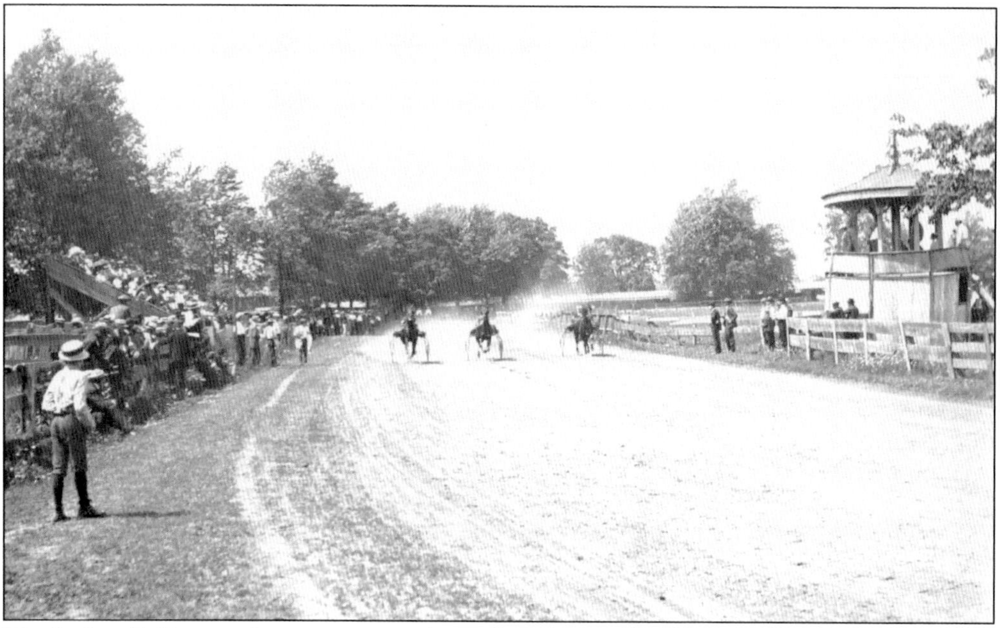

The Rothsville Racetrack at one time was located on a tract of land behind the White Swan Hotel. Between 1886 and 1917, on the seventh Monday after Easter, or "Whit Monday," thousands of people gathered in Rothsville to attend the sulky races. Barrooms had to turn patrons away, and spirits were then dispensed from the backs of wagons and from stands along the track. Once the races had ended for the day, visitors to Rothsville used the track for personal racing and betting. Wages were placed, and oftentimes too much alcohol was consumed, with an occasional fistfight breaking out. Below is a group of spectators at one of these races, with Alvin Deater in the center looking toward the camera. (Above, courtesy of the Robert "Sketch" Mearig collection; below, courtesy of Sharyn Deater.)

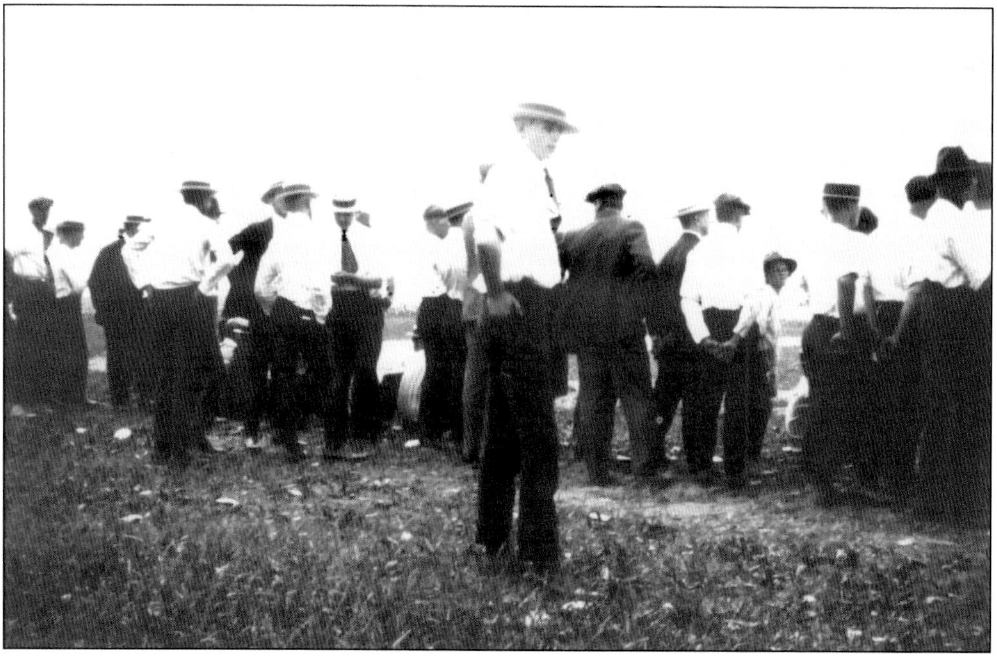

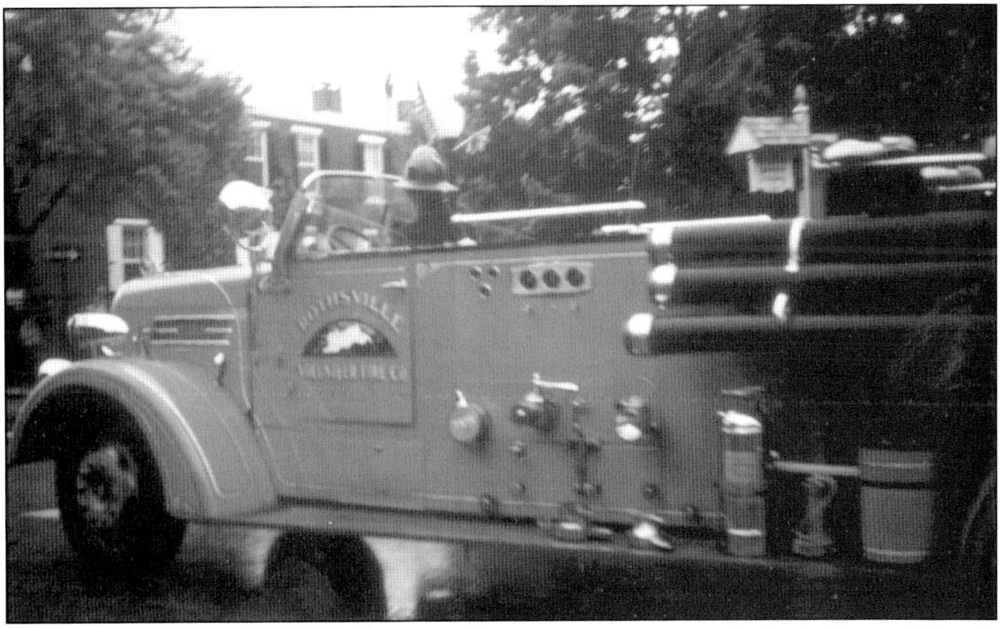

The Rothsville Fire Company truck pictured here is participating in the Lititz Firemen's Parade of 1957. The fire company was established in 1888 by Jefferson Usner. Rothsville's first pumper was purchased about 1900. A two-bay firehouse was erected in 1909 on the property of Henry Myers. The Rothsville Volunteer Fire Company was chartered in 1917, with the first fire chief being Frank M. Bowman. (Courtesy of the Robert "Sketch" Mearig collection.)

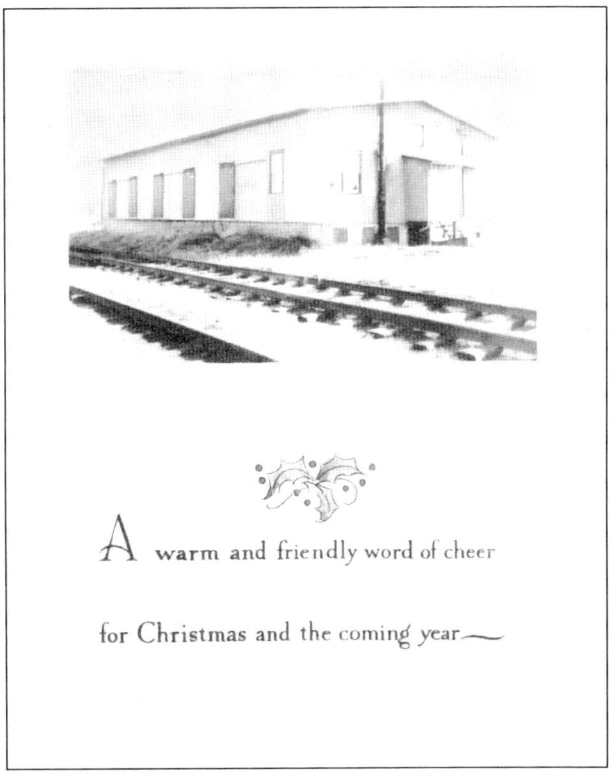

Wallace M. Zook and Son specialized in coal, flour, feed, grain, fertilizer, and cement, which was located next to the railroad tracks at Rothsville Station. On March 2, 1932, a tremendous fire broke out, with neighbors quickly assisting by forming a bucket brigade. Lost in the fire that day were the warehouse, Zook's home and two barns, and the nearby Binkley home. (Courtesy of the Robert "Sketch" Mearig collection.)

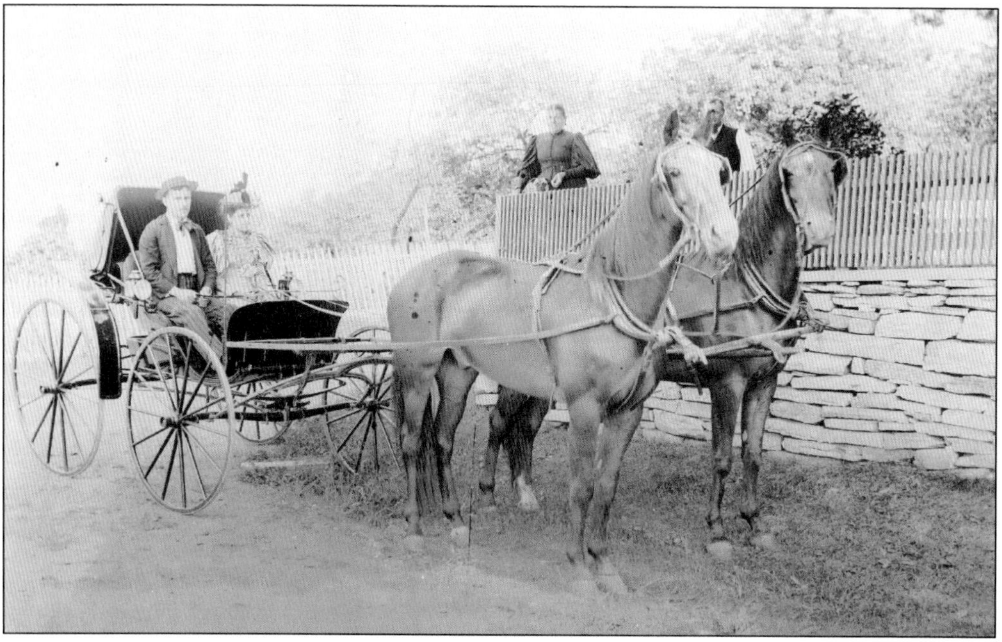

The image above, taken by P. B. Koser of White Oak, Pennsylvania, shows a happy couple out for a pleasant ride in Pine Hill. Mr. and Mrs. David M. Graybill are in the carriage, and standing behind the fence are Mr. and Mrs. Henry Erb and their dog. Pine Hill, located over the hill from Brunnerville, is mostly just a small group of houses, but they did have a school named the Lookout School. In 1894, it was taught by Cyrus R. Gibbel. The village of Pine Hill could also boast having a hotel. Below is another beautiful scene of a well-dressed family taking a ride through Pine Hill. (Both, courtesy of the Robert "Sketch" Mearig collection.)

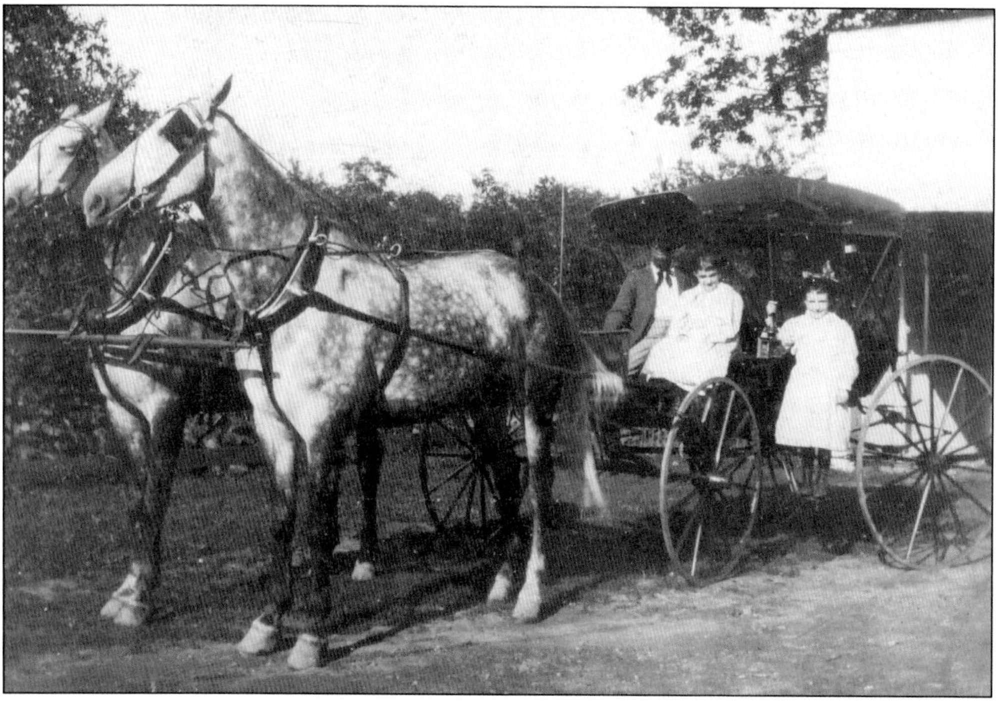

Two

PEOPLE

In the heart of any state, city, or neighborhood, it is certainly the everyday people that make it such an extraordinary place to live. The people of Warwick Township, past and present, young and old, have all played a vital part in making the township what it is today. It has a unique charm all its own and presents the opportunity to enjoy country life to all who want to partake. Whether it is putting in a long day's work, playing on a sports team, or enjoying the countryside, there is much to be said about the township's unique diversity of residents. Many people in this area continue to work long hours in order to provide for their family, volunteer their time with various charitable and nonprofit organizations, or spend long summer and winter hours enjoying their beautiful surroundings. Truly, it is not one individual person, but an entire community as a whole, that has always banded together and looked out for one another during a time of need. The photographs in the following chapter paint a landscape of everyday people and their extraordinary lives in Warwick Township.

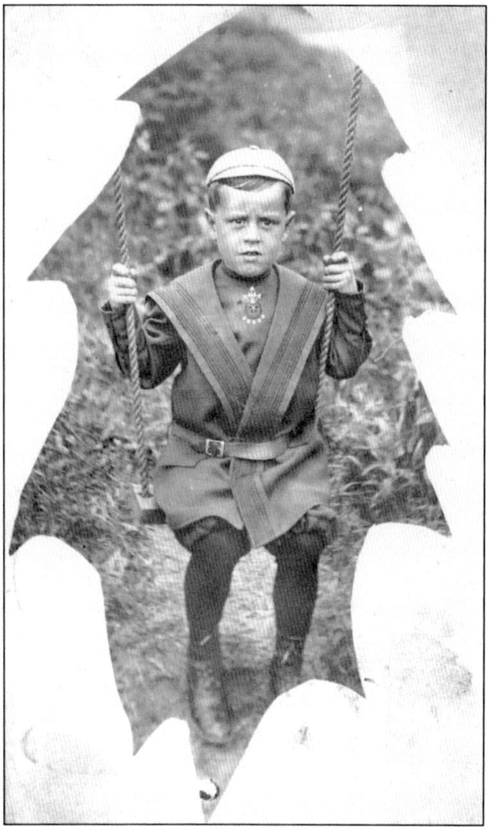

The back of this postcard is dated September 7, 1907, and was cancelled at Millport. Addressed to Rose E. Dauns of Caister, New York, the message written was, "I am coming to see you Rose–Lev." Postcards were a common way of sending a quick message to a friend or relative, whether they lived in another state or just over the hill. (Courtesy of the author's collection.)

The 4-H program began at the start of the 20th century. In this photograph taken in the mid- to late 1930s are Mary Brubaker of Brunnerville (left) and three unidentified members of the Lititz Junior Garden Club. Mary's brother Milton Brubaker served with the 4-H Ayrshire Jersey Brown Swiss Club for 35 years before retiring about 1988. (Courtesy of Dana Clark.)

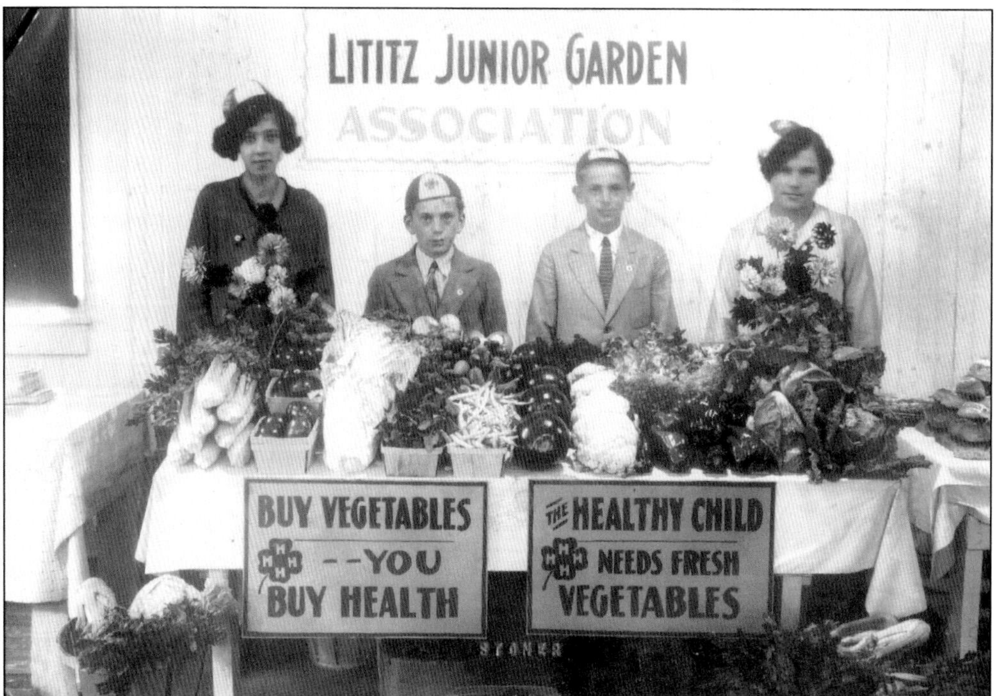

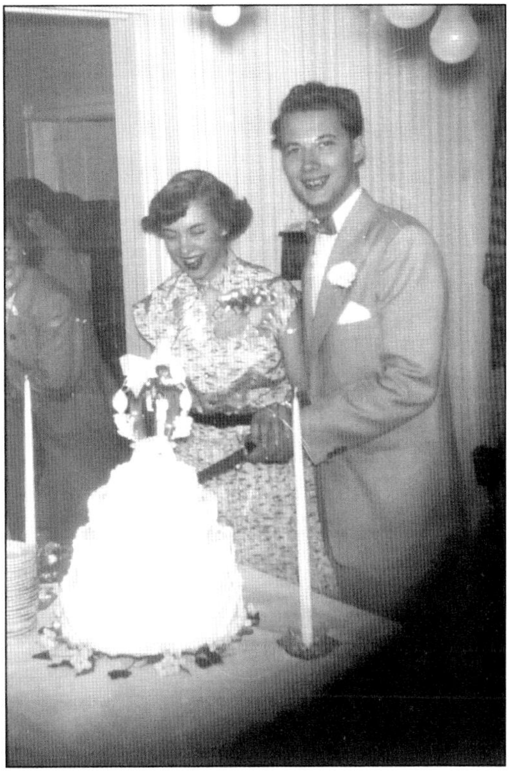

A wedding reception is an occasion filled with joy and love, and this happy couple's day is no exception. Pictured at right on May 24, 1945, are Joe and Jan Galls celebrating their recent vows. The reception was held at 823 Pine Hill Road in Pine Hill. Seen below are the Sheaffer kids, posing by the side of this same house in the flower garden. When this picture was taken (about 1944), the house was owned by the Long family. From left to right are Julie, James, Jan, and Joan Shaeffer. (Both, courtesy of Julia Buch.)

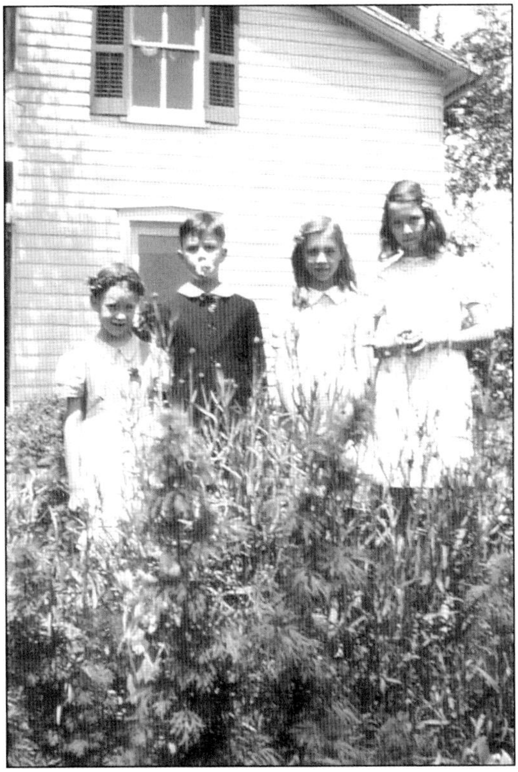

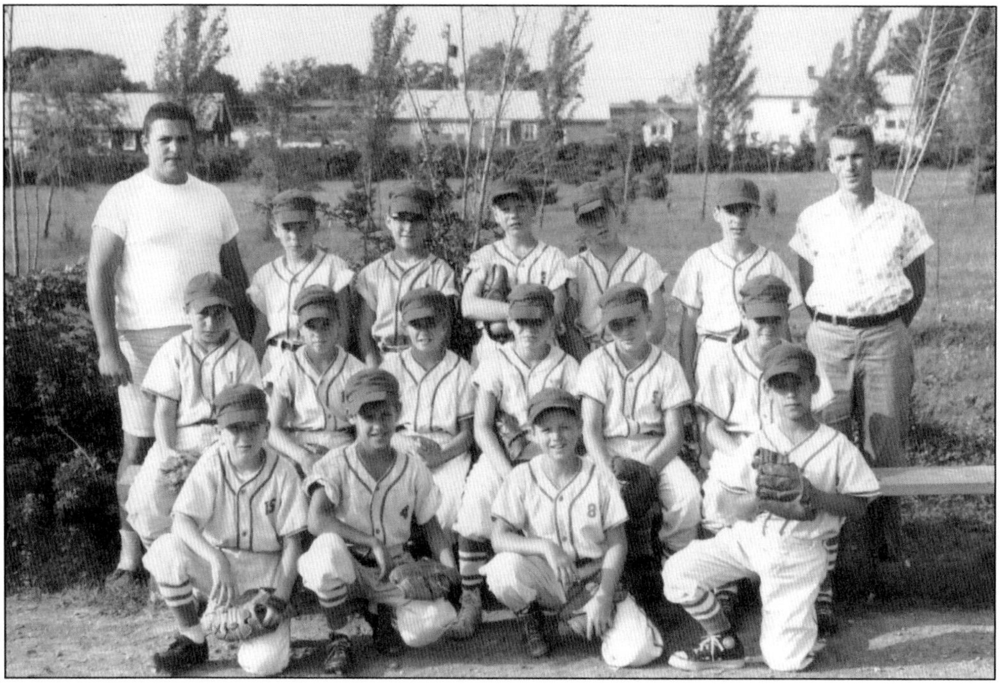

These Little League players are all dressed for the big game. The 1960 Brunnerville Braves are, from left to right, (first row) Barry Todd, Craig Hacker, Bobby Derr, and Keith Hacker; (second row) Mike Chernich, Barry Ober, Tom Risser, Jay May, Dennis Webster, and Neil Meiskey; (third row) head coach Barry Erb, Ray May, John Clark, "Pork" Shank, Gene Worley, Neil White, and assistant coach Wilbert May. (Courtesy of Dana Clark.)

DIED.

Clayton M. Adams, died on Sunday, February 28, 1926, at 8:00 o'clock, P. M. Aged 58 years and 3 days.

Funeral will take place from his late residence in Rothsville, Pa., on Friday, March 5th, at 9:30 o'clock, A. M., at the house, with further services in the Lutheran Church, Rothsville, and interment in the adjoining cemetery.

Yourself and family are invited to attend the funeral and requested to inform friends.

Automobiles will meet the morning train at Millway, Pa., and the 8:45 trolly at Lititz, Pa.

THE FAMILY.

In earlier days, death notice cards like these were sent to family and friends of the deceased to notify them of a sad passing. This particular card declares that Clayton M. Adams of Rothsville had passed away. The card contained the information about where the funeral was to take place and the time of the service: at his home on Friday, March 5, at 9:30 a.m. (Courtesy of the author's collection.)

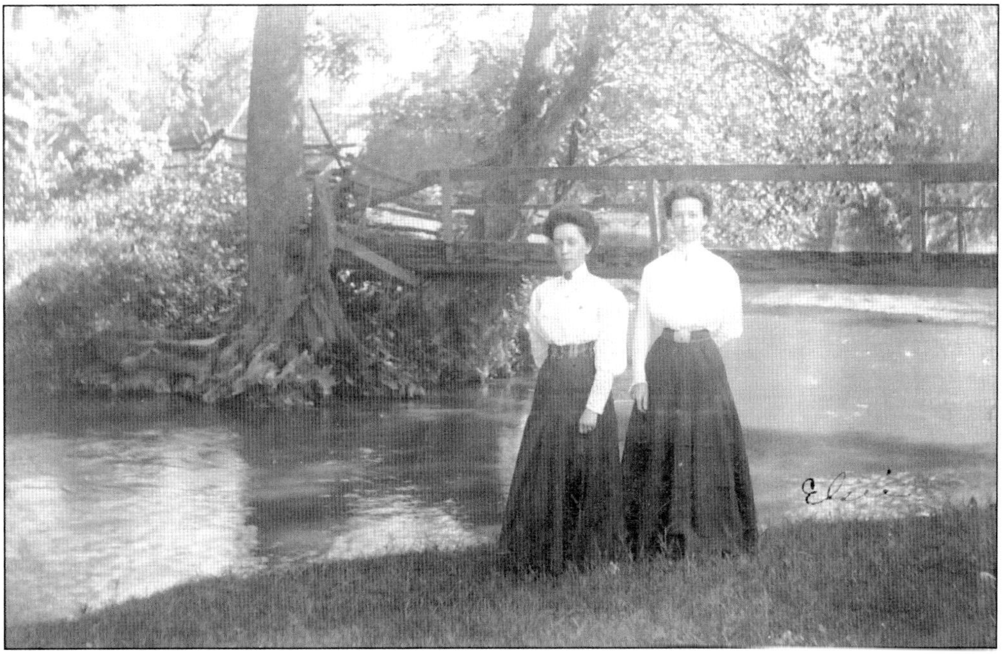

These well-to-do women are standing beside the Cocalico Creek in Millway. The postcard, sent to Ethel Zook of Lititz, has a postmark from the Millway post office and is dated June 8, 1909. The message states, "Dear cousin Ethel, I am sending you a picture I had taken while here. Sincerely, Elsie Ruby." Elsie can be seen standing to the right. (Courtesy of the Robert "Sketch" Mearig collection.)

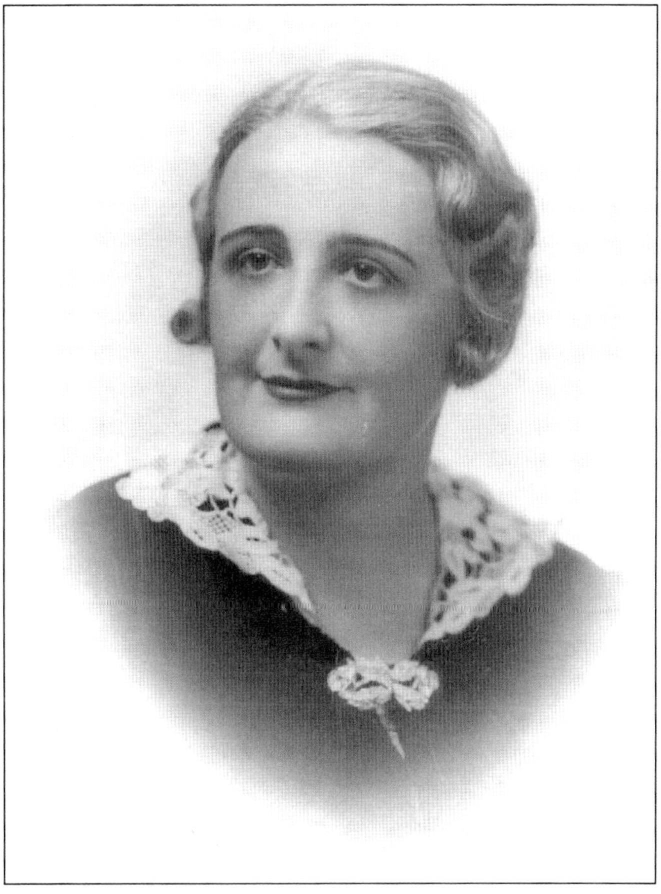

Anna Weber was known far and wide for her delicious crab cakes, which were her specialty when she owned the White Swan Hotel in Rothsville with her husband in 1945. After her husband, Albert, passed away in 1948, she became the sole proprietor of this popular restaurant. (Courtesy of Sharon Deater.)

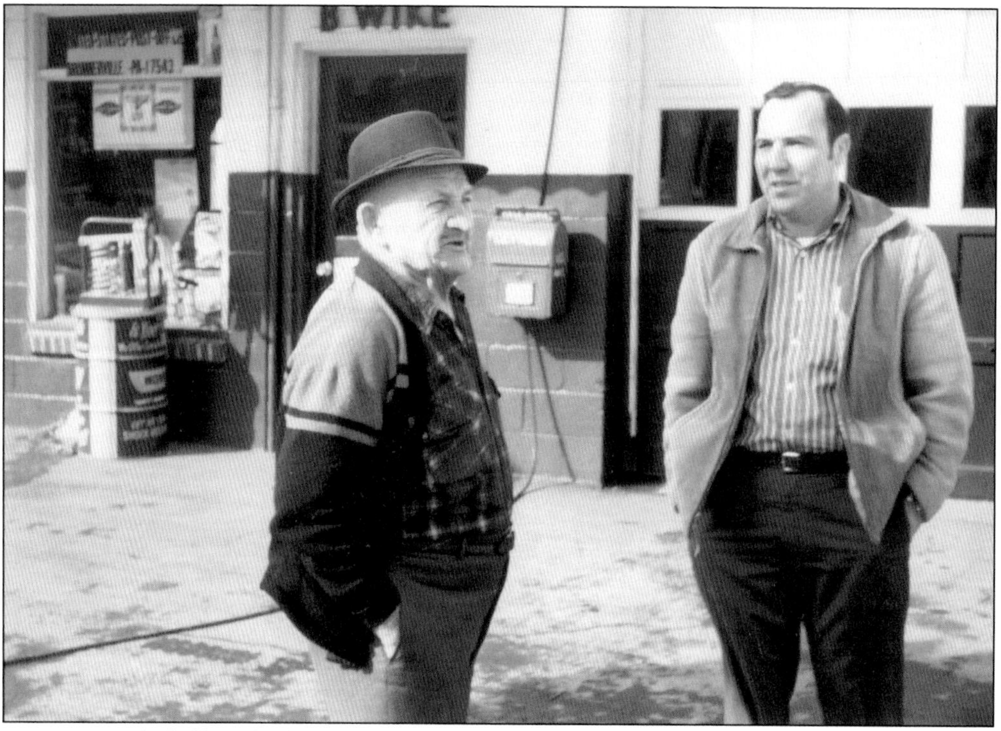

Norman Steely (left) and Clifford Keith (right) pose in front of Bruce Wike's Brunnerville Garage in 1971. Although the Brunnerville Garage has now moved across the street, local residents still gather there in the morning to drink coffee and to discuss the local and not-so-local items of the day. Steely (1889–1978) was an ice dealer and also dealt in furs. When sportsmen around Lititz and Warwick Township trapped small game, Steely would buy the skins. He was also known to purchase skins from skunks, raccoons, and muskrats, among others. Norman's son Vernon ran Steely's store in Brunnerville. Below is one of Steely's business cards that he handed out to his customers. (Both, courtesy of Tom Hackman.)

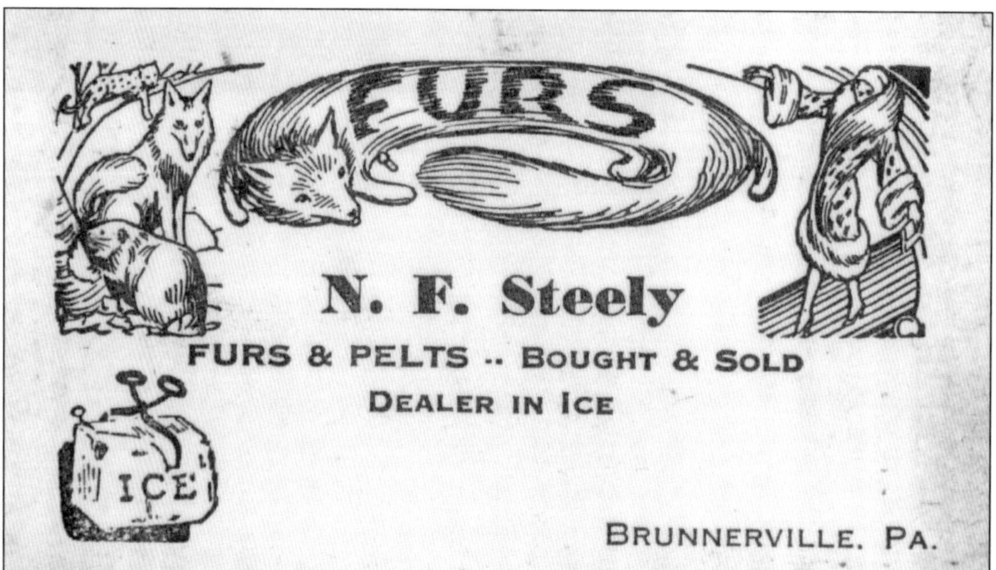

Galen Balmer of Brunnerville lived the country life. Born in 1895, he was orphaned early. In 1916, he decided to ride the rails, earning about $5 a week. He then enlisted in the U.S. Army as a private in Company G, 315th Infantry Regiment, 79th Division. From 1931 to 1970, he ran his family's farm, which was part of the land originally deeded to his ancestors from William Penn. He was known throughout Lancaster and Lebanon County as "The Watermelon Man." He also rolled his own cigars from tobacco he grew. At right is Galen on his 100th birthday, smoking one of his cigars. His barn is seen below. Galen lived to be 101 years old, and at the time of his death, he was one of Lancaster County's last remaining World War I veterans. (Both, courtesy of Bruce Balmer.)

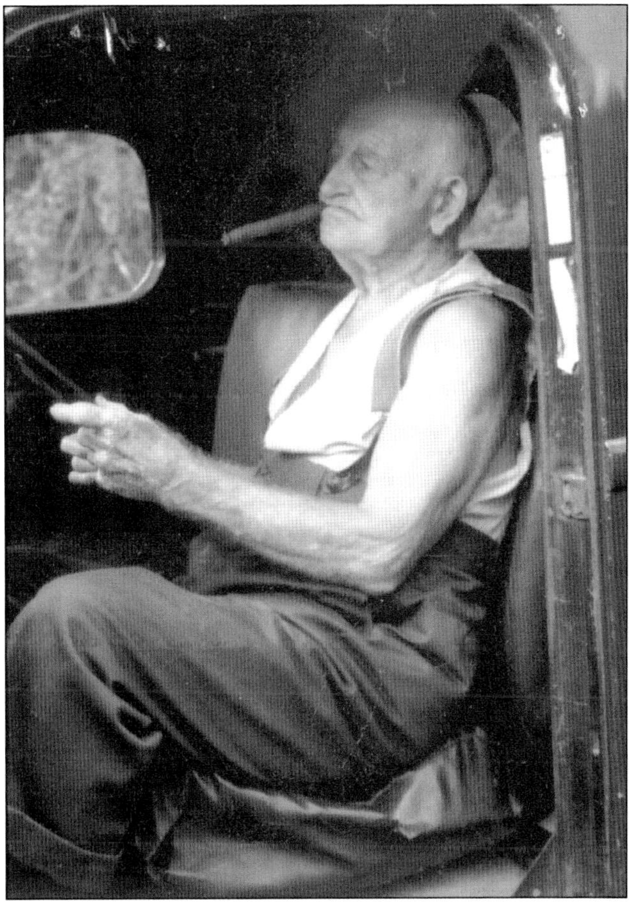

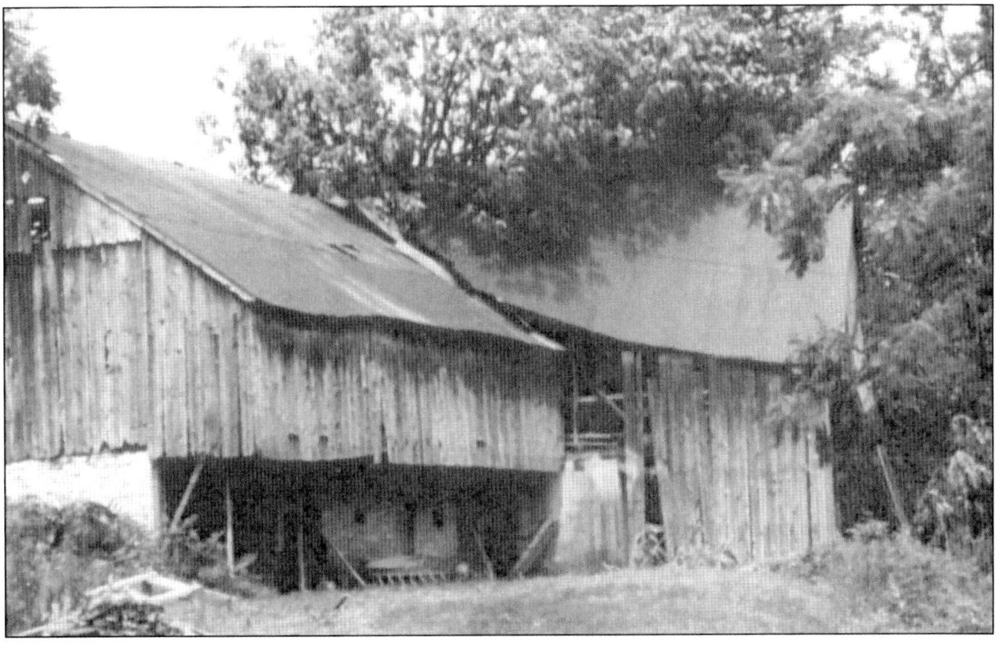

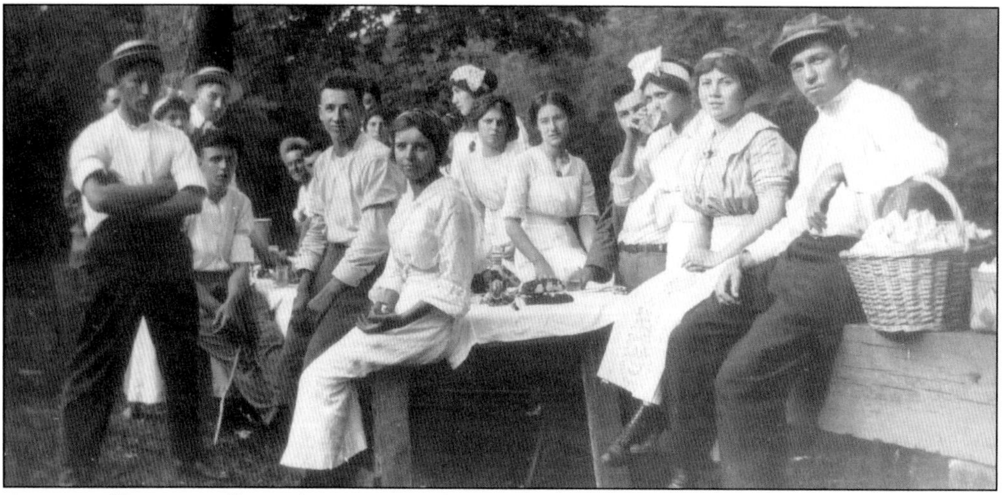

A group of Brunnerville residents enjoys a lovely day for a picnic. The photograph is undated but was taken prior to World War I. The gentleman at far left with his arms folded is George Irwin, who was killed in World War I. Also enjoying the picnic are Clarence Hoffer, Clayton Keith, Bertha Hoffer, Catherine Irwin, Ralph Keith, and Gertrude Hackman. (Courtesy of Tom Hackman.)

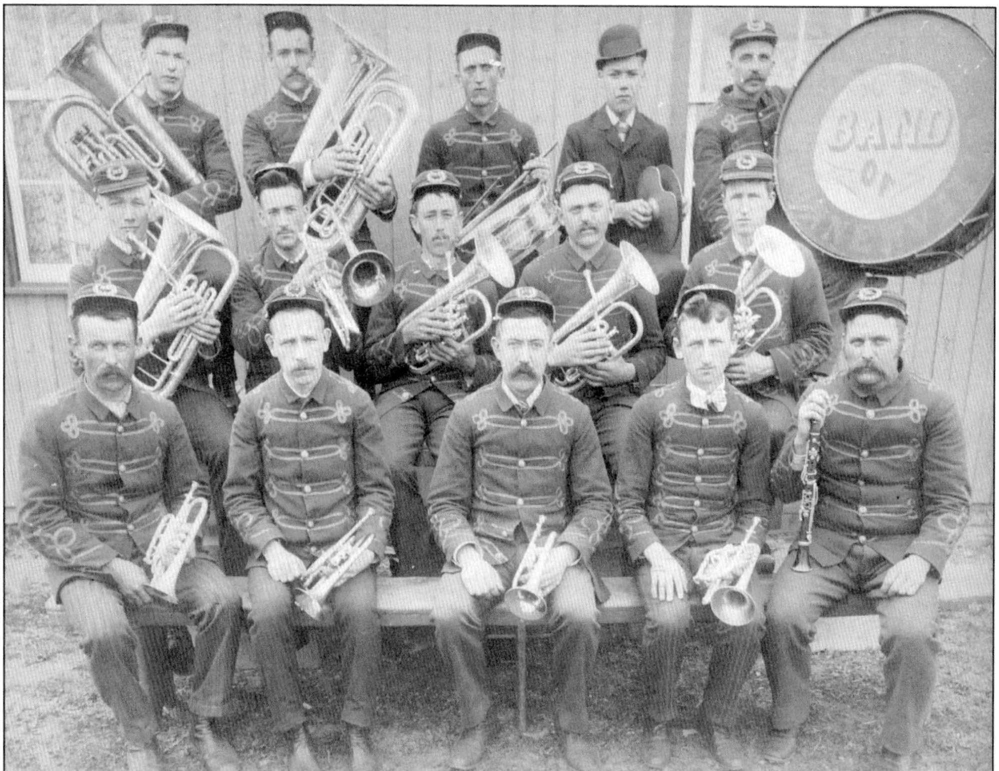

From 1885 to 1900, the Brunnerville Band played occasions like Memorial Day observances and community events. From left to right are (first row) Urias Balmer, George Keith, John Carpenter, Adam Becker, and John Warner; (second row) George Hackman, Cherry Buchter, Rudy Carpenter, Rolandis Longenecker, and Ammon Hollinger; (third row) George Bowers, Grant Buchter, Chester Enck, Clayton Shultz, and Peter Althouse. (Courtesy of Tom Hackman.)

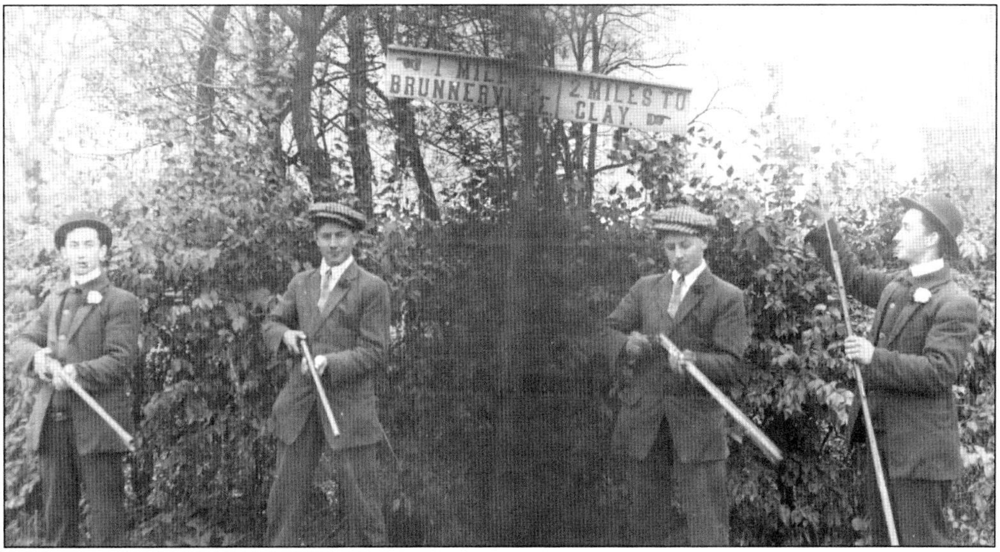

For generations, hunting has been a popular activity for sportsmen everywhere, including residents of Warwick Township. These four men posing with their rifles certainly look like they are having a great time. Look closely at the sign above them. It points one mile to Brunnerville and two miles to Clay, meaning this photograph was most likely taken in the Lexington area. (Courtesy of the Robert "Sketch" Mearig collection.)

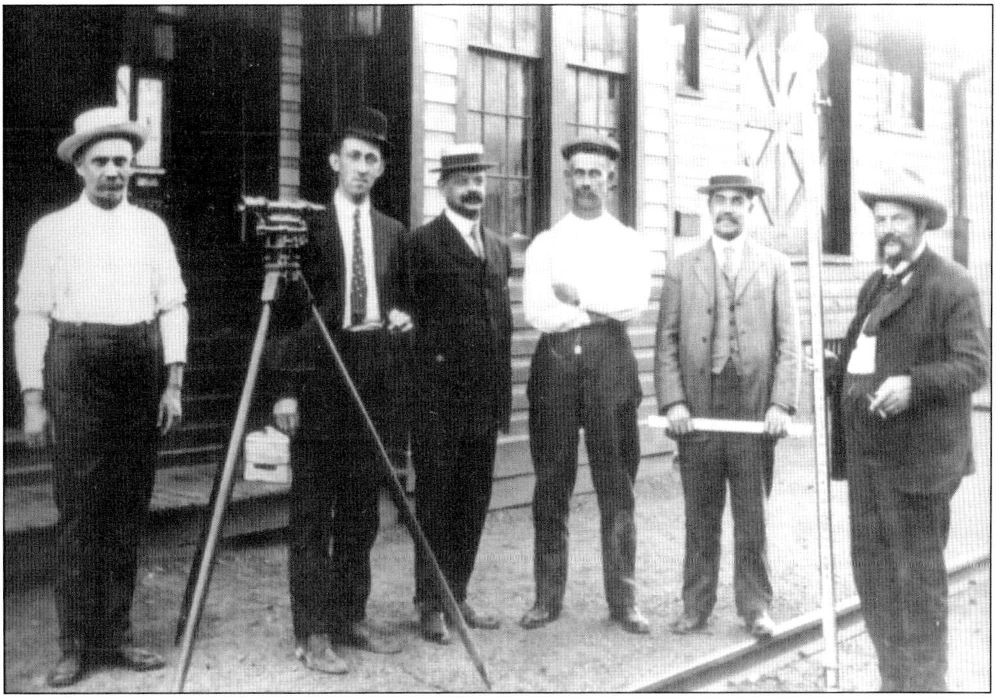

This is the Reading and Columbia Railroad Survey Crew at Millway Station. Standing far left is S. J. McPoland, who in 1913 served as the foreman for the oil station at Millway. Survey crews such as these were important because they researched and investigated topographical road conditions (in this case railroad lines), seeing where improvements could be made to its infrastructure. (Courtesy of Ron Reedy, from the John Denny collection.)

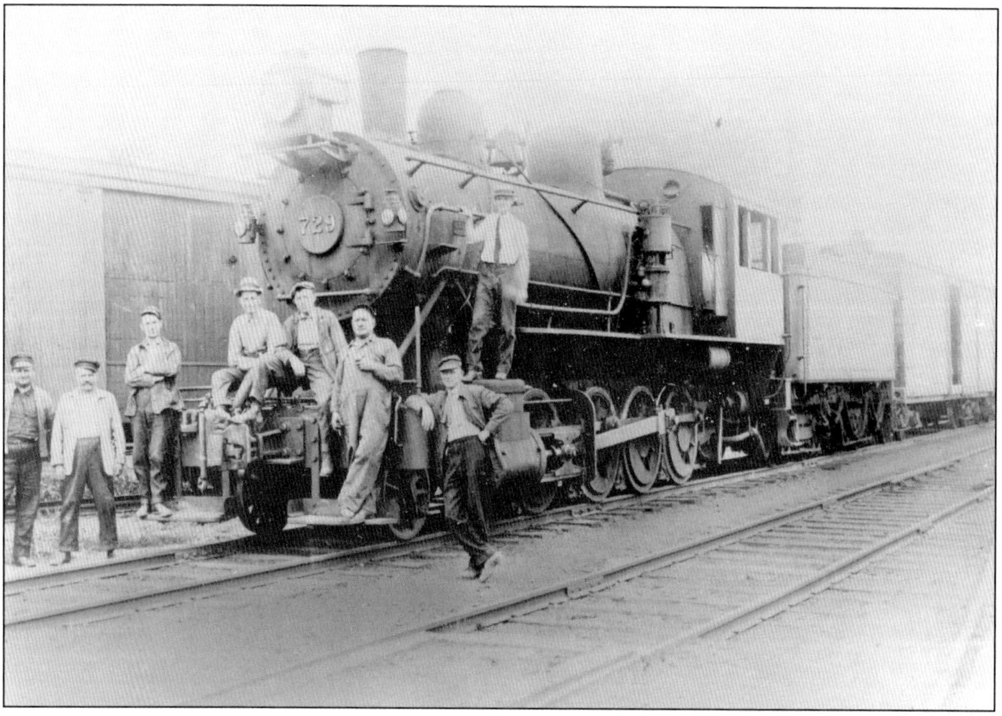

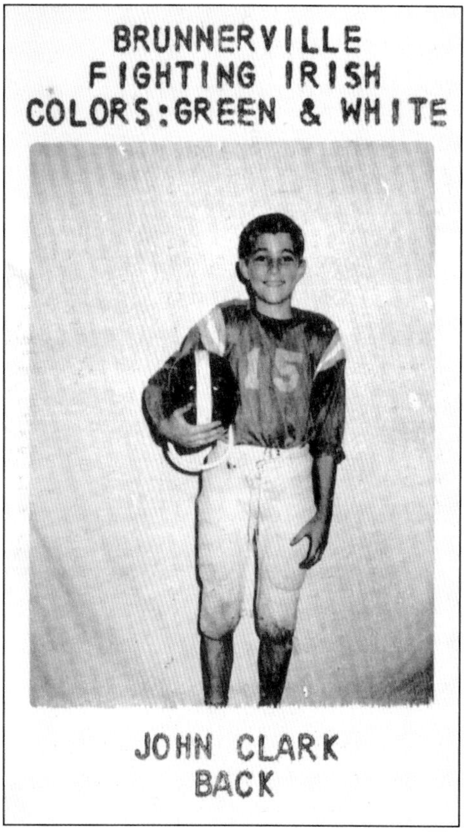

Reading and Columbia Railroad train car No. 729 2-8-0 and crew are seen here in 1913, stopping along the Millway line. On the right is E. E. Leisey standing on the train wearing the straw hat. The locomotive soon thereafter left Millway, carrying either passengers or freight to its next destination. (Courtesy of Ron Reedy, from the John Denny collection.)

In 1960, John Clark posed for this football card while playing for the Brunnerville Fighting Irish. To support the Warwick Midget Football League, cards like these were sold. Other teams within this league were the Rothsville Lions, the Lititz Red Raiders, and the Lititz Junior Giants. The head coaches of the Brunnerville team that year were Austin Weimer and Ray Huber. (Courtesy of Dana Clark.)

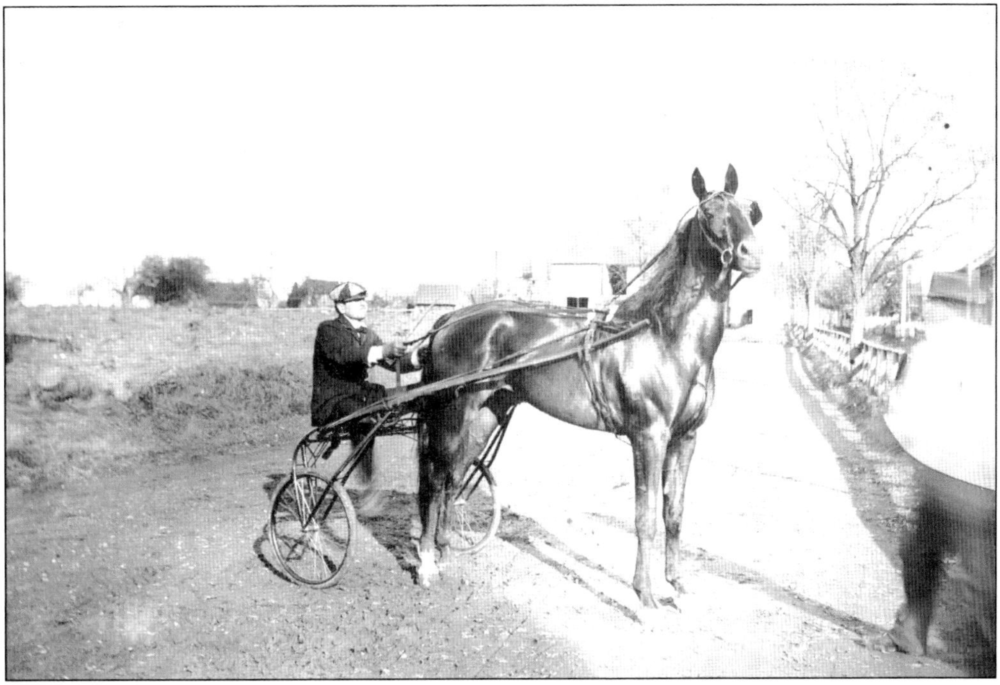

"Joe Patton" was the fastest horse ever to race the Rothsville Race Track. Here is that champion horse with his handler M. C. Frey, who was the owner of the White Swan Hotel in 1909. In the background are the stables and a barn that once sat behind the hotel. To the left in the background, Newport Road can be seen. (Courtesy of the Robert "Sketch" Mearig collection.)

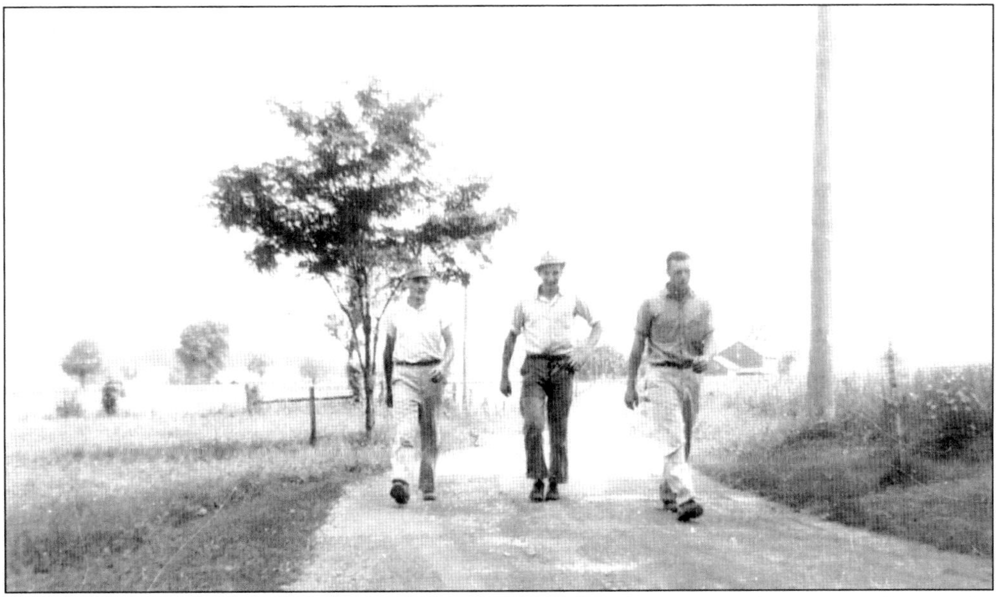

The Amand brothers—Clair (left), Frank (center), and Hen—are seen here on an August day in 1948 in Kissel Hill. When this photograph was taken, Hen was having trouble with his 1938 Chevrolet, and it needed to be pushed by the men in order to get it started. They are pictured walking back toward their farm, which was located on what is now Buckwalter Road. (Courtesy of Clair Amand.)

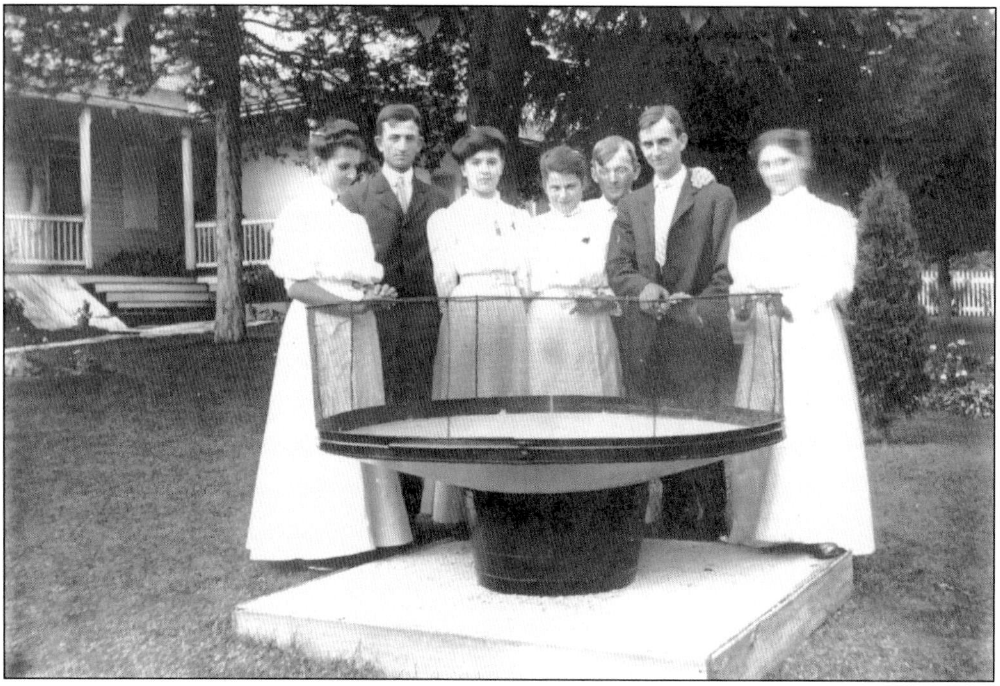

Many dinners and celebrations were held on the grounds of the Becker Family property in Pine Hill. For generations, this property also had a working distillery on its acreage. Here people are gathered around the property's natural spring, making for a very beautiful countryside backdrop. (Courtesy of Warren Becker.)

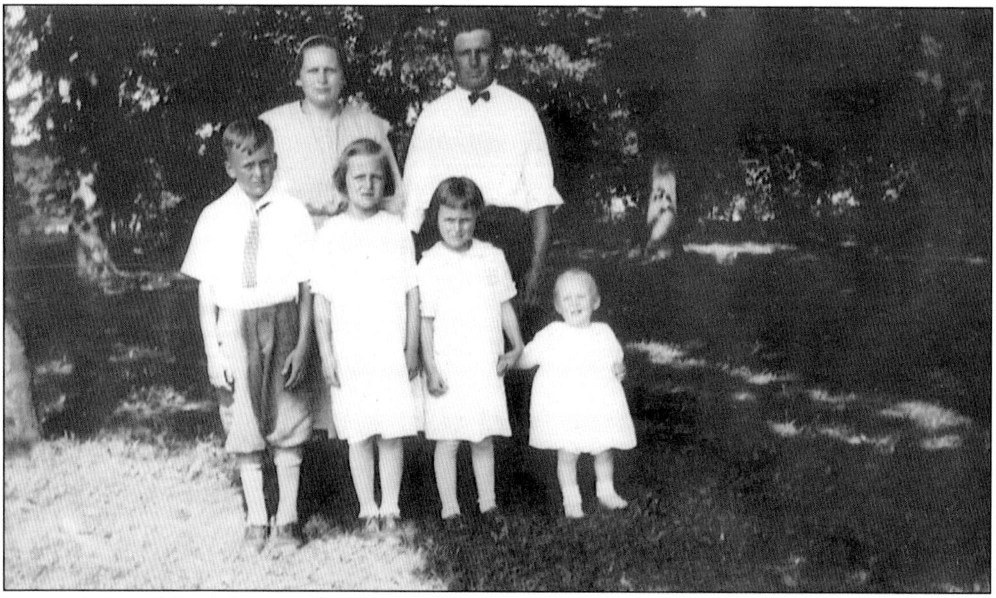

Located along East Newport Road, this property, which was once the site of Jacob Huber's Tavern, was owned by the Hershey family for about 20 years. Paul and Susan Hershey are standing with their children (from left to right) Richard, Jane, Lois, and Mildred from the early 1930s. David and Susan were married on Christmas Day in 1922. (Courtesy of Forgotten Seasons Bed and Breakfast.)

Three

Transportation

Beginning with Newport Road, travel and transportation throughout the years have proven both economical and convenient for trade throughout the township. The Reading and Columbia Railroad, spanning the township from east to west, added to this advancement and made travel by rail a pleasurable and memorable experience for many families. Goods of many kinds could now be transported in larger quantities at a quicker pace. The Conestoga Traction Company's trolley cars traveled through Kissel Hill, making excursions to Lancaster and other connecting communities a reality. Passengers on this trolley system could travel through scenic countryside to go shopping, meet family or friends, attend a special outing at an amusement park, or visit a serene lake for a memorable fishing trip. Once the automobile came into vogue, families would take Sunday drives to the countryside or load up the car to visit friends in other parts of the county or state. With all of this advancement in transportation, certainly the world became smaller. The photographs in this chapter offer a unique glimpse of the diversity of travel in days gone by throughout the township.

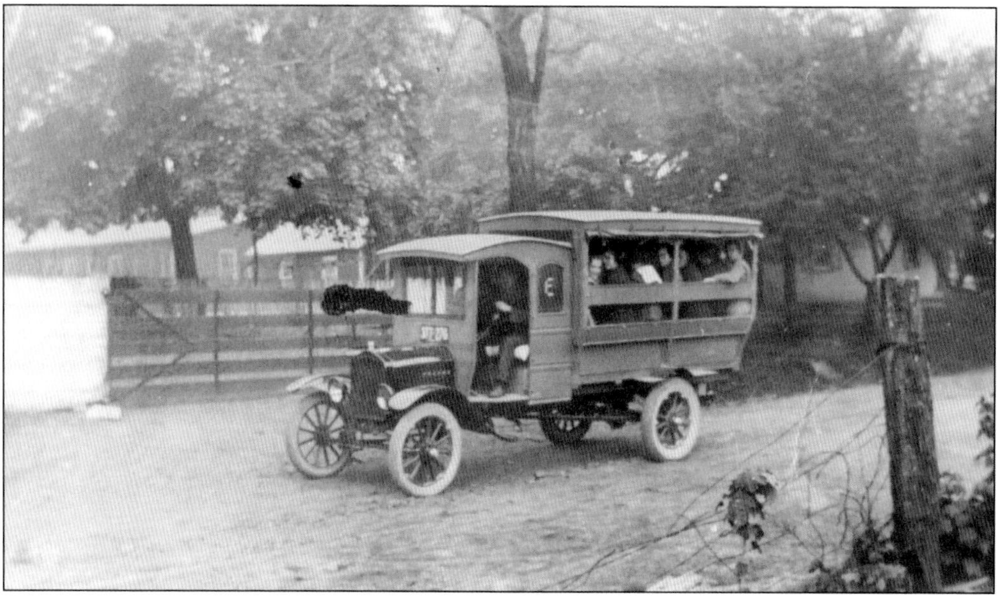

In March 1920, employees who worked for the Eby Shoe Company and the Keystone Knitting Mill of Lititz who lived "out in the country" were transported to and from work each day compliments of their respected employers. This photograph was taken in front of where the Brunnerville Fire Hall stands today. The rear of the Brunnerville Iron Foundry can be seen in the background. (Courtesy of Tom Hackman.)

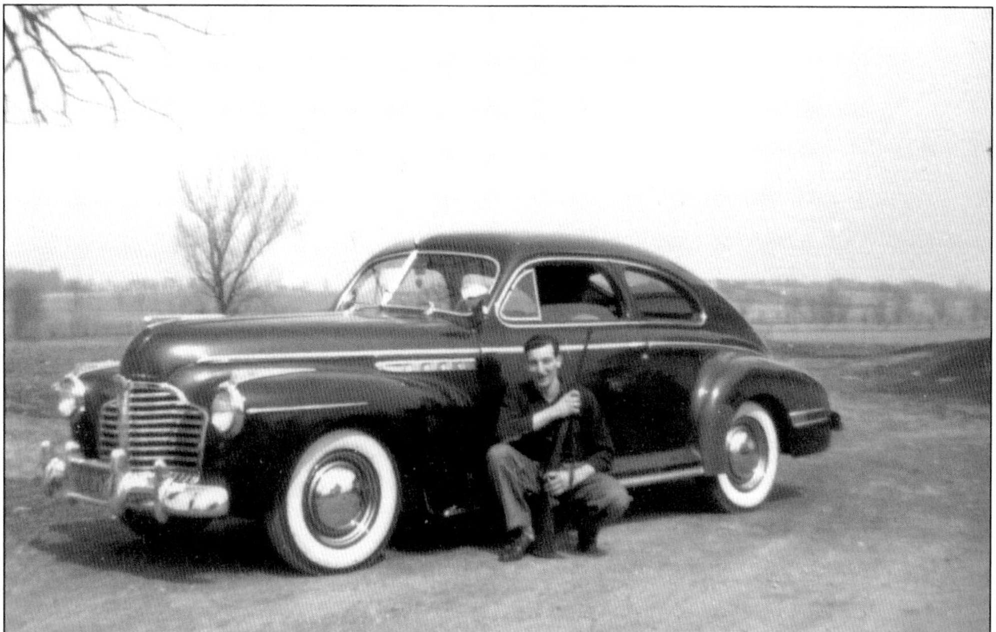

Frank Amand of Kissel Hill was very proud of the new paint job on his 1941 Buick, and he and his brother decided to take several pictures of it. Frank is shown here holding his rifle, posing with this beautiful old car in 1948. The photograph was taken by his brother Clair on their parents' farm. In the background is Kissel Hill before it was developed. (Courtesy of Clair Amand.)

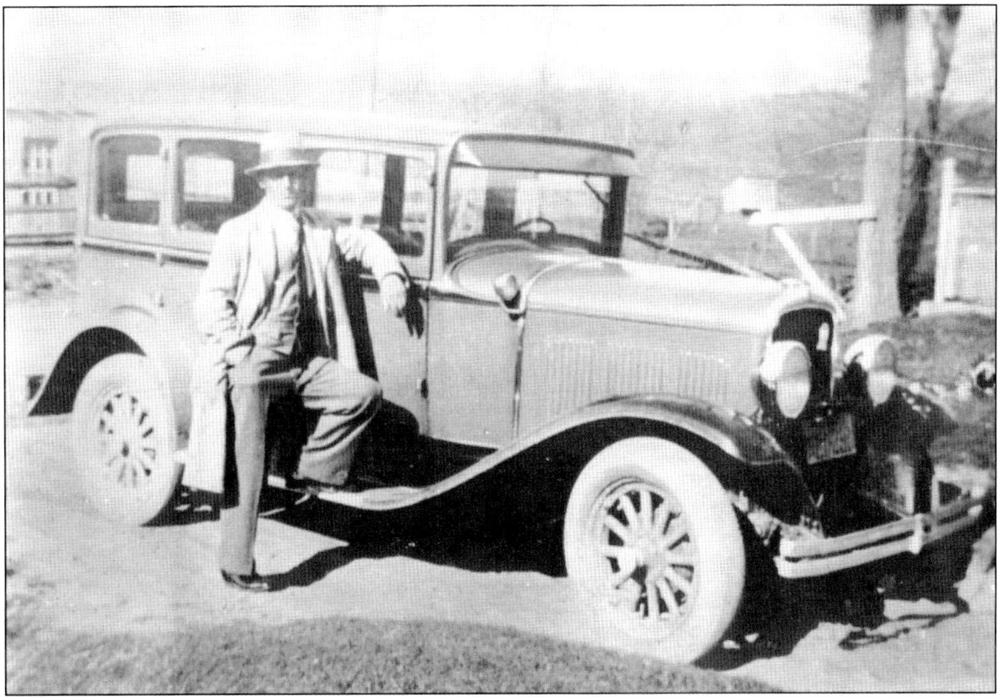

Roy Hoffer (1893–1965) is dapperly dressed, complete with a fedora, and seen here standing next to his car. Hoffer owned the Brunnerville Hotel during the 1920s and operated the business for several years. When cars were first commercially introduced, only the more well-to-do citizens of the community could afford to purchase them. (Courtesy of Catherine Hoffer.)

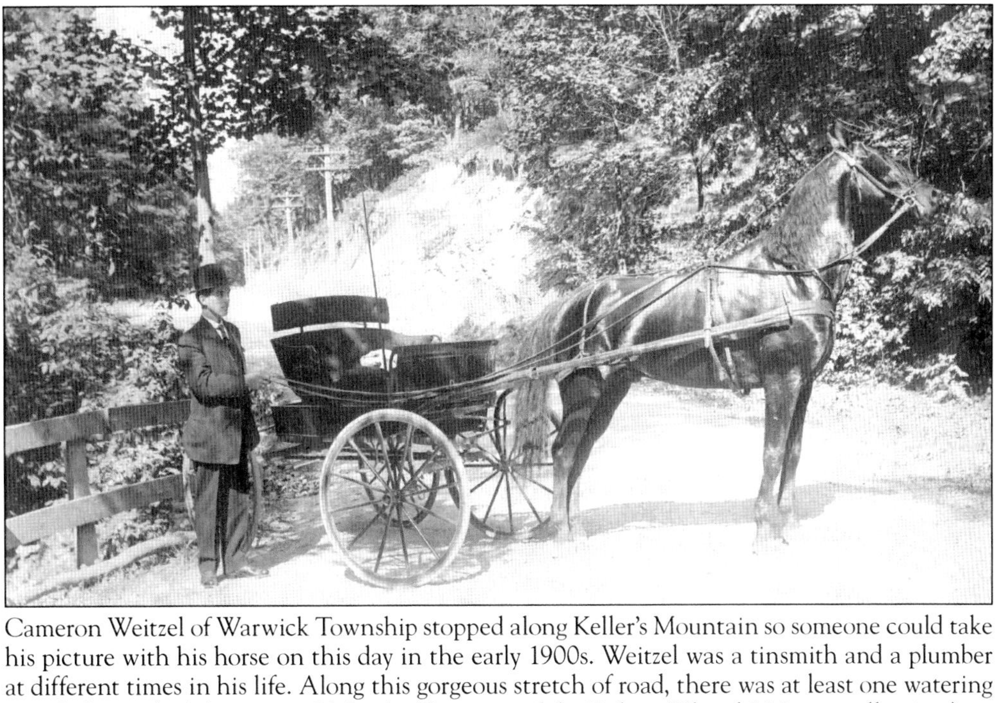

Cameron Weitzel of Warwick Township stopped along Keller's Mountain so someone could take his picture with his horse on this day in the early 1900s. Weitzel was a tinsmith and a plumber at different times in his life. Along this gorgeous stretch of road, there was at least one watering trough from which horses could drink. (Courtesy of the Robert "Sketch" Mearig collection.)

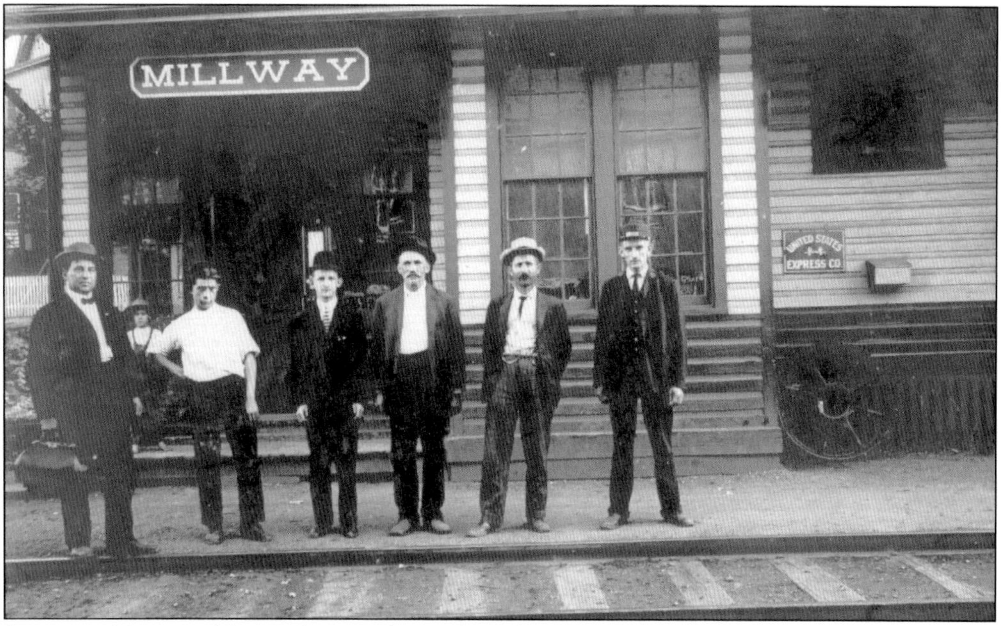

Serving as Moore and Reitz's shipping depot, the Millway passenger and freight station also provided a very important service for neighboring residents. It was here that the mail for Rothsville was picked up and sent off every day. Joe Usner of Rothsville was in charge of this task for several years. After leaving Millway, trains would head toward the next destination, the Ephrata station. (Courtesy of John David Wissler.)

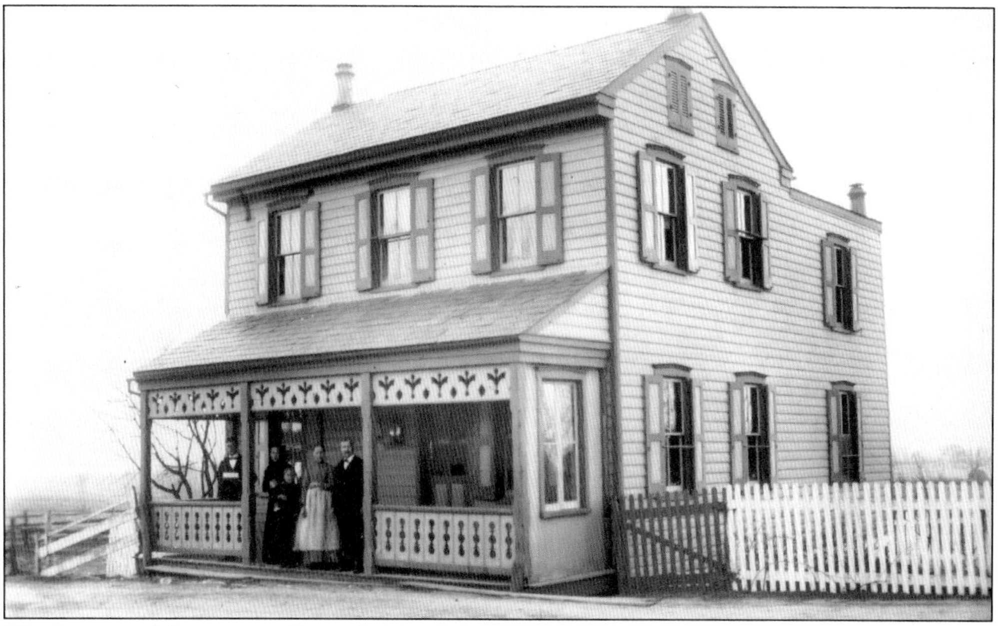

The Lititz and Lexington Turnpike was created in 1882 at a meeting at the Kemper House in Lititz, where a stock company was also formed. This tollhouse was built on the southwest corner of the intersection of Newport Road and Lititz Pike. If the motorist went through this toll and eventually came back the same way, the total was 9¢. (Courtesy of the Robert "Sketch" Mearig collection.)

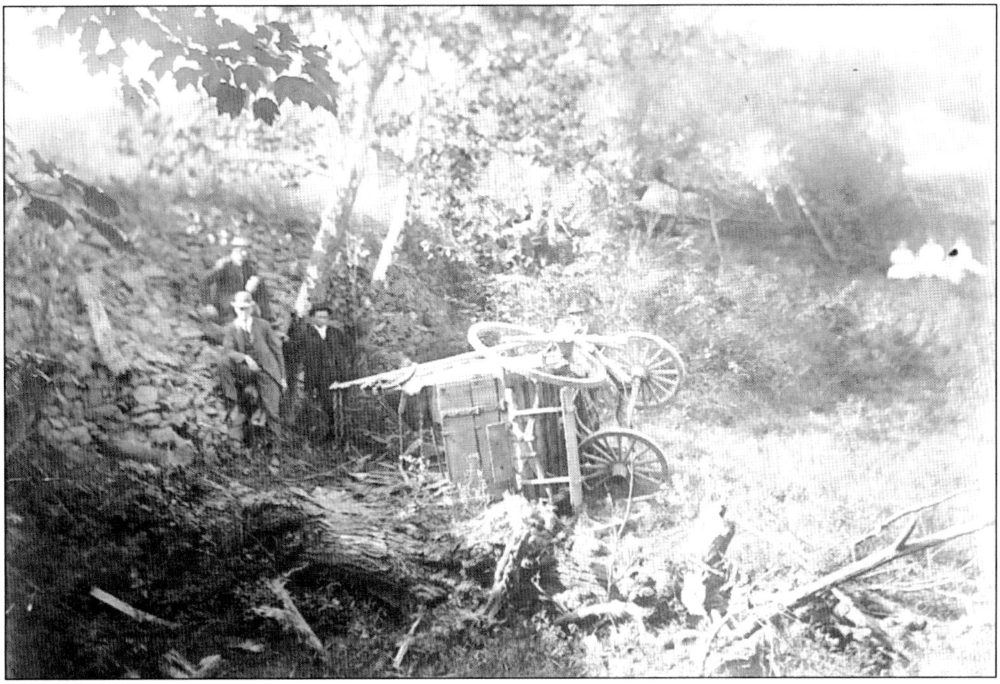

Educator Nathan "Dad" Reist took many pictures of the township, including those of mills, schools, and everyday life in the early 1900s. He even happened to capture the wreck of this wagon when the driver lost control and the wagon rolled down the embankment along the road to Brunnerville near Yerger's Ice Dam. (Courtesy of private collection.)

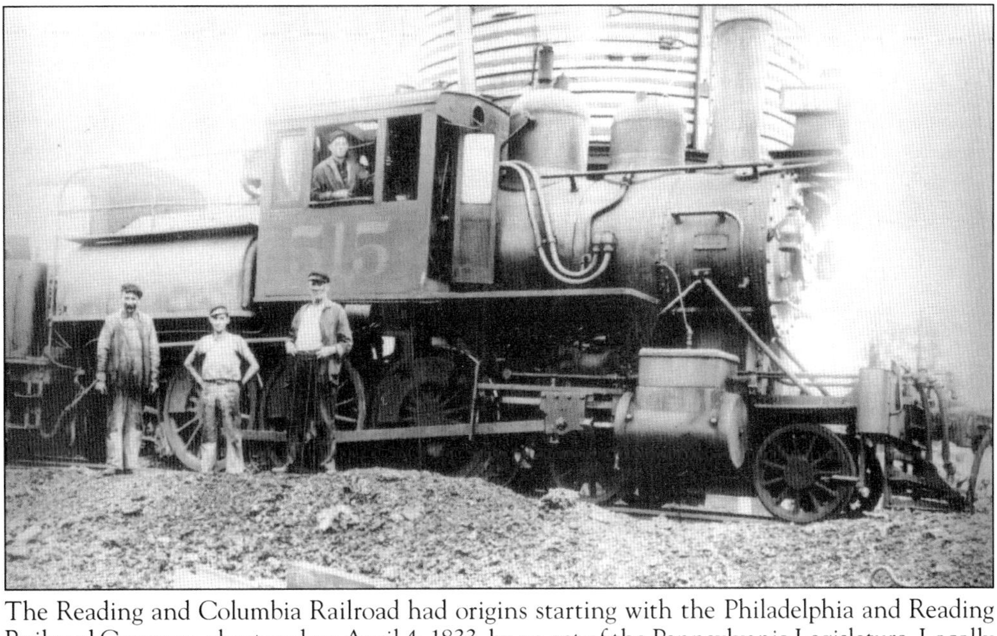

The Reading and Columbia Railroad had origins starting with the Philadelphia and Reading Railroad Company chartered on April 4, 1833, by an act of the Pennsylvania Legislature. Locally the idea of a railroad system was first thought of by Joseph Konigmacher of Ephrata. Engine No. 515 4-6-0 and crew gathered around 1905, stopping beside Millway's water tank as seen above. (Courtesy of Ronald Reedy, from the John Denny collection.)

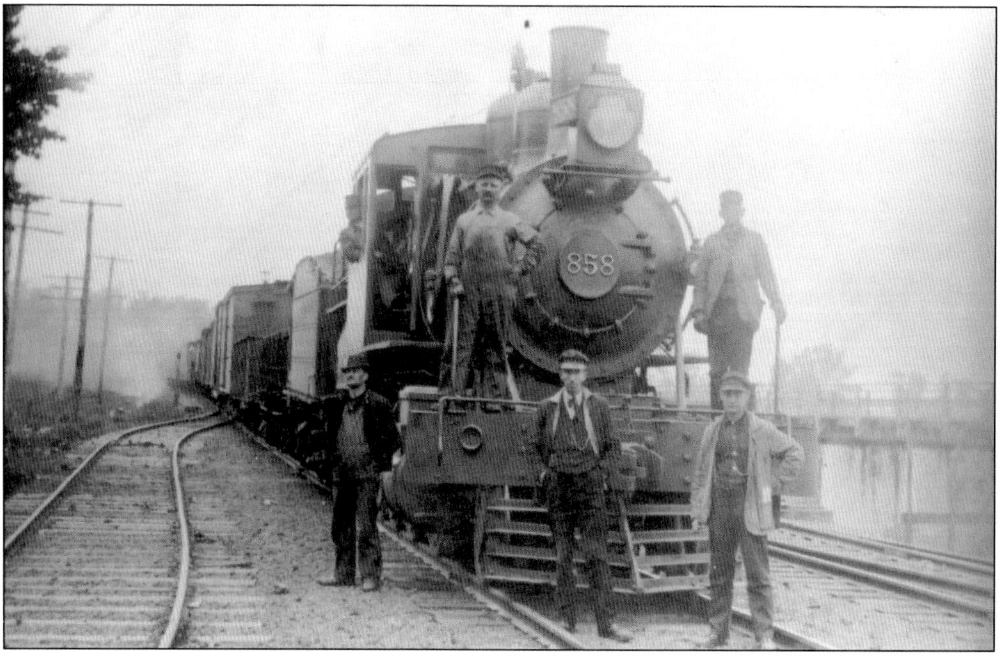

Signed by Gov. James Pollock on May 19, 1857, the Reading and Columbia Railroad line was officially chartered, and by December 1860, the location and survey of this line was completed. Train No. 858 carried local freight into Millway from Lititz. The station's track can be seen at far left, with the passing side to the locomotive's immediate right. (Courtesy of Ronald Reedy, from the John Denny collection.)

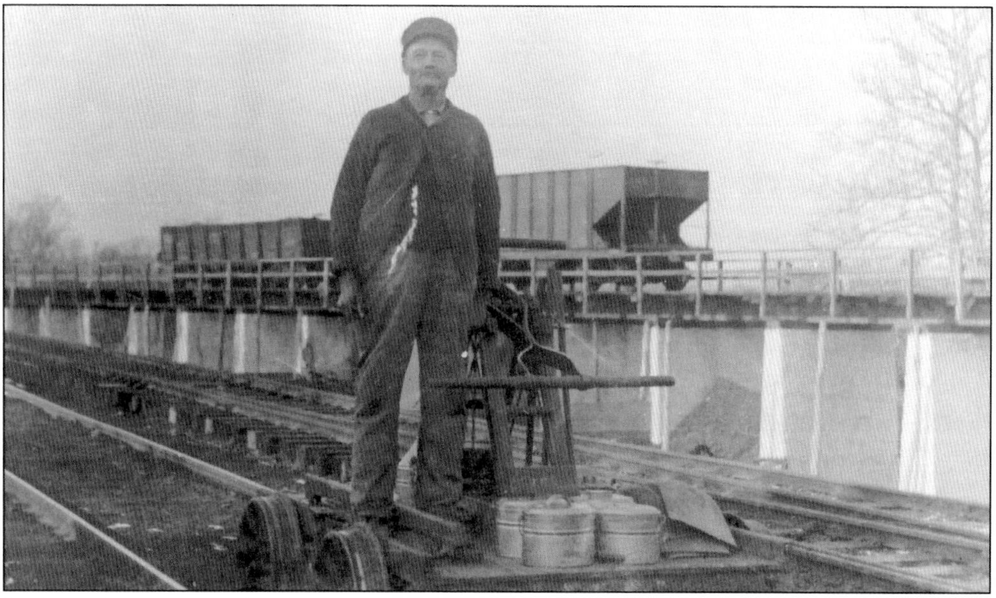

Sinking Spring was to be the starting point of this new rail system, for it was at this location where it could connect with the Lebanon Valley Railroad. The line would then run to Reinholds, Stevens, Ephrata, Akron, Millway, Rothsville, Lititz, and Manheim, continuing on to Columbia. Section foreman Dan Smith often operated the handcar at Millway in the early 1900s. (Courtesy of Ronald Reedy, from the John Denny collection.)

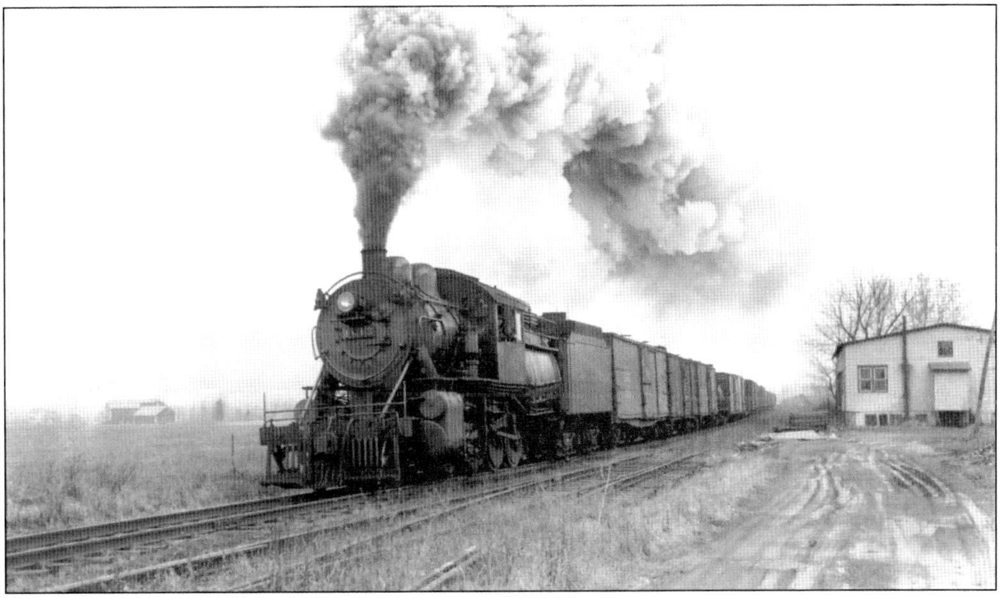

In February 1941, with smoke billowing from its stack, the "Night Buck" or Camel Back No. 1613 engine left Rothsville Station heading toward Lititz. Facing more modern transportation methods, including automobiles and the evolving mass-trucking industry (which could carry heavier loads) and several merges, the Reading Company, which owned the Reading and Columbia Railroad, went bankrupt. (Courtesy of Ronald Reedy, from the John Denny collection.)

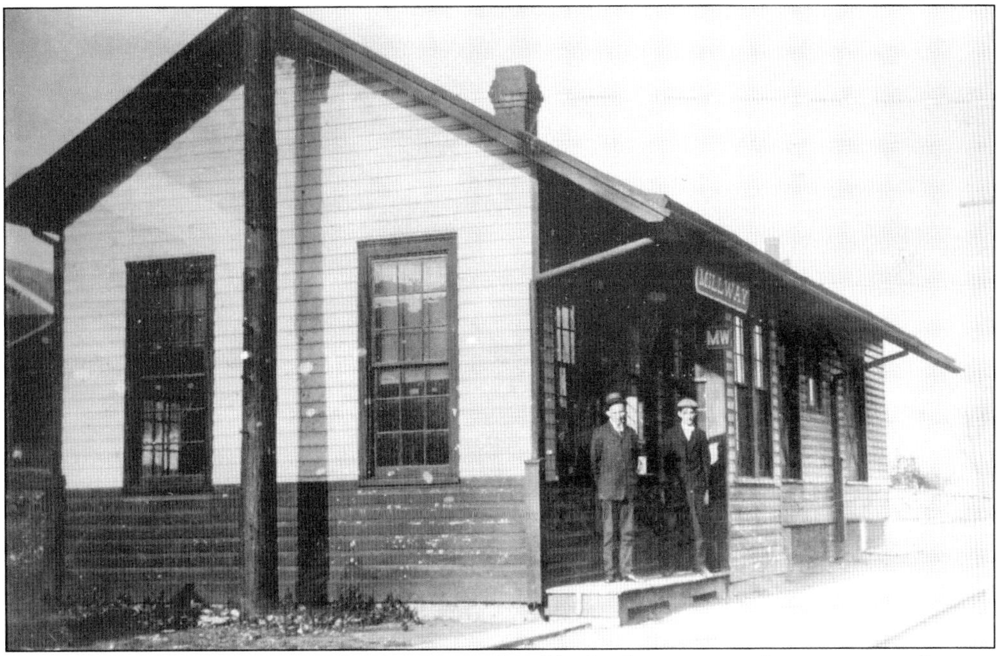

Each stop along the Reading and Columbia Railroad had a depot station. In some cases, the stop was only to pick up freight, and in other cases freight and passengers were picked up. Millway station served both purposes. This photograph was taken between 1906 and 1908 and shows acting Millway agent Ralph Holland on the right. (Courtesy of Ronald Reedy, from the John Denny collection.)

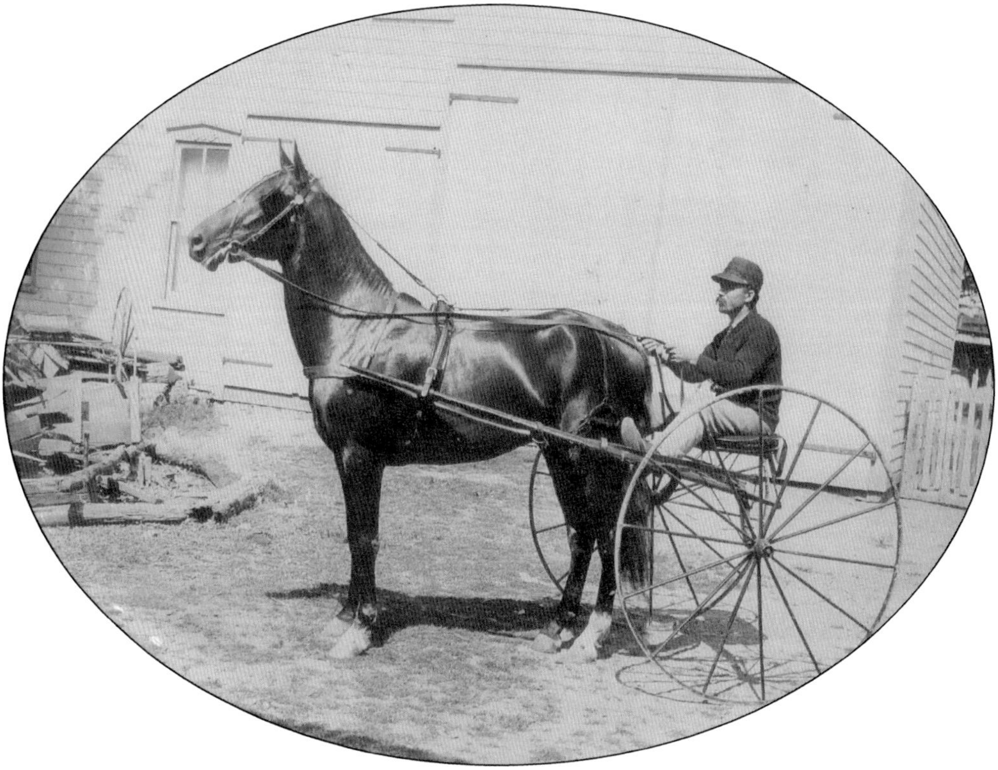

This early transportation method certainly got a lot of attention. Constable Allen Butzer is at the helm, ready to serve and protect the citizens of Rothsville. Born in 1862, by 1900 and spanning over 10 years of his life, Butzer worked as one of the many cigar makers in the township. The setting of this photograph is behind the Rothsville Carriage Works. (Courtesy of Sharyn Deater.)

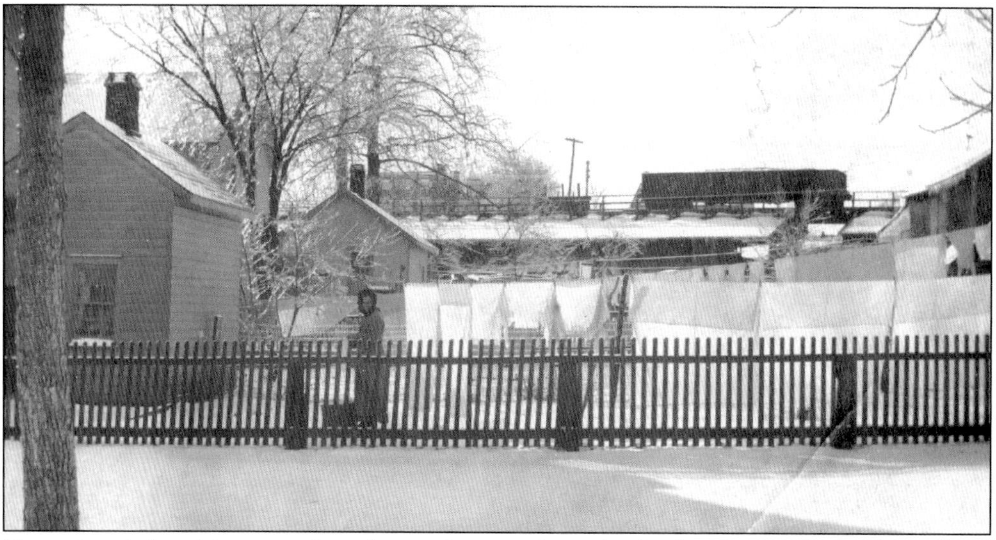

On a winter's day, this woman hung her wash out to dry in her backyard in Millway. The Millway train can be seen passing through the town. Goods had to be delivered and picked up even in the coldest of conditions. Although the train was a great convenience to the community, the sound at night no doubt woke many residents. (Courtesy of John David Wissler.)

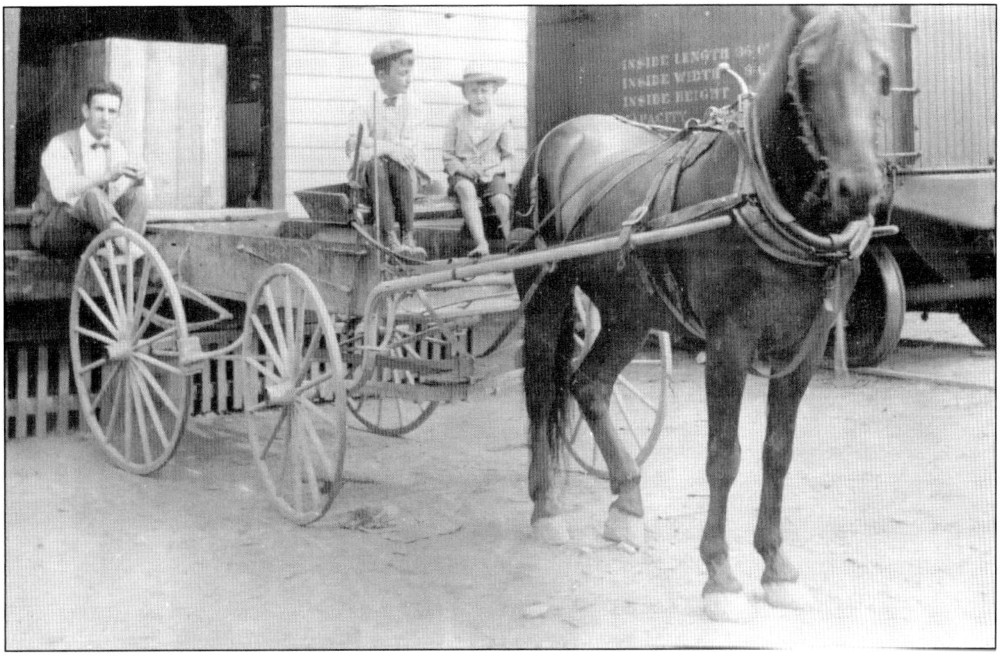

Two boys sat at the front of this spring wagon in front of Millway Station. The wagon was most likely driven there by the gentleman sitting alongside the dock. It is unknown whether the case of tobacco that can be seen on the dock was dropped off by the train or being readied to be shipped off to a cigar manufacturer in a neighboring community. (Courtesy of Ron Reedy, from the John Denny collection.)

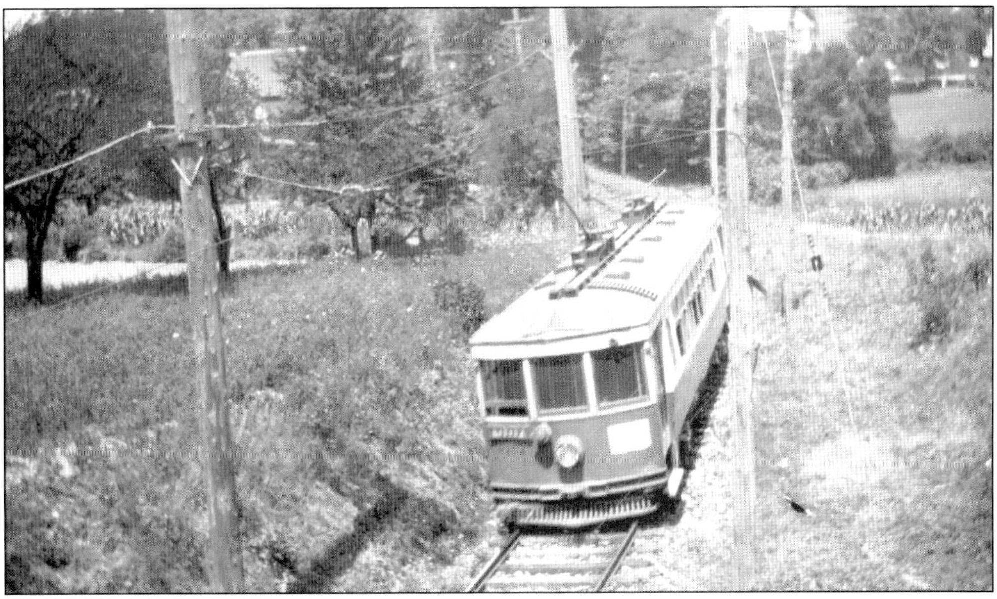

A Lititz car passes through Kissel Hill. A group of citizens met on February 6, 1890, to consider establishing a trolley line to run from Lancaster to Lititz. The Lancaster Traction Company, chartered on March 7, 1893, was an effort to combine and operate numerous street railways around the county. By 1894, this company leased the Lititz and Lancaster Turnpike for 999 years. (Courtesy of Ronald Reedy, from the John Denny collection.)

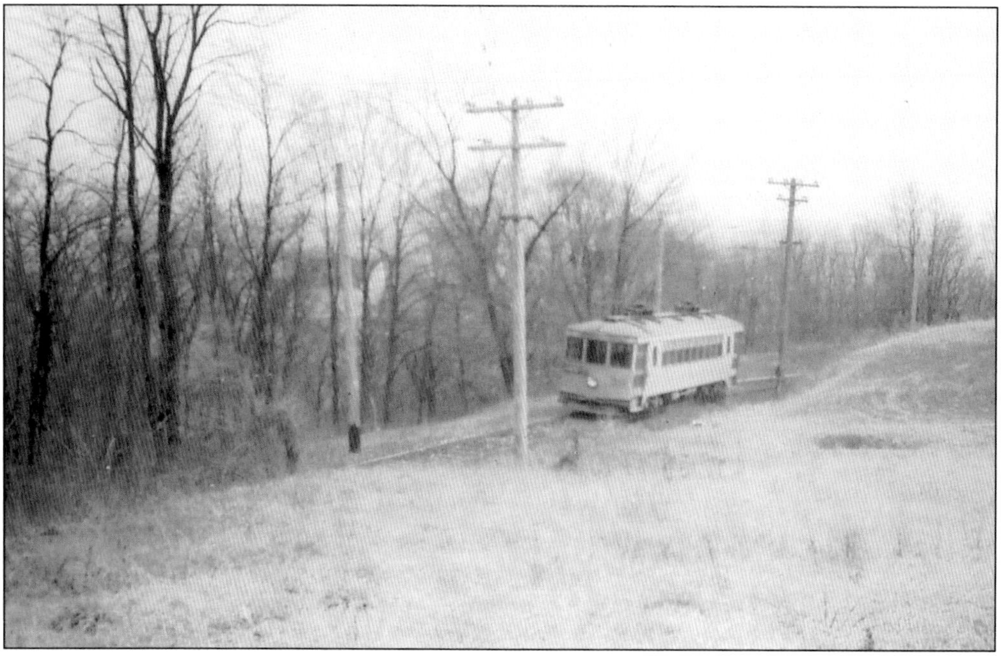

The Kissel Hill portion was completed by April 30, 1895. Trolley cars lacked much horsepower, therefore cars traveling through Kissel Hill had to be rerouted around scenic woods along Lititz Pike in an "S" curve. It veered to the east and then crossed over East Woods Drive, arriving at the bottom of a small hill where, a trolley stop was erected. (Courtesy of the author's collection.)

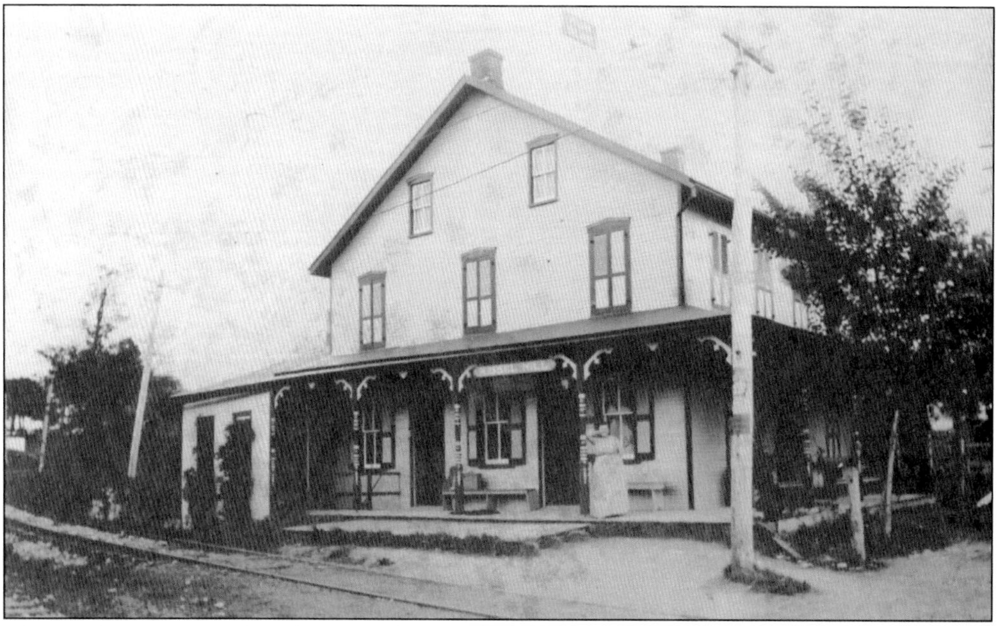

This trolley stop served as the post office and general store for Kissel Hill. It was operated by Andrew Dunlap and his wife when this photograph was taken. It also was a stopping place for the night, as travelers could rent a room at the Kissel Hill Hotel and then purchase supplies at Dunlap's before continuing on their trip. The post office closed on December 31, 1918. (Courtesy of Polly Garner.)

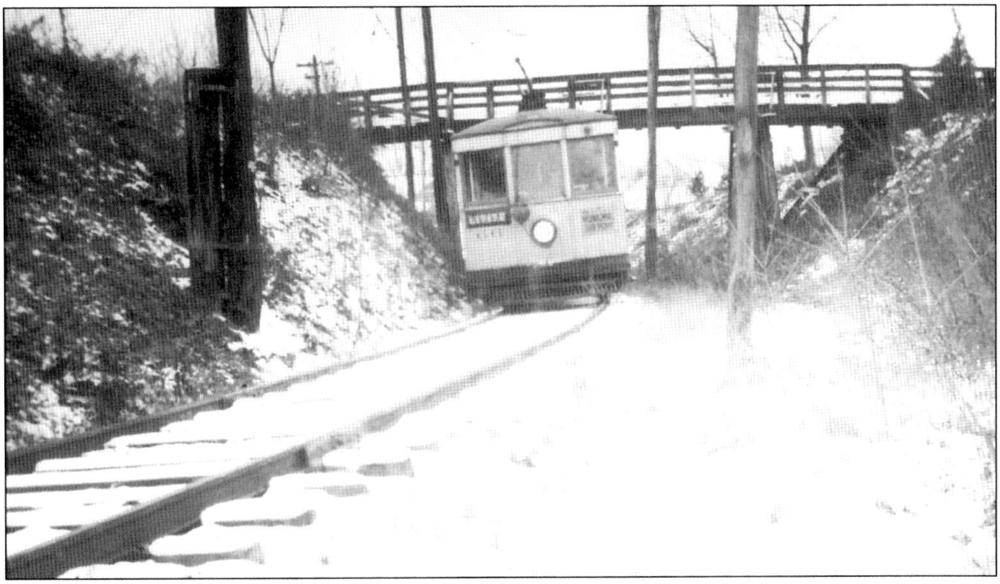

The trolley proved to be an effective and popular method of transportation. In 1900, several members of the Conestoga Traction Company discussed a proposal to extend the Lititz line north to Lexington. This idea never came to pass, and it can be assumed that the hill on the road connecting Lititz to Lexington proved to be too steep for transportation. (Courtesy of Ronald Reedy, from the John Denny collection.)

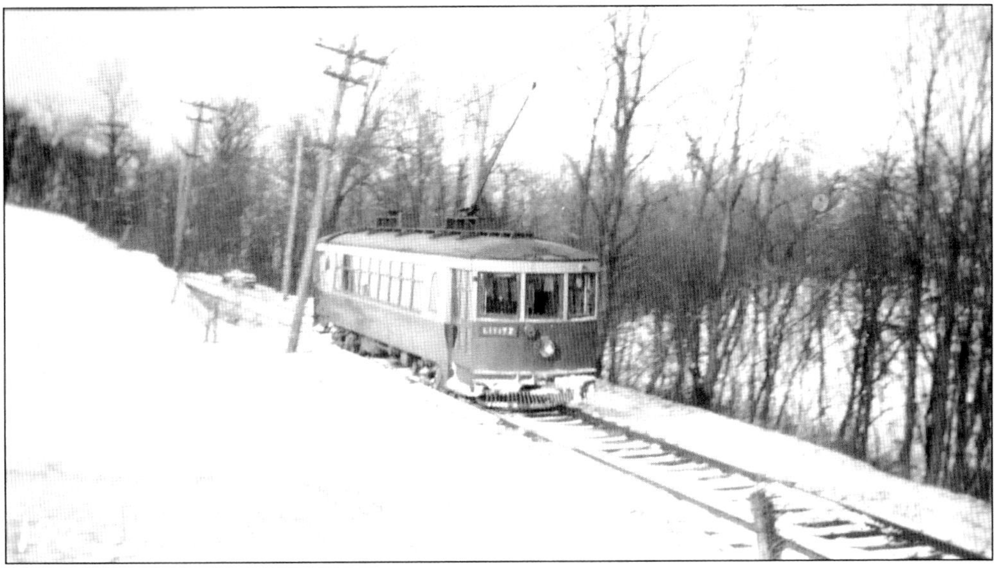

By 1932, the Conestoga Transit Company (the name by which the company was now known) replaced trolleys with buses all over the county. This more modern means of transportation, which did not depend on overhead electric wires and tracks in the roadway, proved to be a safer method of travel. The year 1938 saw the last trolley run through Kissel Hill. (Courtesy of the Robert "Sketch" Mearig collection.)

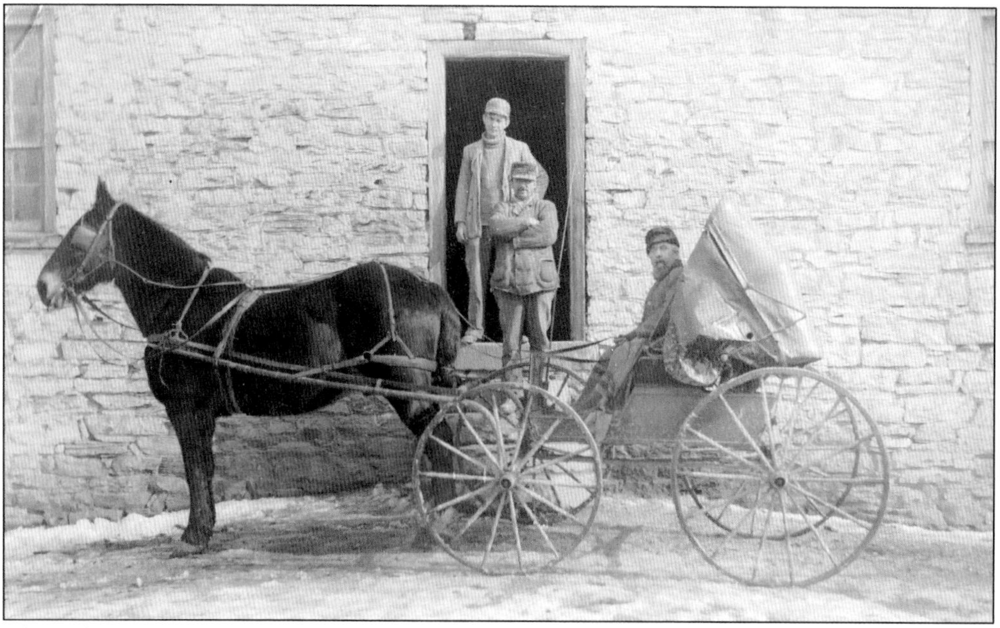

These three men were the hardworking employees of the mill located in Millway. Owners of companies often delivered their own goods to their customers around the county. Oftentimes thin wagon wheels would break from the roughness of the unpaved dirt roads. Delivery would be delayed as the operators walked back to their businesses to get another wagon to finish the delivery. (Courtesy of John David Wissler.)

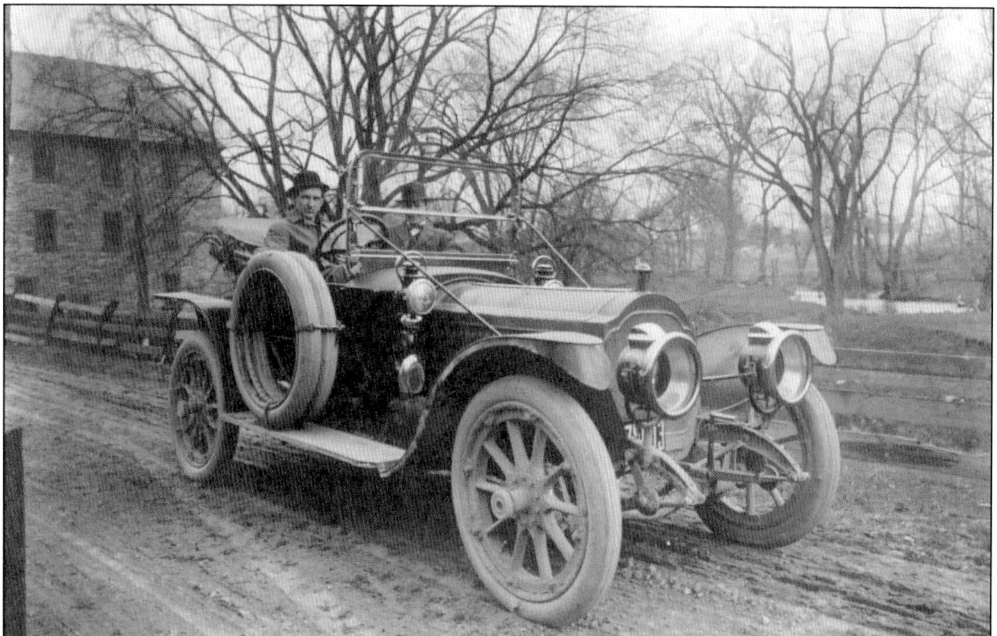

Shown in detail are the dirt roads and rough terrain that were traveled on every day by both horses and automobiles. This photograph of men dressed in suits and bow ties in an old-fashioned Packard car was taken by A. R. Holland of Millway. Note the old wooden fence located along the edge of the road with the mill in the background. (Courtesy of John David Wissler.)

Four

BUSINESSES

As more and more people settled in Warwick Township, trading and commerce began to play an important role in the area's economic growth. In the early years, businesses such as gristmills and sawmills began and prospered. Farming, including the raising of grain and foods as well as the planting, harvesting, and eventual sale of tobacco for smoking or chewing, played a key role. As more and more families grew into established villages, the demand was created for more products that could be purchased. Skilled laborers and craftsmen worked long hours at dangerous jobs to satisfy the needs of their customers and neighbors. Whether it was operating a round-the-clock hotel, pouring molten iron into molds, tending to livestock and milking cows early in the morning, or running the corner store, it can certainly be stated that businesses within the township were diverse.

As more modern machinery and new patents were developed through the years, it either meant more income for a company or it caused its downfall. One example is the cigar industry. For many years, the manufacturing and hand-rolling of cigars employed a large number of the residents. Once an automatic rolling machine was developed and patented, skilled human hands were no longer needed, and companies found themselves having to lay off hundreds of employees. The mom-and-pop corner stores suffered the same fate when more modern 24-hour gasoline stations and warehouse-sized grocery stores began to open.

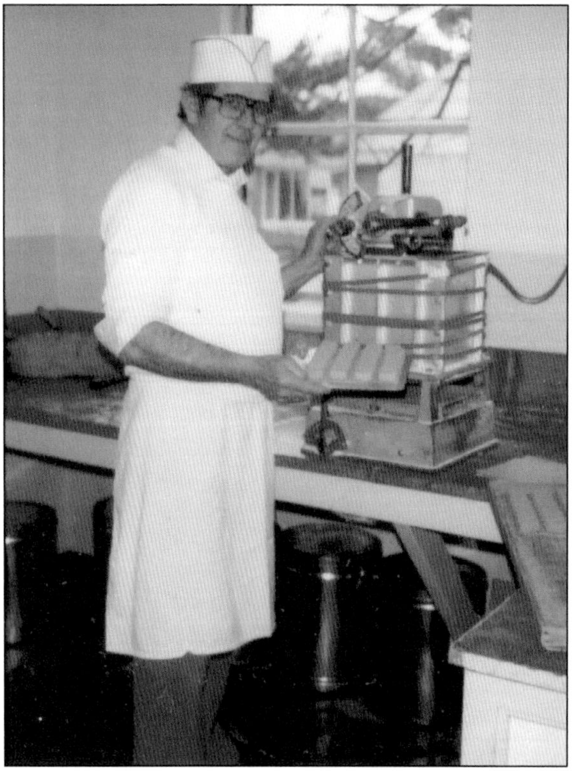

Kline's Candy was started by Norman B. Kline in Lancaster in the early part of the 20th century and eventually relocated to Lexington. There they produced seasonal candy, including peppermints, peanut chews, chocolate Easter eggs, vanilla butter creams, peanut clusters, chocolate covered marshmallows, and other treats. In the beginning, all of the sweet treats were hand dipped, but as the business began to thrive, modern machinery was added to the operation, including a chocolate enrober. At the height of the business, seven people were employed, including five girls who packed the candy. Ken Zook and his wife, Dorothy, are pictured here working long hours to create these delicious confections. During one Easter season, a huge 25-pound egg was specially made for a man to give to his special girl. (Both, courtesy of Dorothy Zook.)

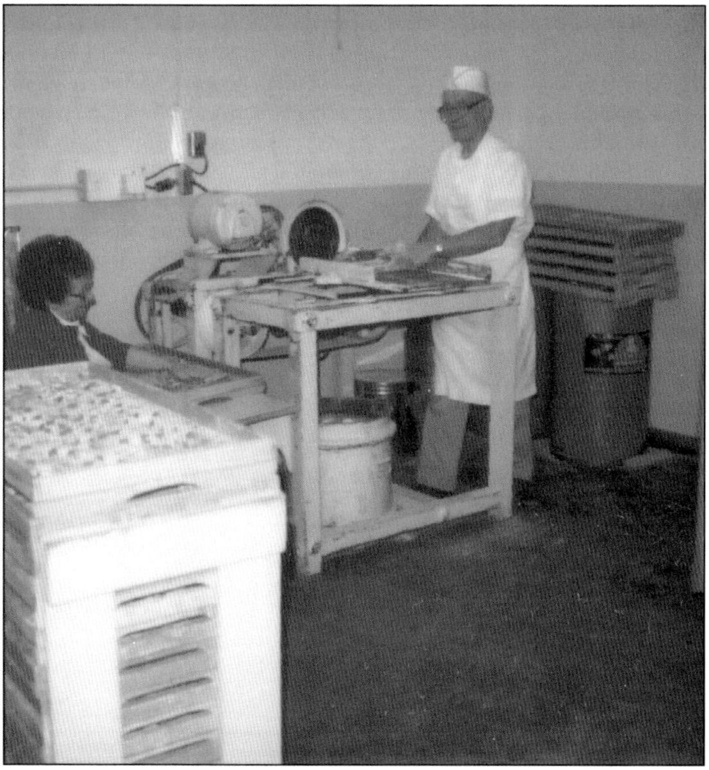

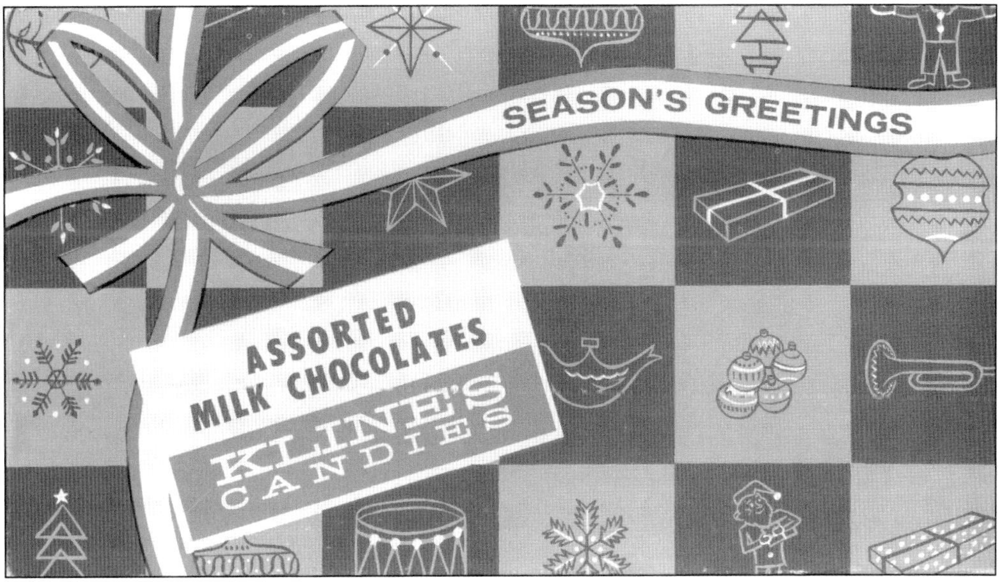

In summer months, potato chips and popcorn were produced. Norman Kline, Norman Kline Jr., and Ken Zook eventually became the three owners to the business. The operation was closed in the mid-1980s when the owners decided to retire. Christmas was a very busy time for the business, and this beautifully decorated box of assorted chocolates was sure to please somebody special during the holiday season. (Courtesy of the author's collection.)

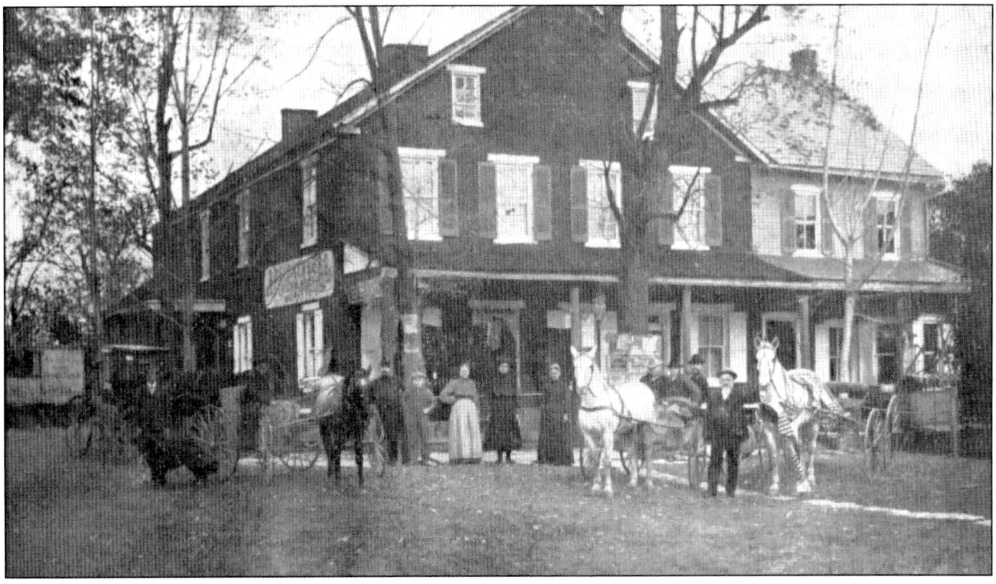

Eichenberg's Store in Millway supplied local farmers and residents with household and personal goods of many kinds. Simon Eichenberg (1848–1918) owned this operation for many years, with the business coming to an end on January 18, 1918, when he died. An advertisement in 1913 stated "Eichenberg's carries one of the largest stocks of general merchandise to be found in a country store." (Courtesy of the Robert "Sketch" Mearig collection.)

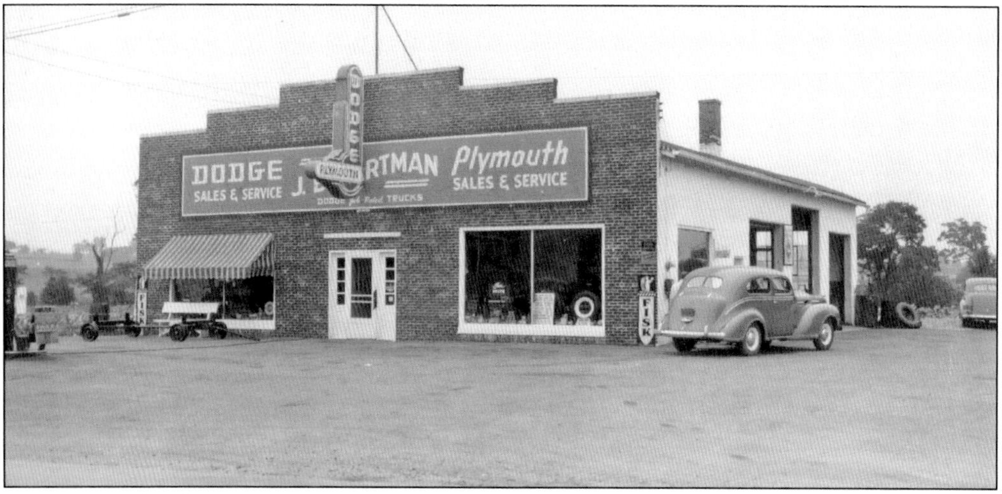

Zartman Dodge, located on Route 501, was opened in the summer of 1945 by John B. Zartman. Originally selling Dodge and Plymouth automobiles, by 1960 it was a Dodge dealership exclusively. John's son Glenn started working there in 1967 washing cars, eventually becoming owner. The business prospered for many years, and in 2006, it was sold to Keller Brothers of Lititz, another car dealership in the area. (Courtesy of Glenn Zartman.)

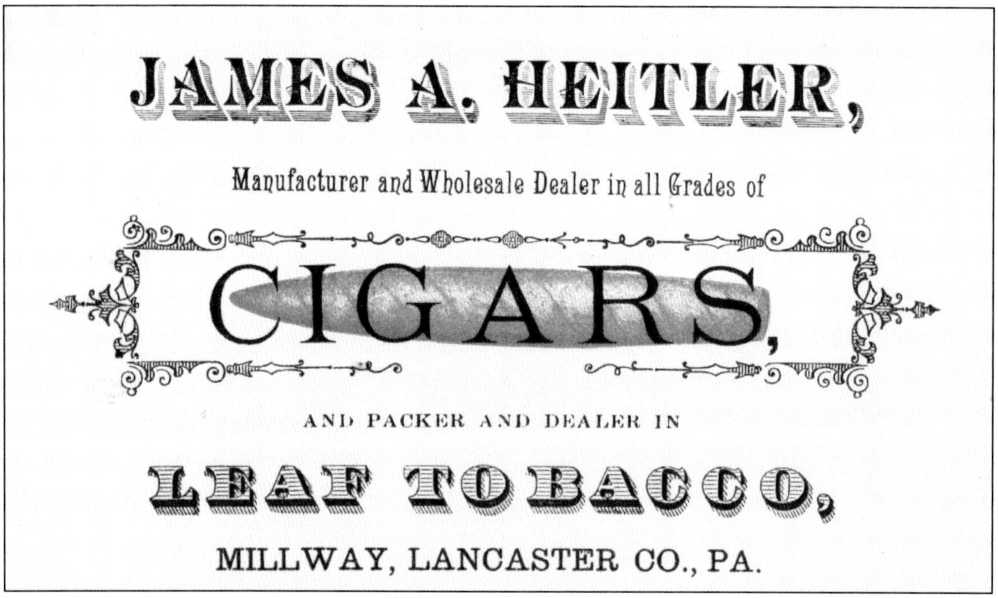

James A. Heitler rolled, packed, and sold his own cigars in Millway. He moved to Rothsville in the 1880s and became a well-rounded businessman, at different times owning a store, manufacturing furniture, and serving as an undertaker and a photographer. Somehow, he even found time to become the minister of the United Zion Church of Rothsville. (Courtesy of the Robert "Sketch" Mearig collection.)

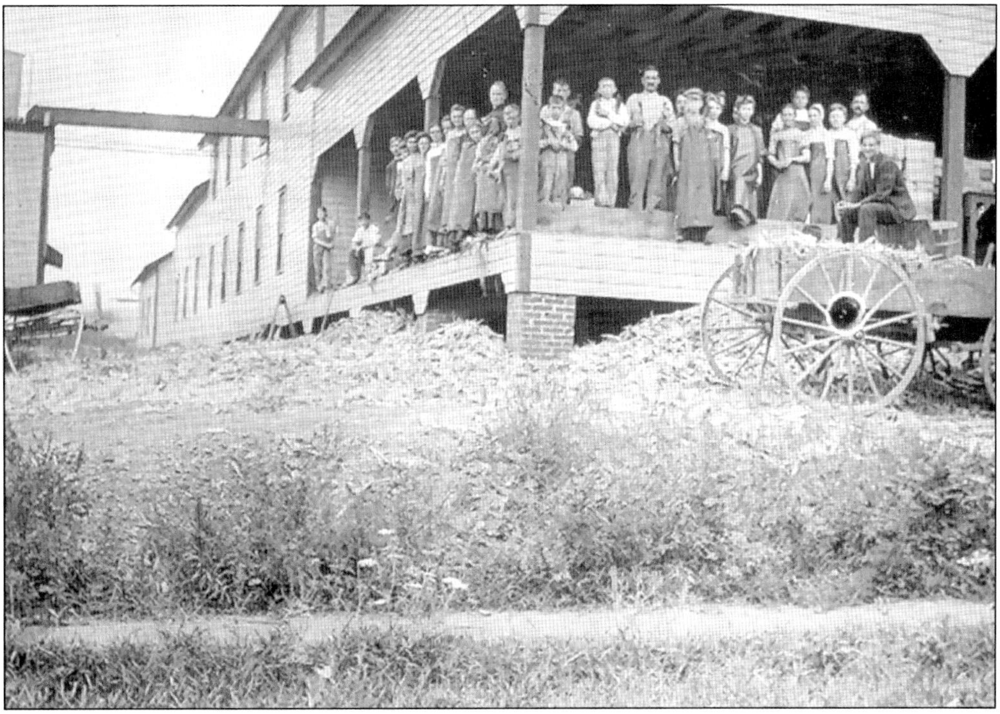

The Ideal Canning Company in Rothsville was founded in 1904. Some of Rothsville's most prominent businessmen, including Jefferson Usner, John F. Ruth, Noah G. Hess, and Tobias H. Snavely, invested in this business to help get the company started. The plant processed and packed Our Favorite Brand tomatoes and Cuckoo brand corn. By 1905, the company showed signs of financial problems, with money becoming so tight that the owners paid treasurer Samuel Ruth in canned goods instead of real dollars. In 1907, the company was able to pay off all of its debts with the exception of that which was owed to Hiram Buckwalter, who was one of the founding investors. Instead of payment, Buckwalter took over the building, which he converted to a tobacco distribution and processing plant. (Above, courtesy of private collection; below, courtesy of the author's collection.)

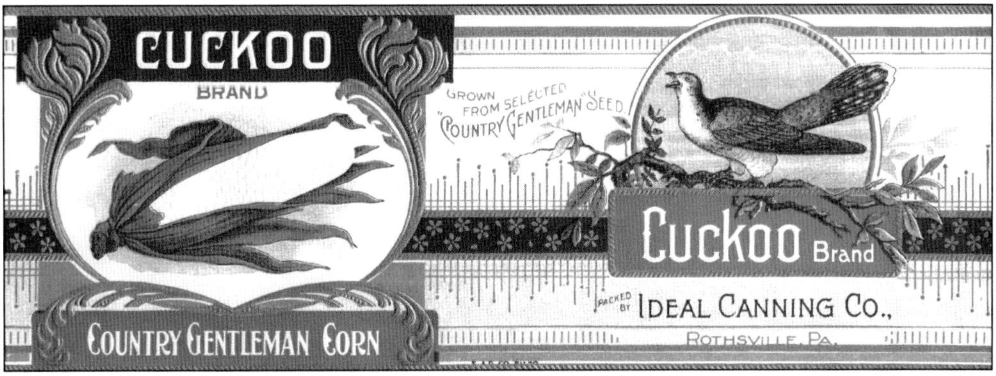

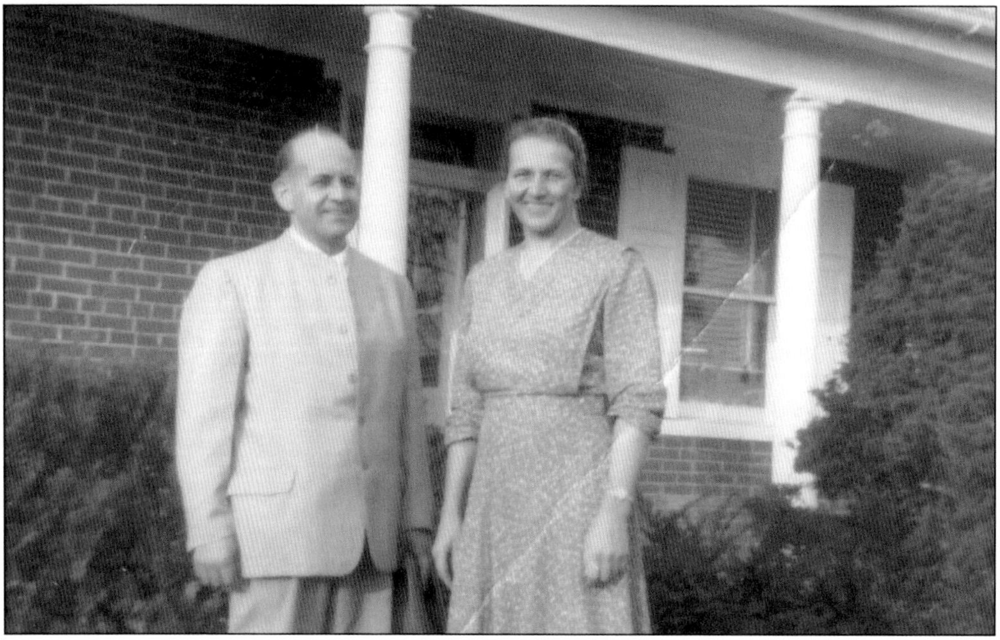

Born and raised on the Stauffer fruit farm in Warwick Township, Roy M. Stauffer Sr. operated a fruit stand on the south side of Kissel Hill. In 1937 the stand was destroyed by fire. That year, a front yard stand was opened on the grounds of the Stauffer property, and cantaloupes and watermelons were added to the inventory. The business grew, with a store eventually built at 813 Lititz Pike. Products, including flowers, shrubs, and trees, were added to their inventory during this time. Eventually, several employees, including family members, were added to the payroll to help with the ever-increasing customer base. In 1952, Roy underwent surgery and died the following year. In Roy's absence, his wife and children continued to operate the business under the management of Roy Jr. (Both, courtesy of Stauffer's of Kissel Hill.)

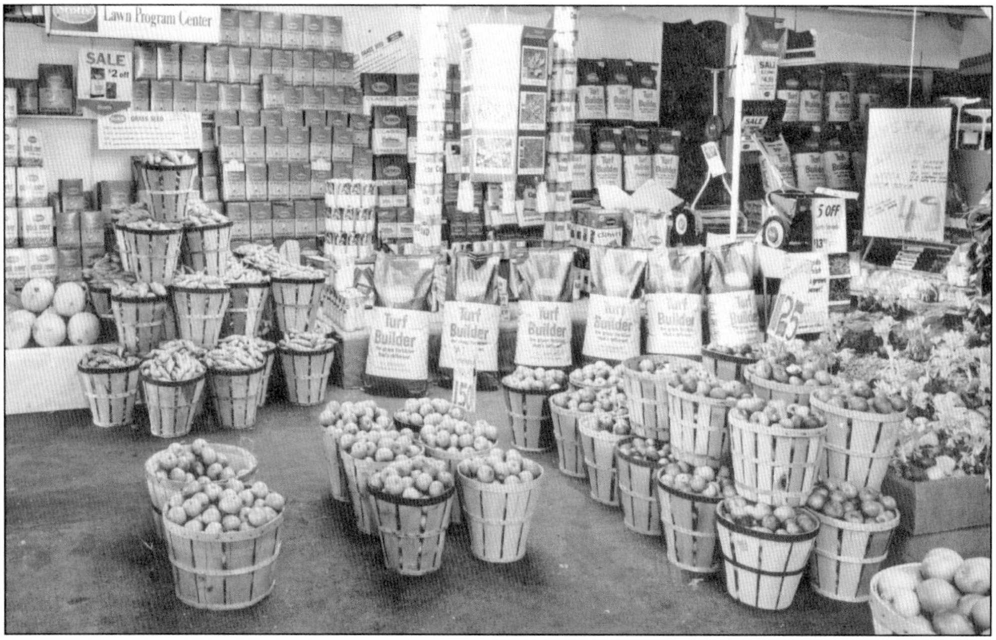

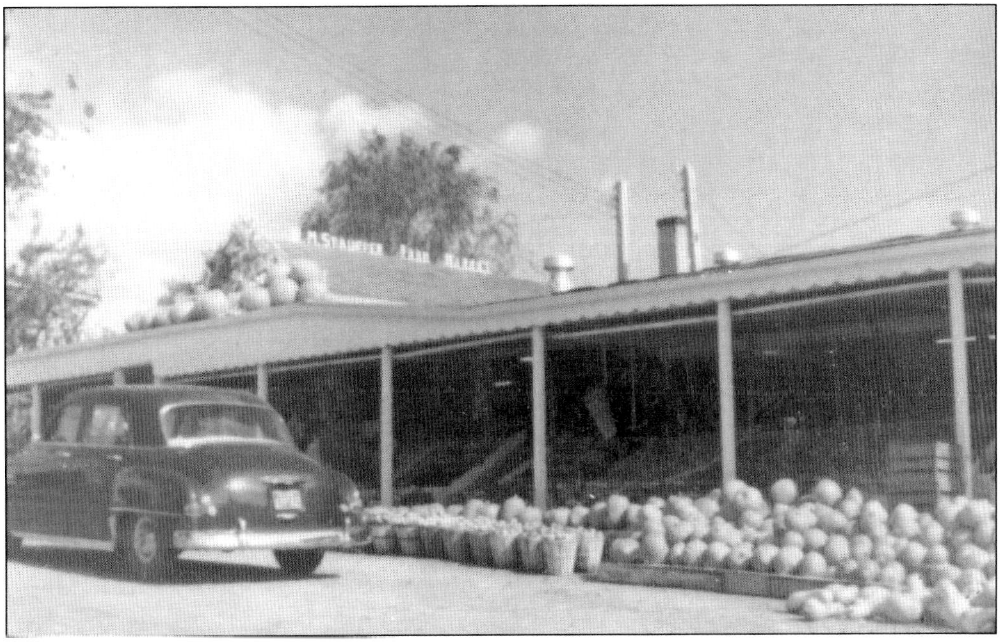

In 1956, Roy Satuffer Jr. and Jay Oberholtzer formed a partnership and rented the business. Stauffer's continued to prosper, with a second store opening in 1964 on the Oregon Pike near Lancaster. In 1983, a 20-acre plot of land was purchased on the northwest corner of Lititz Pike and Millport Road. This larger location was opened in 1985, replacing the older store that was located on Lititz Pike. (Courtesy of Stauffer's of Kissel Hill.)

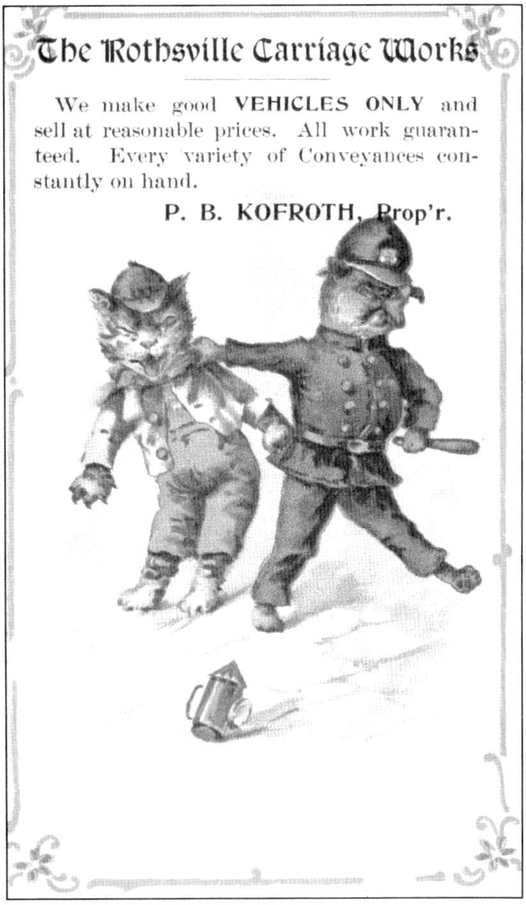

The Rothsville Carriage Works was located along Newport Road. In 1875, John Lowry was the owner of the business, and during that time, he also operated the Rothsville Hotel. By 1878, Preston B. Kofroth was owner, learning the craft of coach making from S. and H. Grosh of Lititz. Under Kofroth's ownership, horse-drawn carriages, firefighting equipment, and sleighs were built. (Courtesy of the Robert "Sketch" Mearig collection.)

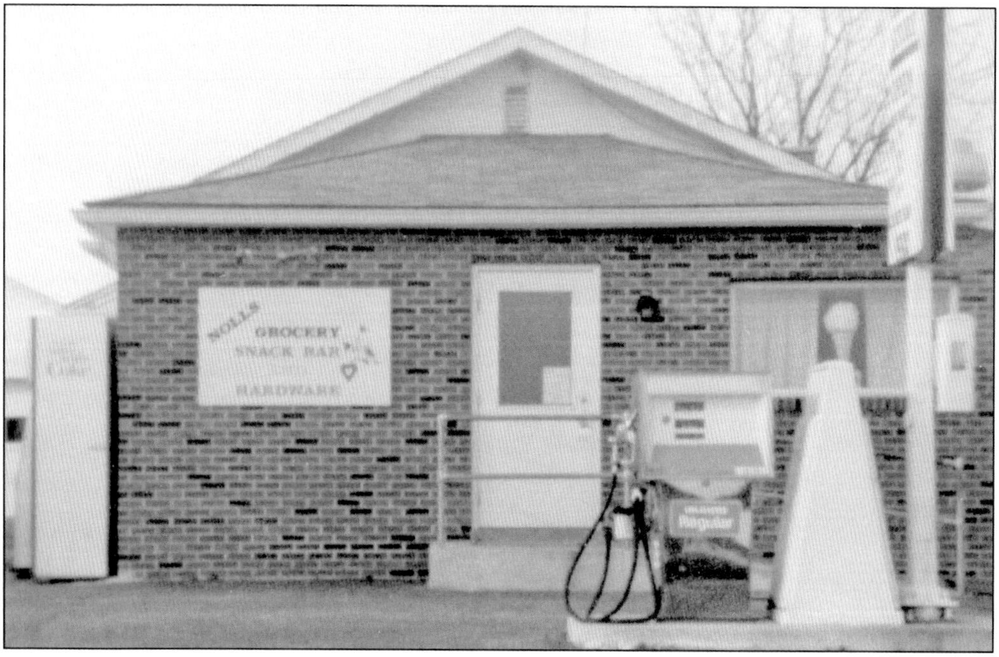

Midway is a small area "midway" between Lexington and Brunnerville. About 1950, a gentleman with the last name of Carpenter opened a store along this road at 305 East Lexington Road. After a few years, the store and adjoining property, which included a house, were sold to the Mann family, with Charles and Violet Noll eventually purchasing the properties in 1977. During Noll's ownership, the store's inventory increased to include hardware, gasoline, candy, and even hand-dipped ice cream. In 1982, the store and home went up for public sale and was purchased by the Metzger family, who ran the store for about two years, eventually selling the property to Richard Haller. Below, a winter storm made for a great picture as Kenneth Noll stands next to a giant snow mound in the early 1980s. (Both, courtesy of Violet Noll.)

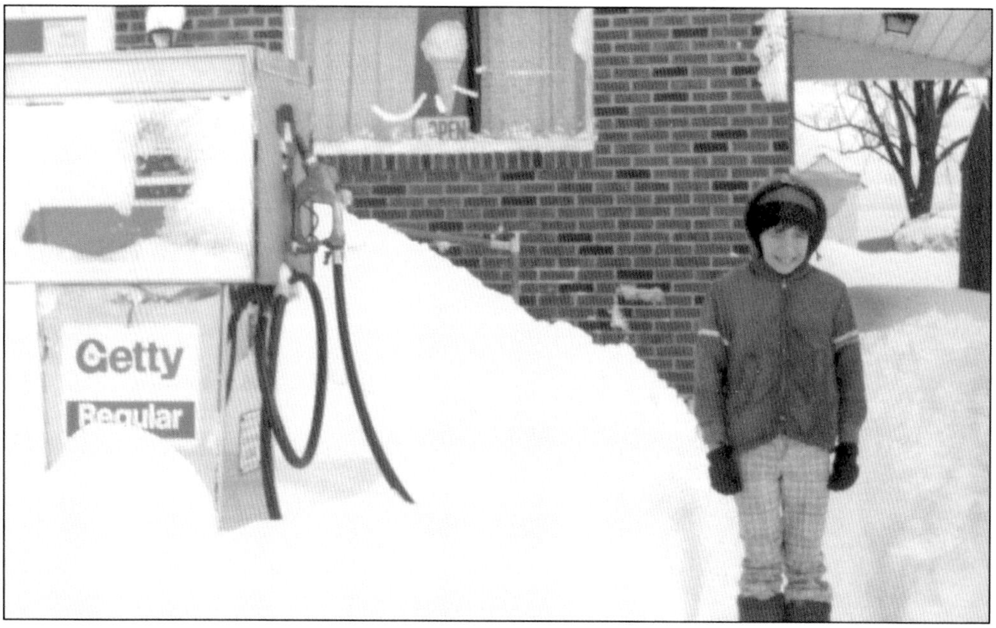

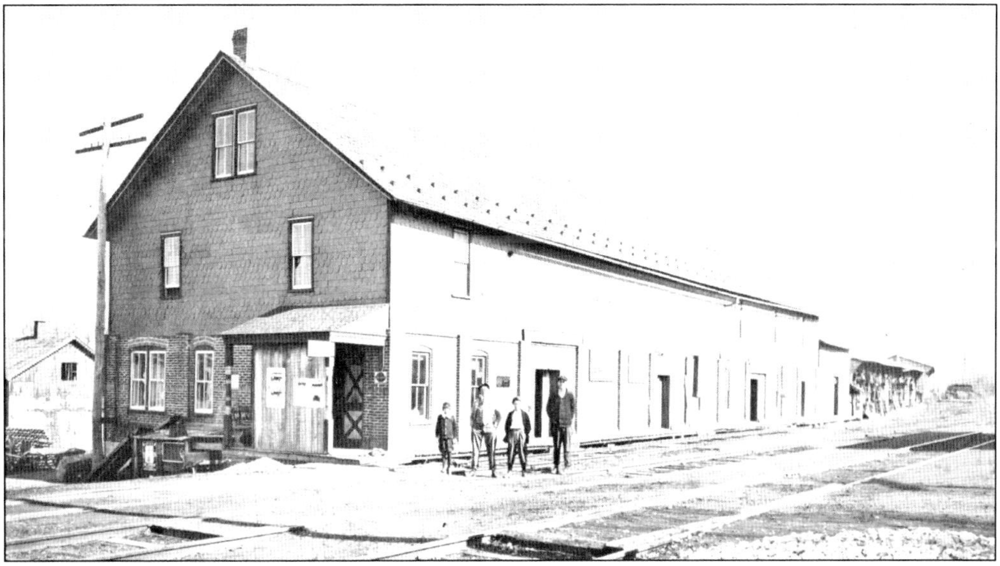

In April 1902, the Moore and Reitz Company of Millway began with partners John H. Reitz and his brother-in-law Elam S. Moore. They offered farm implements, feed, fertilizer, and grain. By 1908, Reitz became full owner and saw the company prosper to great heights. During that same year, a devastating fire destroyed much of the company's inventory and warehouses. (Courtesy of the Robert "Sketch" Mearig collection.)

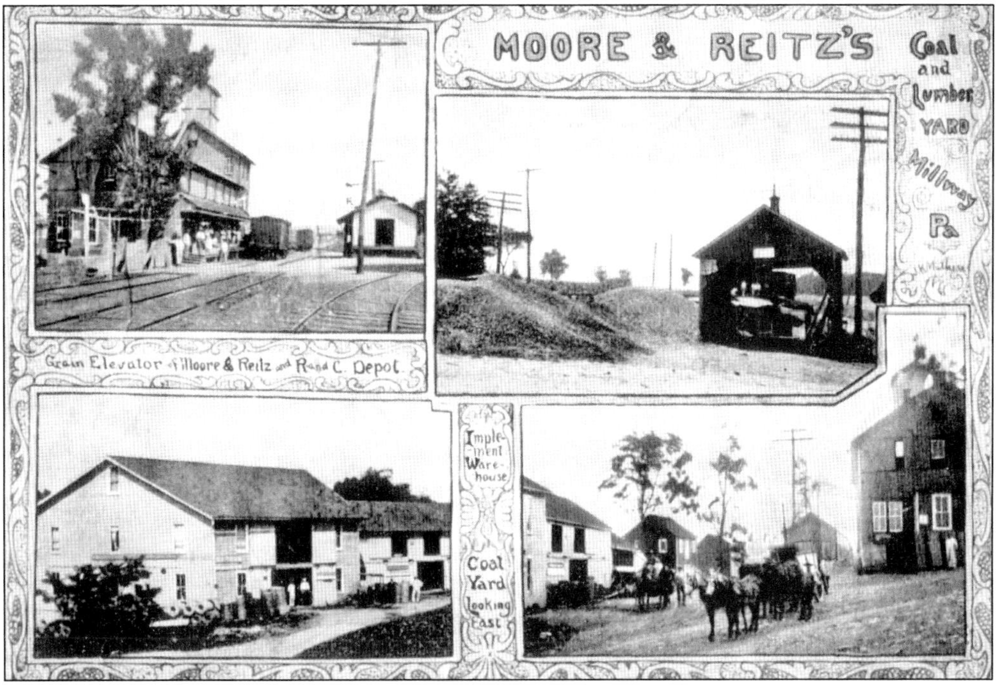

As the newly reconstructed business began to take off, they added coal and lumber to their inventory. The year 1920 saw John's son Chester entering into partnership with his father, and the company's name was thus changed to J. H. Reitz and Son. In 1916, Reitz became the first Purina dealer in Lancaster County, continuing to sell the product until the business was closed for good in 1964. (Courtesy of Richard Reitz.)

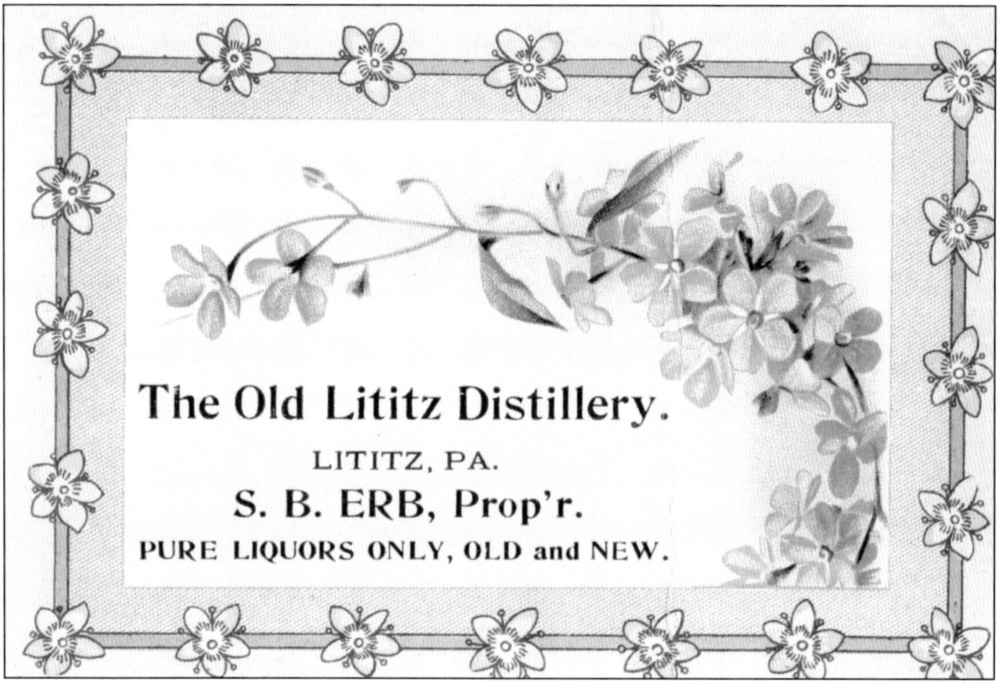

In 1815, Peter Fielis began operation of the Rome Distillery. A four-inch wooden pipe fed water from the Lititz Run downstream into the distillery. In August 1893, when owned by Jacob Hertzler, a group of Prohibitionists set the distillery on fire. Hertzler never fully recovered from this financial burden, and he sold the business in 1896 to Samuel B. Erb. (Courtesy of the Robert "Sketch" Mearig collection.)

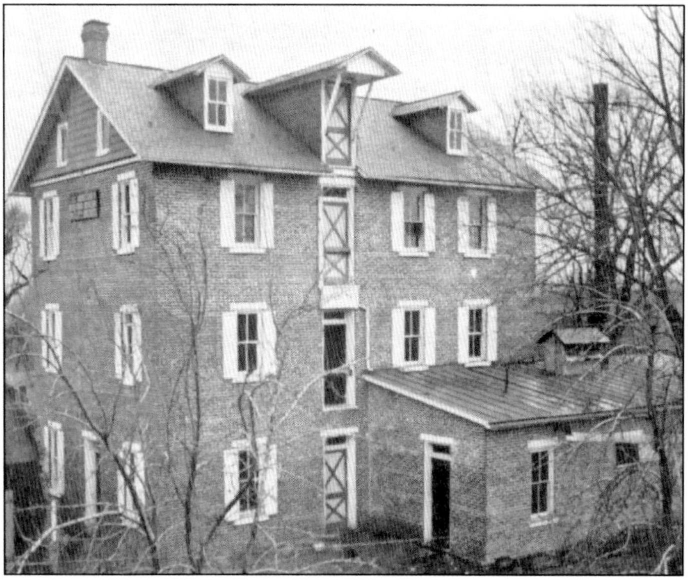

John C. Horting, a successful Lancaster wine and brandy distributor, purchased the business in 1904. Horting was known for his Lititz Springs Pure Rye, Horting's Old Safe, and Lititz Springs Straight Rye whiskeys. In January 1905, Horting tore down the original distillery and built a new three-story modern facility in its place. Once Prohibition became law, the distillery quickly went out of business. (Courtesy of the Robert "Sketch" Mearig collection.)

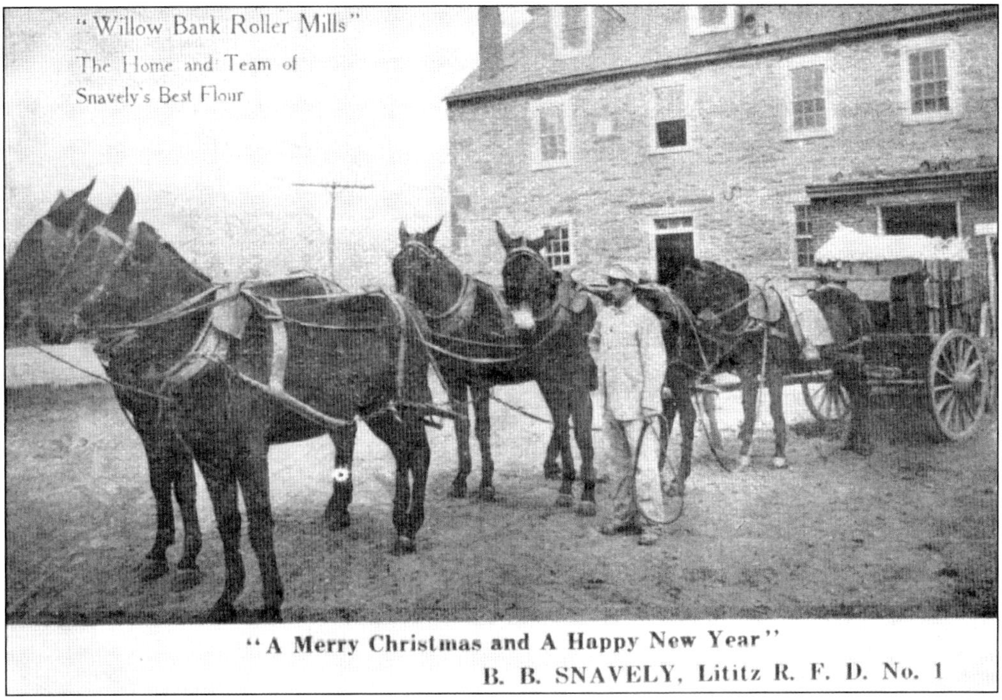

A mill was erected along Hammer Creek in 1850 by Christian Eby. In 1866, the mill passed to Henry Hess, and by 1875, John Snavely ran the milling operation. In 1890, the mill passed hands to John's son David. He installed two turbine water wheels—one a 30-horsepower turbine and the other a 28-horsepower turbine. By 1906, the mill was owned and operated by B. B. Snavely and was known during this time as Willow Bank Roller Mills. It remains in the Snavely family today, producing quality bulk and sacked flour for distribution up and down the East Coast. A total of six semi-trucks help to carry the fresh product to bakeries and other businesses. (Both, courtesy of the Robert "Sketch" Mearig collection.)

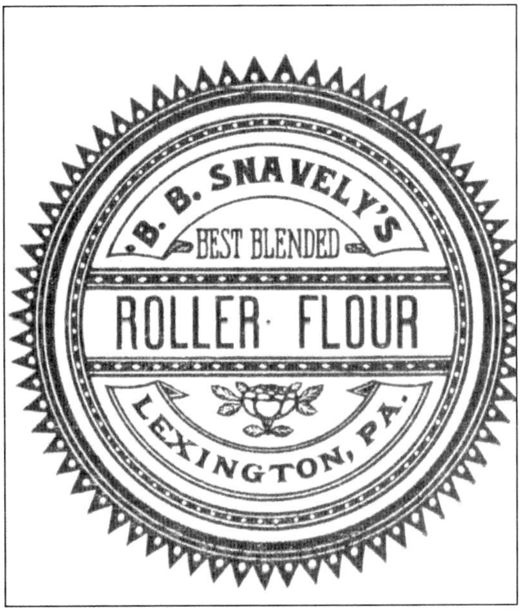

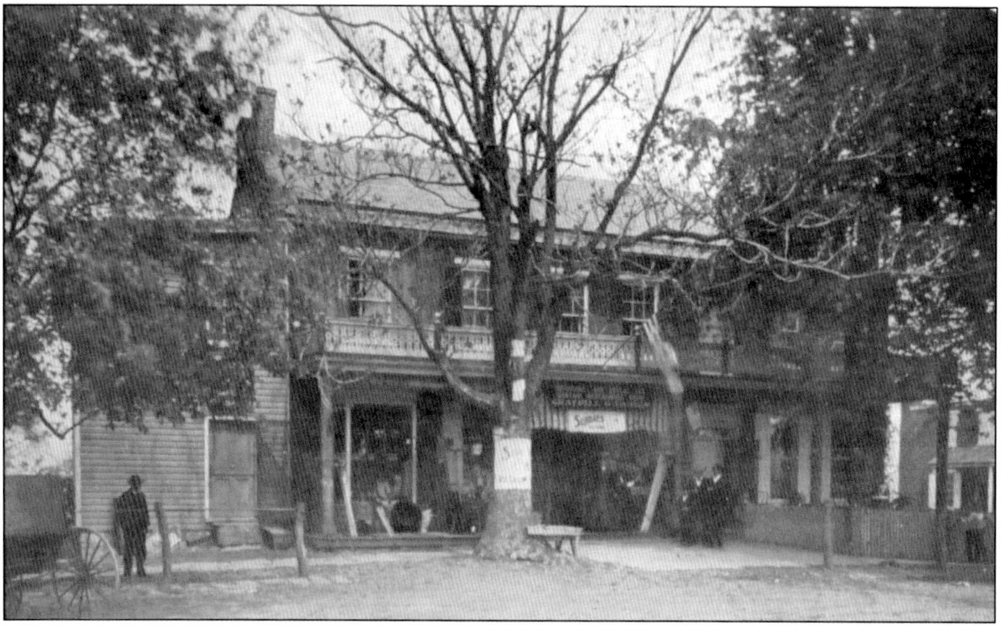

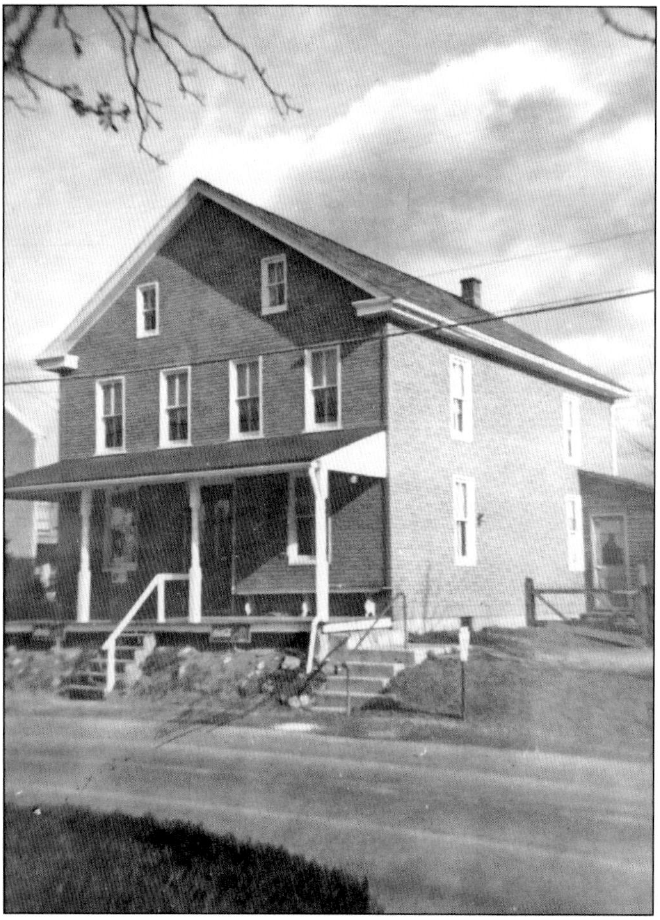

This store was one of the original brick buildings in Rothsville, with Abraham Myers purchasing the land in 1849, building a house and store. It was here in 1851 that he became the first postmaster of Rothsville. In 1875, it was purchased by Susan and Daniel Habecker, who ran it until 1884, eventually selling it in order to purchase the White Swan Hotel. (Courtesy of Robert "Sketch" Mearig collection.)

Located in Kissel Hill, this building became the store of Beaver Stauffer and his wife in 1938. In the early 1950s, they sold the property to a Mrs. Brookmyer, who decided to turn it into a private residence. After her passing in 1972, it was demolished. In 1973, Your Place Restaurant purchased the land and operated a very successful restaurant for many years. (Courtesy of Tim Stauffer.)

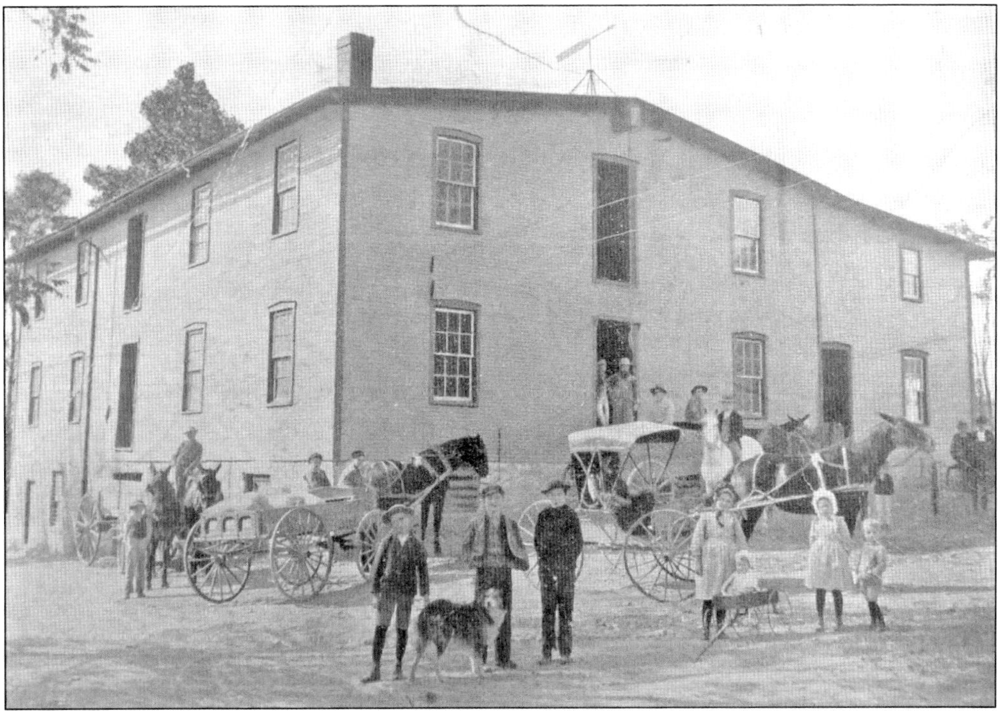

Millport Roller Mills was a very successful operation. The mill dates to as early as 1816, when Joseph Musser first listed a sawmill for sale. By 1822, a three-story stone gristmill and sawmill, measuring 40 feet by 50 feet, was advertised for sale and purchased by Jacob Weis. In 1862, Samuel Fry became the owner, as it continued to thrive. Transferred in 1902 to Wallace M. Zook, the mill continued to do a brisk business for several years thereafter. Seen below is an undated group photograph of the Zook family. From left to right are (first row) Alice, Jacob, Kathryn, and Wallace Sr. (man with beard); (second row) Harry, Emma, Wallace Jr., Elmer (young boy), Lizzy, and Charles. Elmer eventually took over mill operations in 1932. (Both, courtesy of Logan and Lynn Myers.)

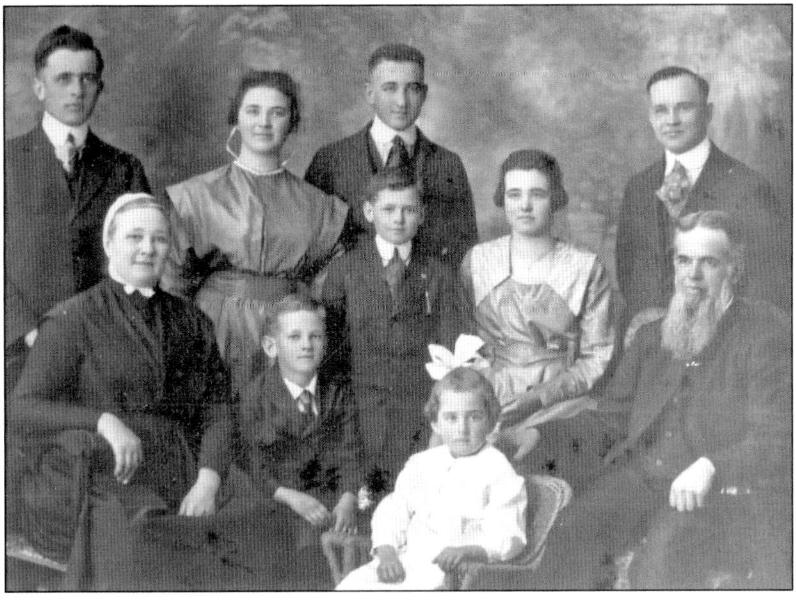

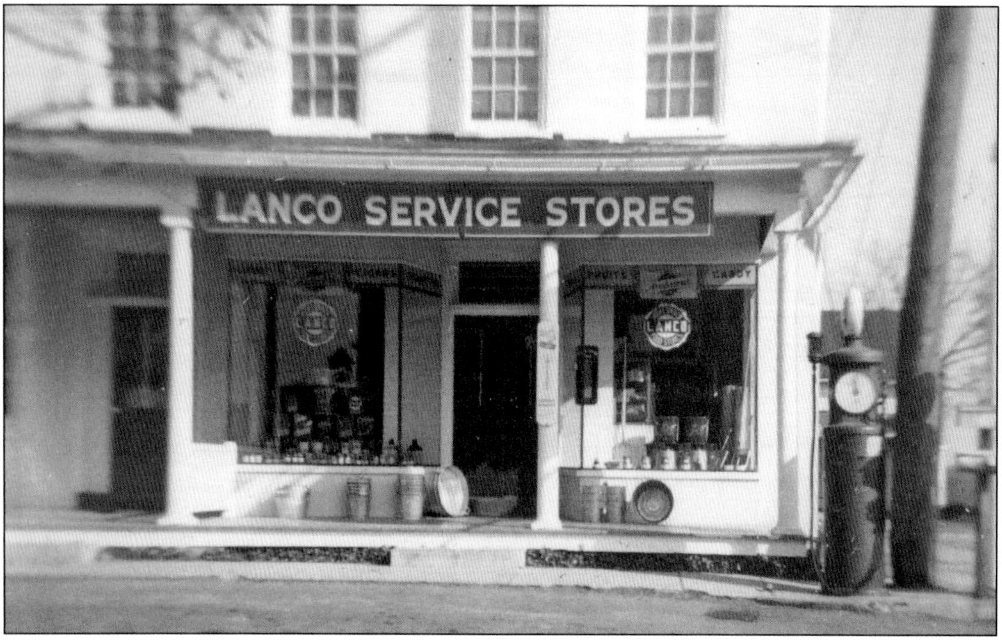

Originally built by Jacob Hershey in 1855, this structure in Lexington sits at the crossroads of Chestnut Street and Elbow Road. By 1894, a post office and general store was in full operation. Then, in the 1940s, The Wise family ran a LANCO (Lancaster County) full-service store here. In 1954 the store was purchased by Robert and Emma Donmoyer who came from Jonestown, Lebanon County. The store was in part of the first floor and the Donmoyers, during their ownership, lived in the rest of the building. After they became the owners they converted it into a self-service store. (Above, courtesy of the Robert "Sketch" Mearig collection; below courtesy of the Donmoyer family.)

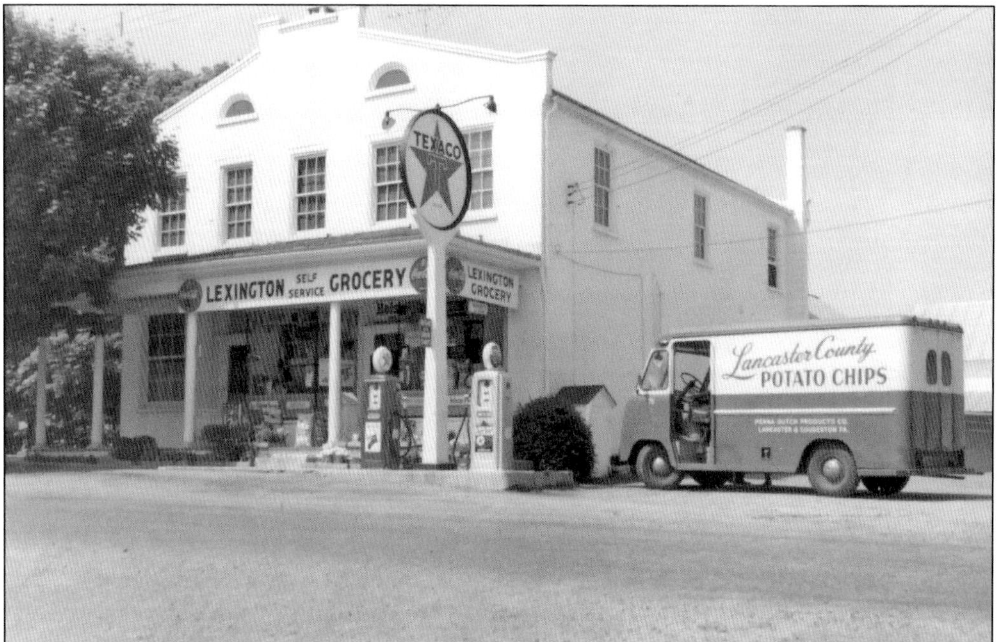

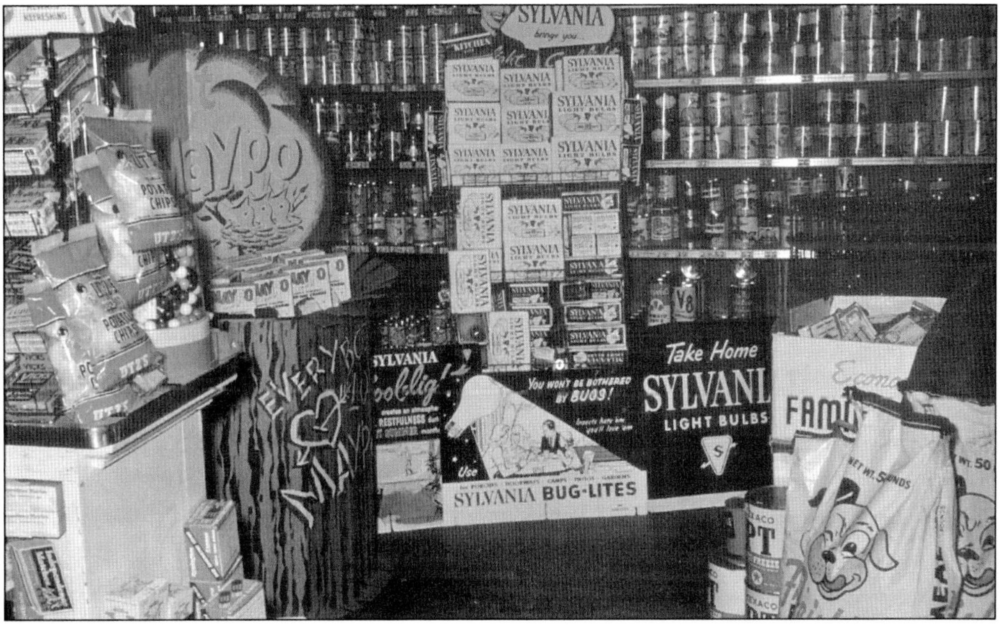

By telephoning 6-8981 ahead of time, a customer could discover the store's current stock of everyday items, a sampling of which is shown here. Along with the Donmoyer family, employees such as Emily Hurst and Mamie Adams worked as clerks in the store. In 1969, the store ceased operations, with the building eventually converting to apartments shortly thereafter. (Courtesy of the Donmoyer family.)

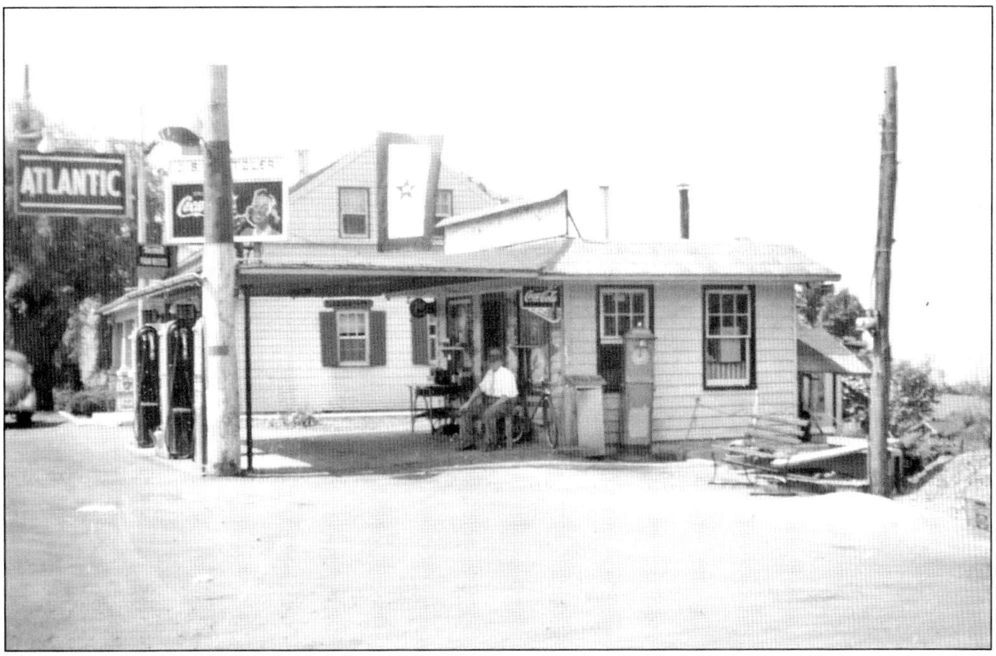

Refreshing Coca-Cola and Atlantic gasoline were just two of the many products that could be purchased at Jerry B. Hertzler's small store and gas station located at the top of Kissel Hill at West Woods Drive. Customers could also buy a newspaper, sip coffee, or catch up with the local news of the day with other residents of Kissel Hill. (Courtesy of Polly Garner.)

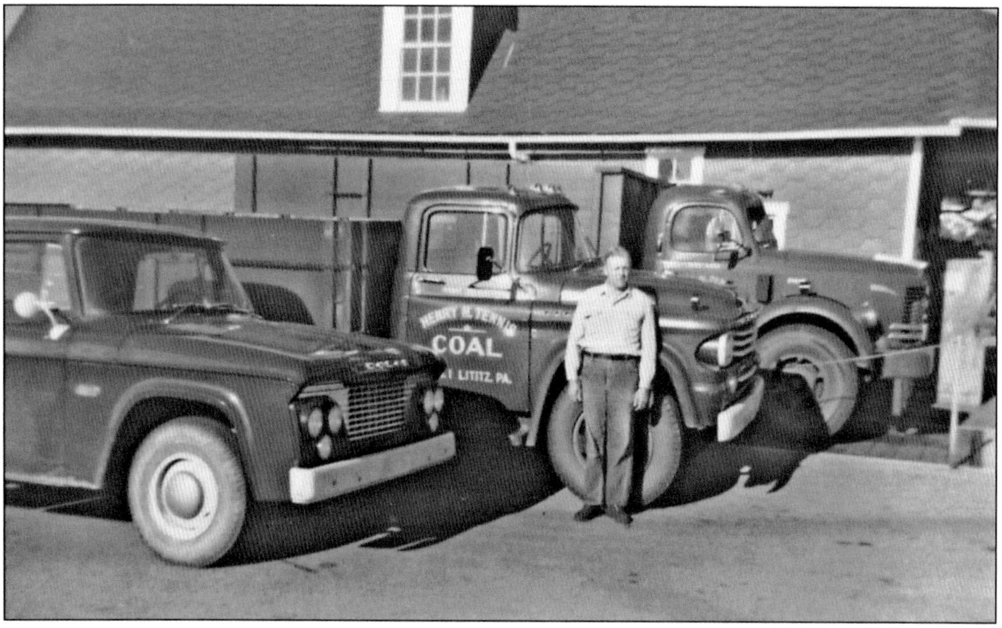

Henry H. Tennis Coal began on April 16, 1945, when Tennis purchased an existing business from Monroe Shreiner. The coal yard was located behind his residence next to United Zion Home on Route 501 just south of Lexington. At various times over the years Henry employed two residents from the home, one neighbor, and several family members to help with the labor. The business was moved to 106 Race Street in Lexington in 1952 when Tennis purchased property at public auction which was formerly owned by "Nanny" Markley. Tennis then renovated the property, adding coal bins behind the barn. A large scale to weigh trucks was also installed. Henry sold Reading and Kocher anthracite coal by the ton or by the bag, which was delivered to his customers in one of his several trucks. (Both, courtesy of Donna Heisey.)

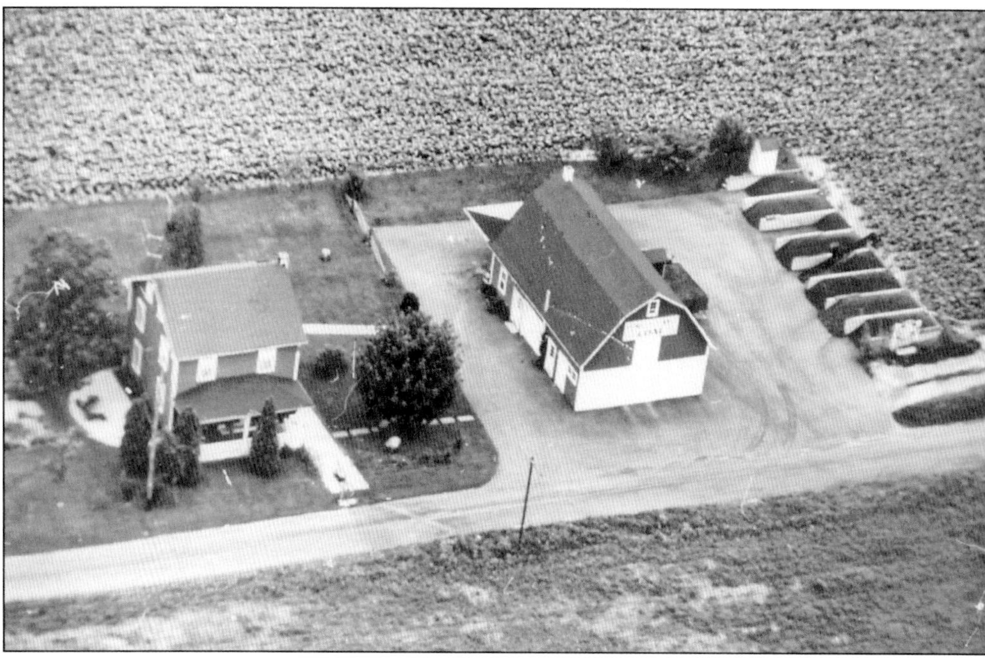

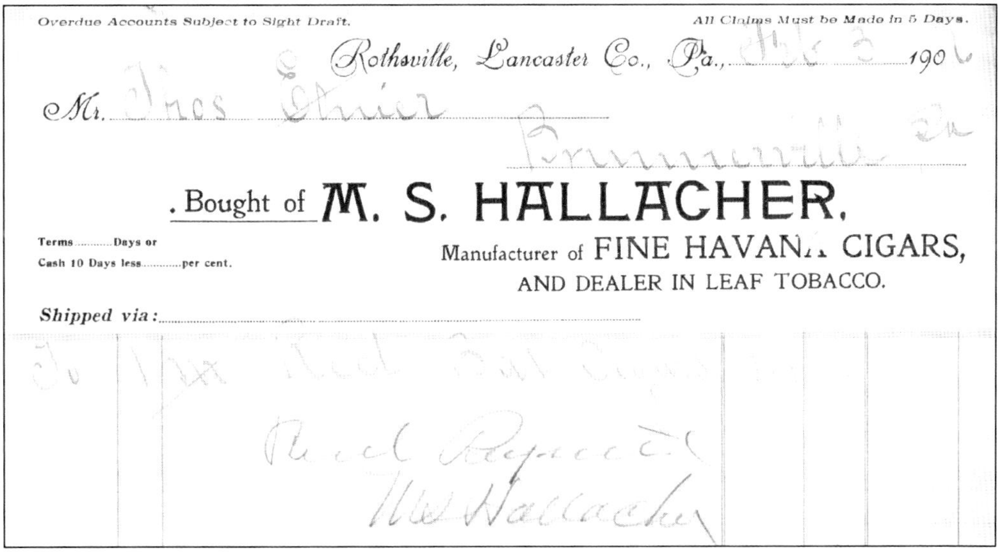
Overdue Accounts Subject to Sight Draft. All Claims Must be Made in 5 Days.

Rothsville, Lancaster Co., Pa., ... 190

Mr. ....

Bought of M. S. HALLACHER,

Manufacturer of FINE HAVANA CIGARS,

AND DEALER IN LEAF TOBACCO.

Terms .... Days or
Cash 10 Days less .... per cent.

Shipped via: ....

Milton S. Hallacher of Rothsville was mostly known for his Lena brand of cigars. He ran a very successful operation from about 1886 to 1930 operating factory number 1058 within the ninth tax district of Pennsylvania. Rothsville was primarily known as a cigar-manufacturing town, with more residents of this village employed by this concern than any other village in the township. (Courtesy of the author's collection.)

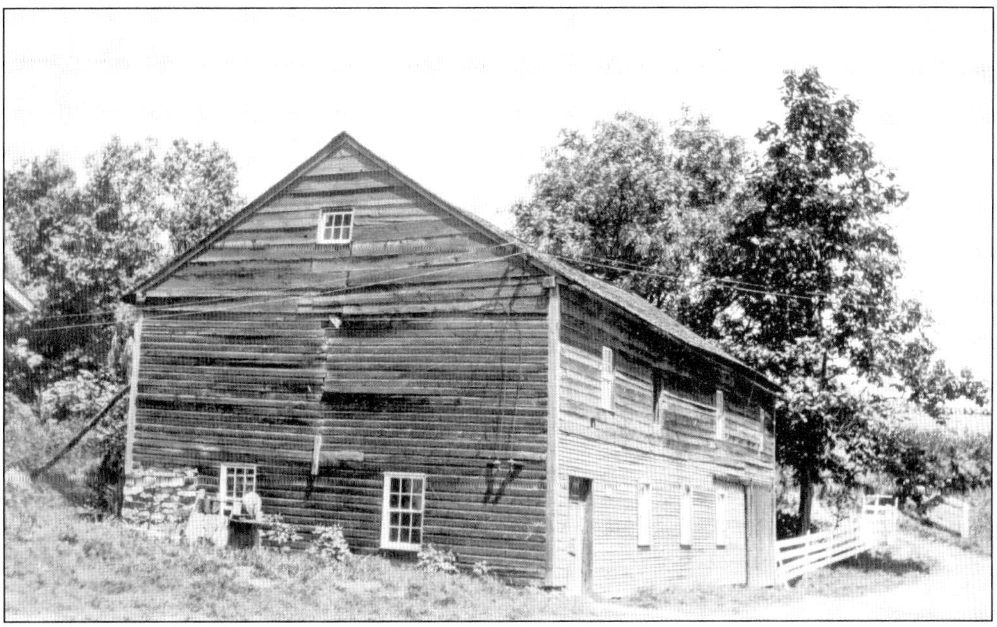

Valentine Becker and his three brothers came to America on the ship *Snow Betsey* from Germany on August 27, 1737. They eventually settled in Warwick Township on a tract of land surveyed and deeded to Valentine on March 25, 1738, by Thomas and Richard Penn. In 1817, Valentine's grandson Henry began distilling spirits at this location on Pine Hill Road across from the family farmhouse. (Courtesy of Warren Becker.)

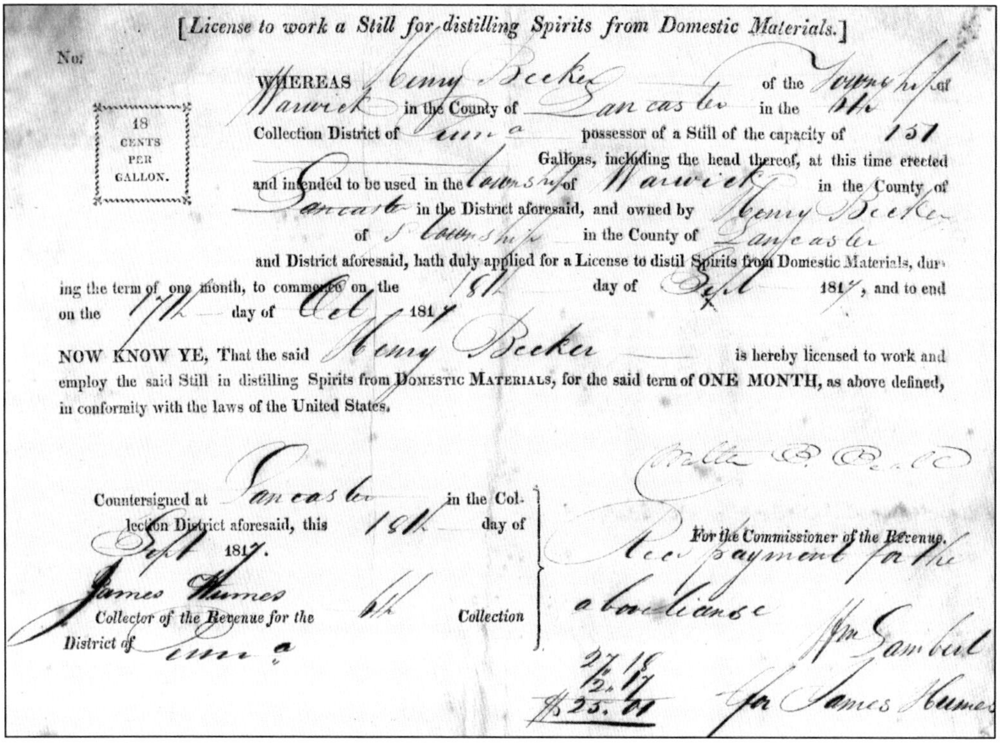

[License to work a Still for distilling Spirits from Domestic Materials.]

No.

18 CENTS PER GALLON.

WHEREAS Henry Becker of the Township of Warwick in the County of Lancaster in the 6th Collection District of Penna possessor of a Still of the capacity of 151 Gallons, including the head thereof, at this time erected and intended to be used in the Township of Warwick in the County of Lancaster in the District aforesaid, and owned by Henry Becker of S Township in the County of Lancaster and District aforesaid, hath duly applied for a License to distil Spirits from Domestic Materials, during the term of one month, to commence on the 18th day of Sept 1817, and to end on the 17th day of Oct 1817

NOW KNOW YE, That the said Henry Becker is hereby licensed to work and employ the said Still in distilling Spirits from DOMESTIC MATERIALS, for the said term of ONE MONTH, as above defined, in conformity with the laws of the United States.

Countersigned at Lancaster in the Collection District aforesaid, this 18th day of Sept 1817.

James Humes

Collector of the Revenue for the 6th *Collection District of* Penna

For the Commissioner of the Revenue.

Rec payment for the above license

27.18
2.17
$25.01

Wm Gambel for James Humes

On September 18, 1817, a license was applied for and issued to Henry Becker to create spirits from a 151-gallon still for a period of one month. The apparatus that was included in this application was believed to be the largest still in the area at that time and was Henry's invention. This whiskey sold for 25¢ to 30¢ a gallon. (Courtesy of the Lititz Historical Foundation.)

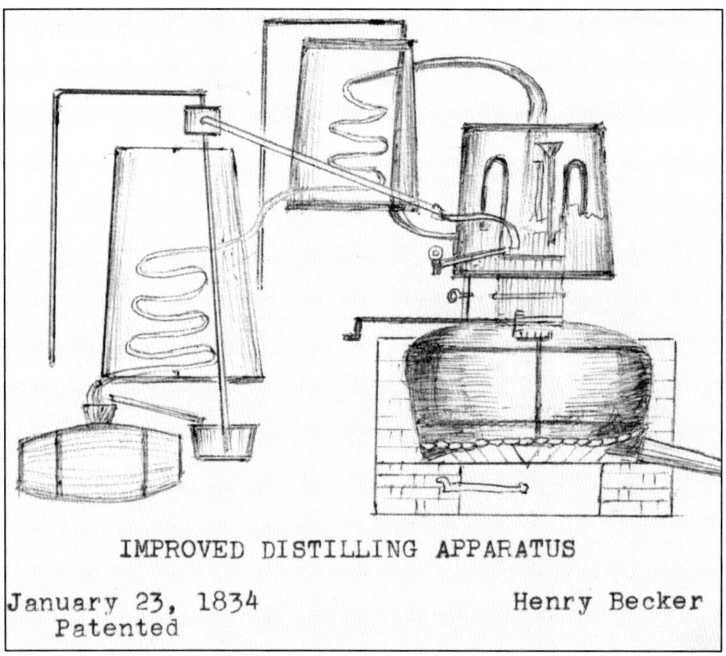

On January 23, 1834, a letter of patent was sent by Henry to the government for improvements in distilling. His patent promised five new improvements in the areas of speed, fuel economy, and faster heating among others. The patent office burned down during the application process, and by the time he reapplied for it, someone had already applied for and been granted a patent for the same process. (Courtesy of Warren Becker.)

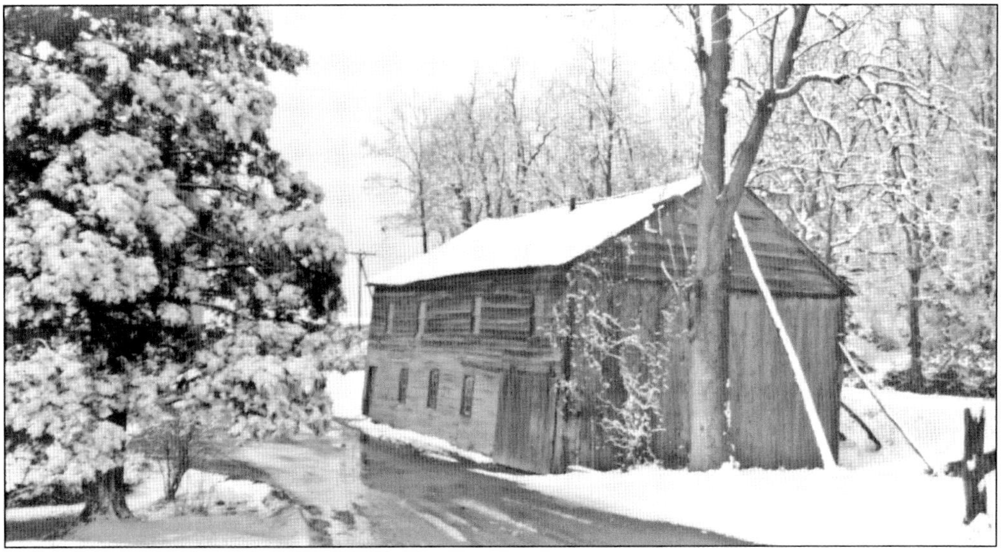

The Becker Distillery operated for a total of 56 years, ending with Israel Becker in 1873. In 1865, an order was placed by a gentleman from Womelsdorf, Berks County, for 400 gallons of whiskey priced at $2.15 per gallon—quite a large order. After the distilling operation ceased, the building became a tobacco barn and eventually was torn down. (Courtesy of Warren Becker.)

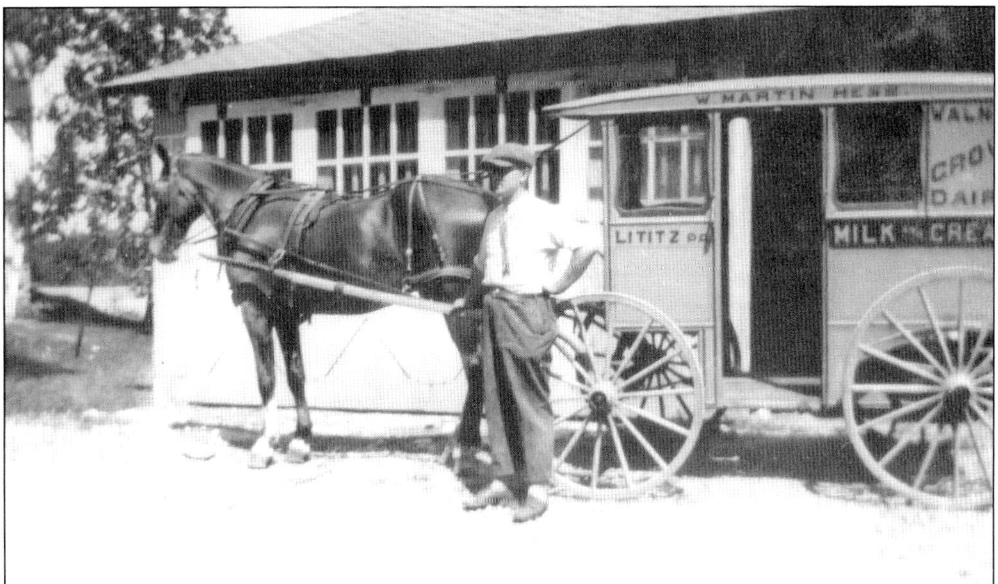

Walnut Grove Dairy was operated by W. Martin Hess. Located in Rome, it was sold from a horse-drawn wagon. "Dawn to dusk-dusk til dawn; our pure milk builds brain and brawn" was the catchphrase spoken by the dairy's mascot Billy Break O'Day in various print campaigns in local newspapers. (Courtesy of the Robert "Sketch" Mearig collection.)

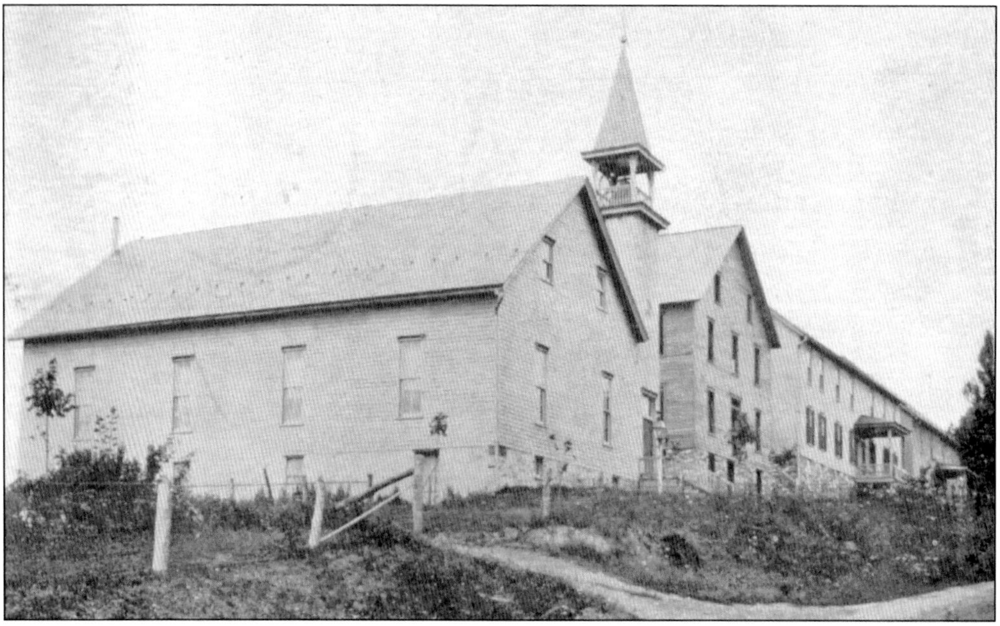

Situated in Lexington is the United Zion Home, which began in 1902, when Barbara and Henry Firestone took five elderly people who needed care into their home. During the United Zion Home's general conference in 1905, it was agreed that the Home for the Poor and Indigent Persons be purchased from them, with the Firestones becoming the steward and matron of the facility. After the paperwork was finalized, this facility was renamed the Home for Homeless of the United Zion Children Church. The living room served as a place for worship, but after dormitories were built, worship was moved to a basement room. A chapel with a bell tower was built, eventually being replaced by a brick building in 1955. Their charter signing was reenacted at the Centennial Celebration, which took place on May 27, 2005. (Both, courtesy of the Robert "Sketch" Mearig collection.)

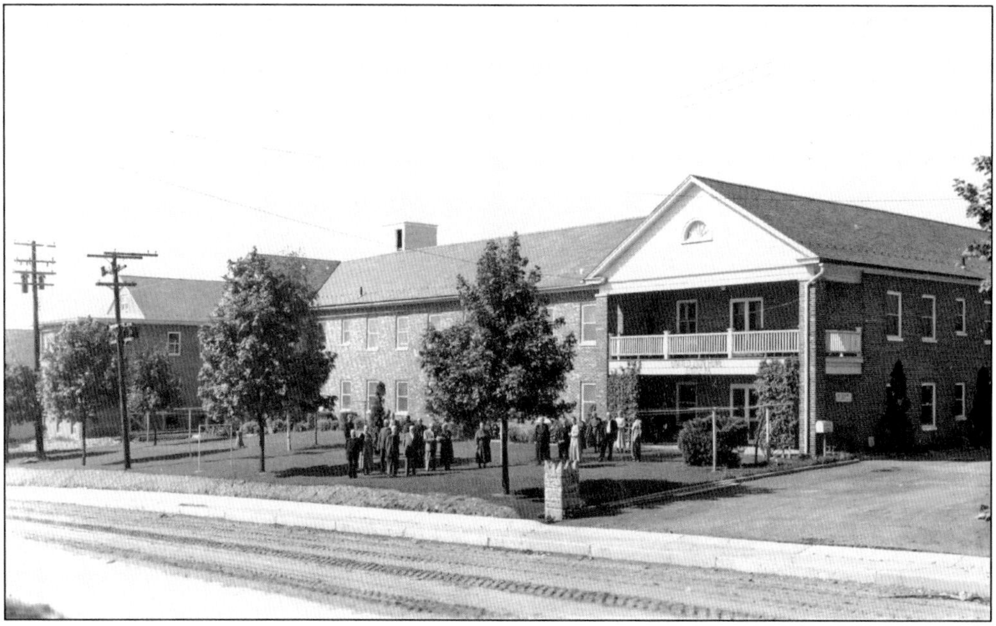

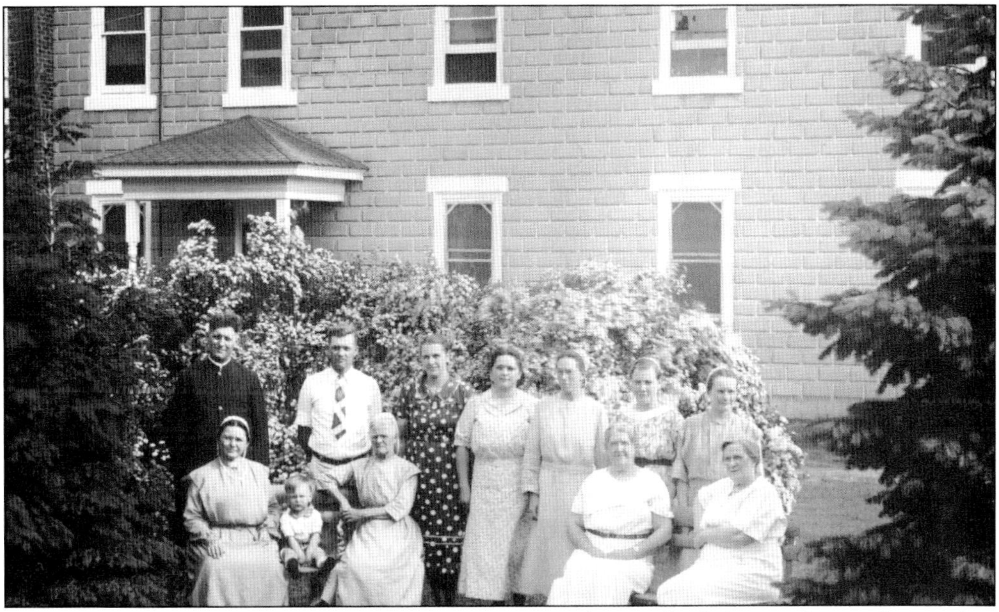

This photograph taken behind the building in 1937 shows all of the employees during that year. Henry Tennis is wearing the tie, and his wife, Ruth, is in the polka dot dress standing to his left. Allen Tennis was the administrator of the United Zion Home and can be seen on the far left dressed in black. Agnes Tennis, his wife, is seated directly in front of him. (Courtesy of Donna Heisey.)

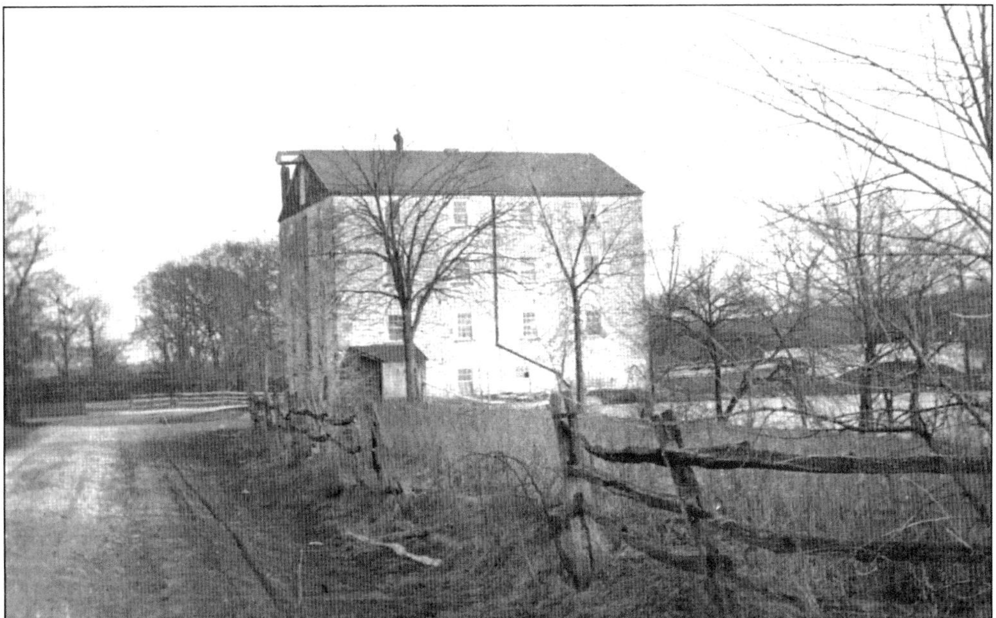

In 1855, this mill was constructed by Martin Grube and served primarily as a flour mill. In 1899, the mill was transferred to Benjamin B. Snavely, who continued to run operations until its closing in 1917. This mill on the corner of Brunnerville and Snavely Mill Roads has been converted into a private residence. (Courtesy of Ron Reedy.)

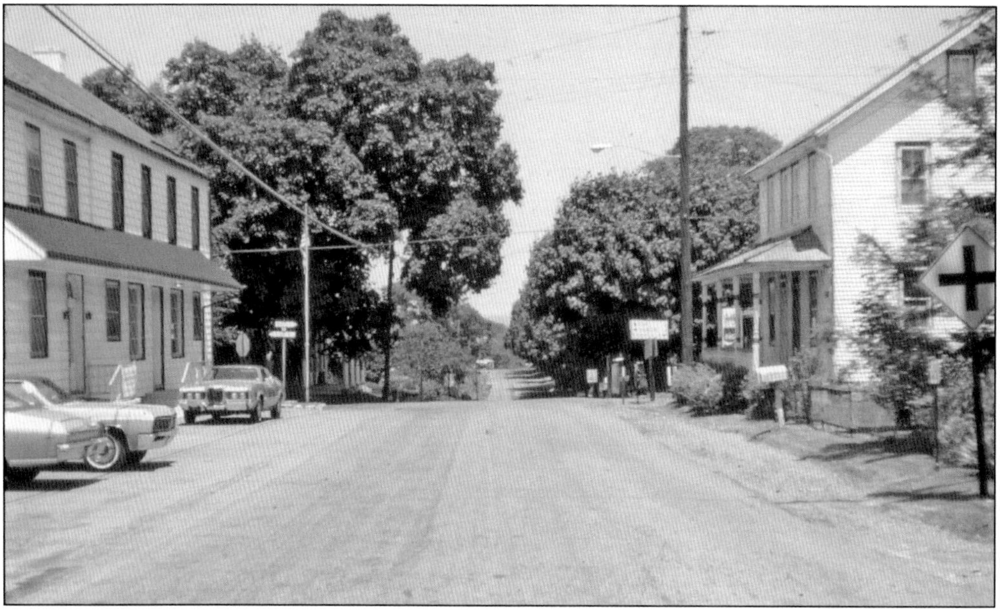

A Mr. Maelhorn originally built an inn and store at the location to the left in 1824. Teamsters stopped here for the night, often choosing to sleep in the hay in the adjoining stables rather than in a bed. It is said that White Hall, the original name of Brunnerville, got its name from the tavern's main room, which had whitewashed walls. (Courtesy of Tom Hackman.)

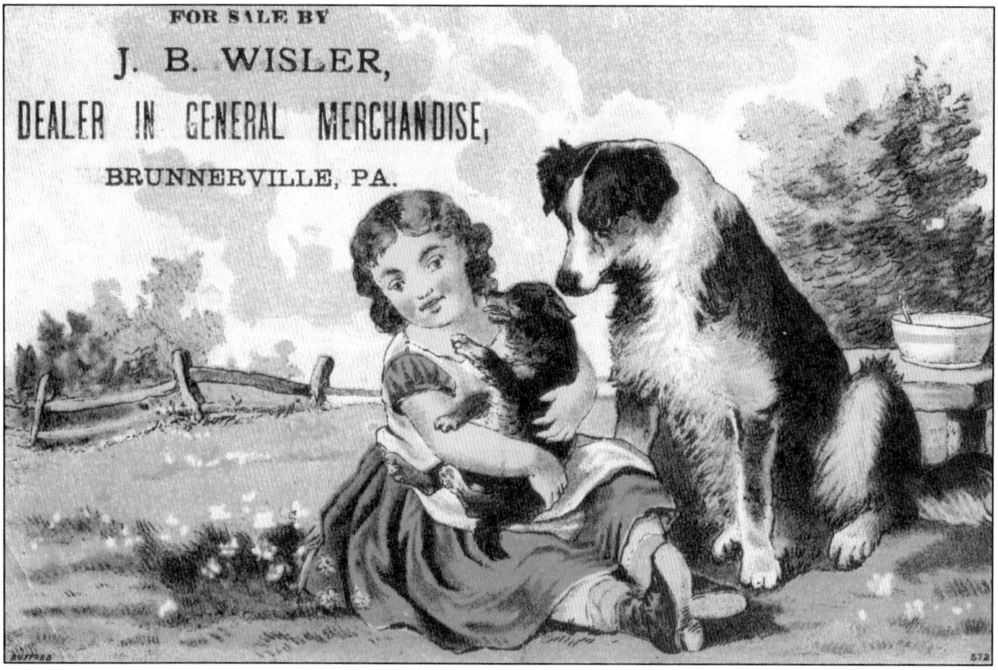

In 1827, the property was sold to Abraham Eichler and his wife. A post office was erected in 1861, while owned by Ezra Wissler. It was during this year that the Brunnerville Hotel was established across the street, and the hotel operations at this original location ceased. John B. Wissler eventually purchased the store from his father on May 12, 1877. (Courtesy of the Robert "Sketch" Mearig collection.)

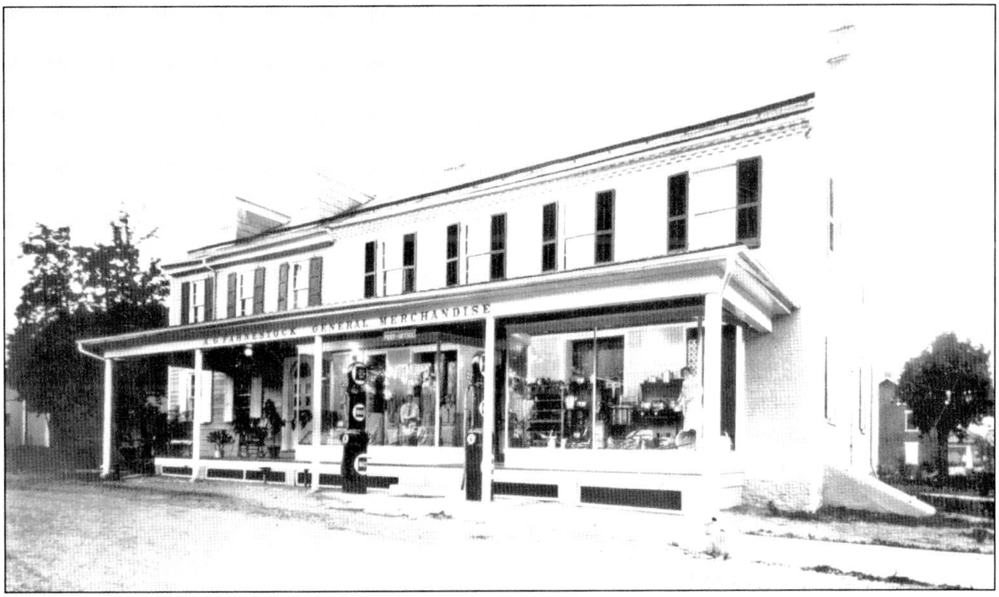

On April 1, 1905, Wissler sold the store to Elmer G. Geyer, an outstanding citizen of Brunnerville. Geyer served as treasurer of the Brunnerville Telephone and Telegraph Company, which was chartered on March 12, 1912. The store was eventually sold to Adam G. Fahnestock on August 6, 1920, with 1926 seeing Fahnestock's Store carrying over 6,000 different items. On August 6, 1938, the store was sold to Martin H. Lauver, who ran it for six years and then sold it to Ivan G. Bushong. Several Bushongs then ran the store from 1944 to 1950, when it was sold to Charles Wolf. In 1960, Wolf sold it to James Varick, who in turn sold it to Russell Keith in 1966. Keith converted it to apartments shortly thereafter. (Above, courtesy of the Robert "Sketch" Mearig collection; below, courtesy of Tom Hackman.)

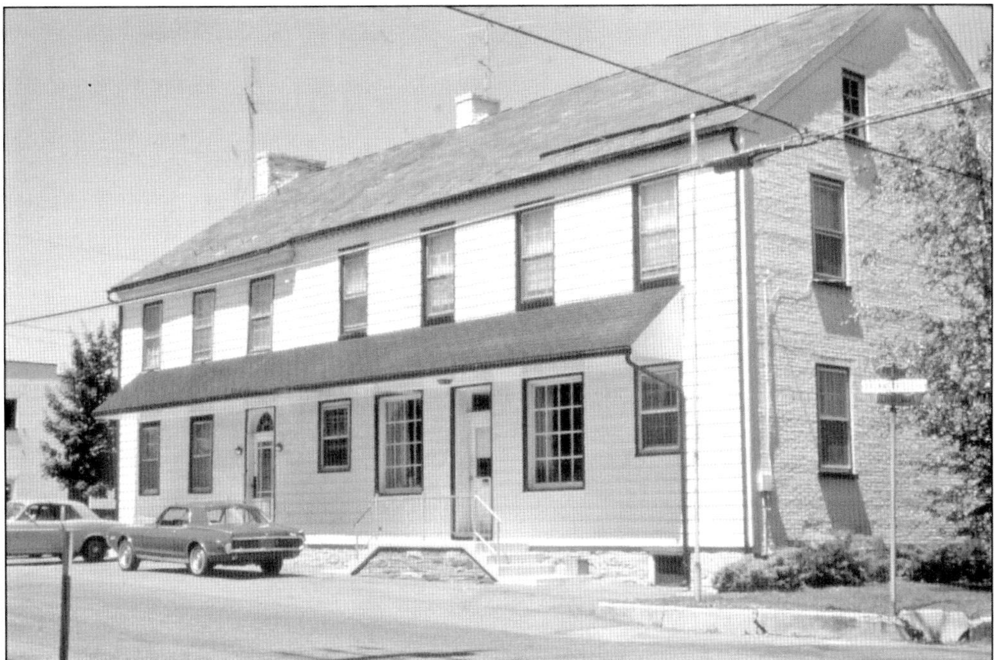

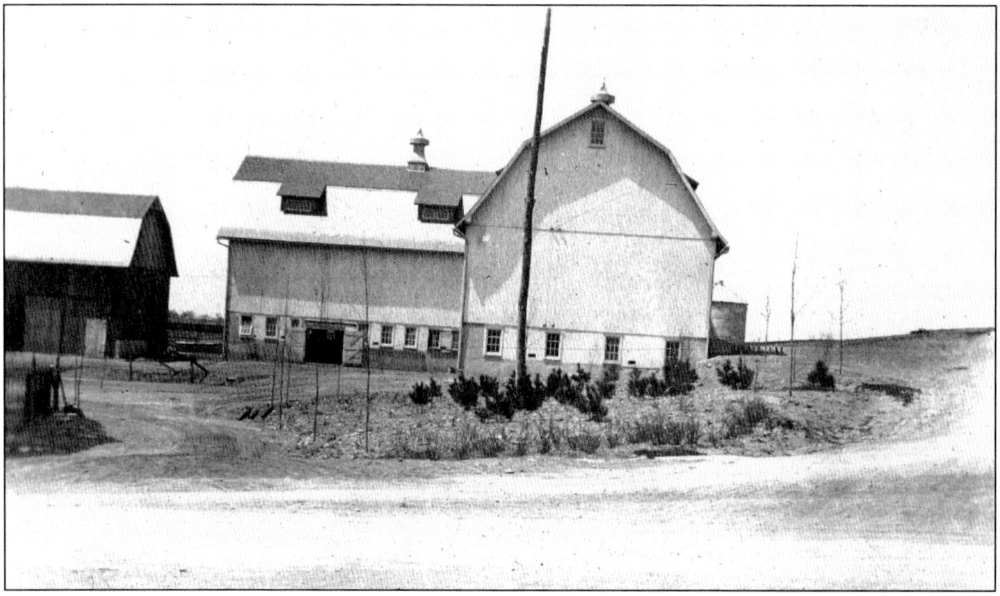

Built by Abraham and Maria Huber in 1836, this was the location of Spruce Villa Dairy beginning around 1905. J. Clayton Brubaker operated this establishment until it was destroyed by fire on November 20, 1916. It was rebuilt in 1917 by J. Clayton and his wife, Florence Moore Brubaker. For years this dairy in Brunnerville sold various dairy products to the community. The products were delivered fresh throughout the township including the town of Lititz. On May 3, 1958, the barn burned again but was rebuilt the same year. The business eventually passed down to Mary and Milton, the children of J. Clayton and Florence. It continued as it passed into the hands of the third generation when John Clark (Mary's son) took ownership. (Above, courtesy of Ron Reedy; below, courtesy of the Robert "Sketch" Mearig collection.)

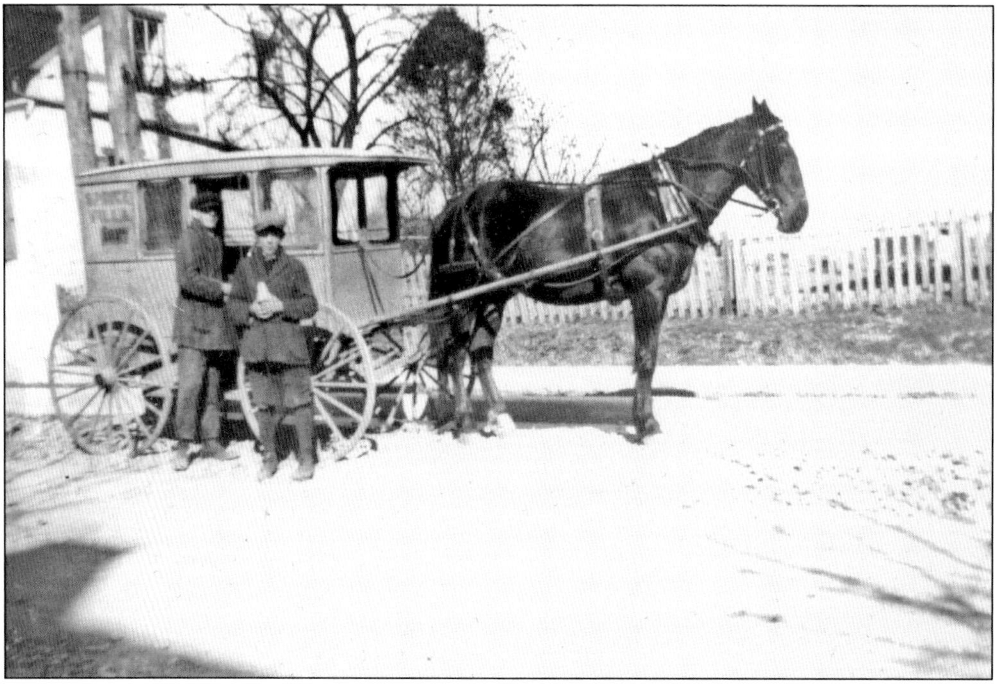

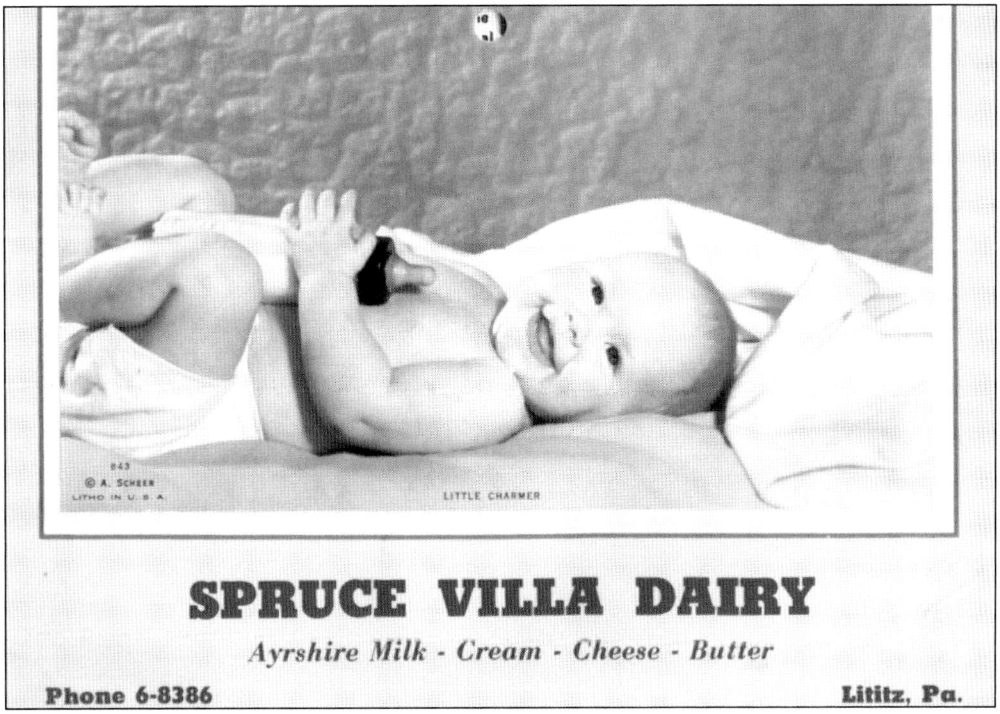

Many advertising items were produced by the family in an effort to help promote their growing business, including this calendar from the year 1955. By the early 1980s, with the mounting pressure of increasing modernization, the dairy was closed. Today, Spruce Villa Dairy bottles command upwards of several hundreds of dollars at local public auctions and antique shops. (Courtesy of the Robert "Sketch" Mearig collection.)

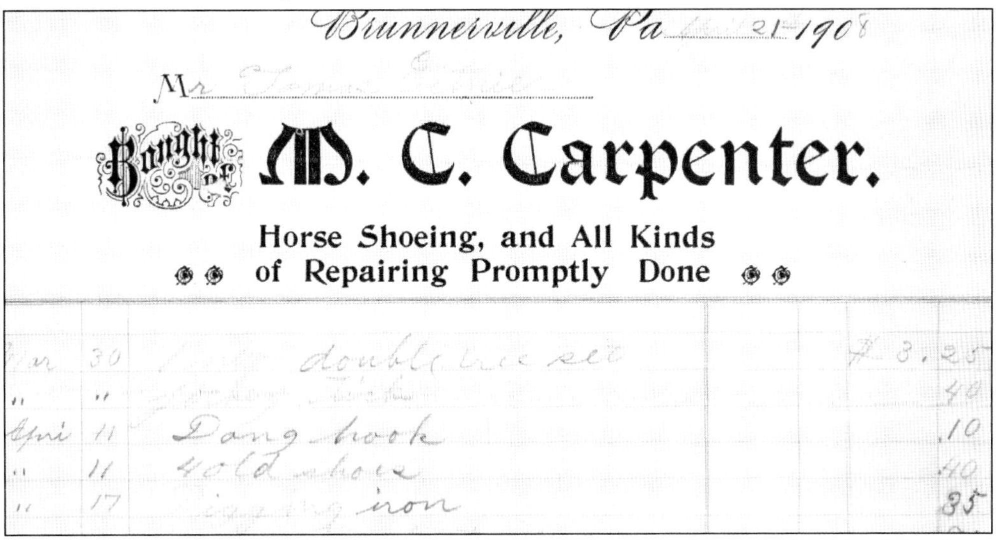
Brunnerville, Pa 21 1908

Mr

Bought of M. C. Carpenter.

Horse Shoeing, and All Kinds of Repairing Promptly Done

Morris Carpenter learned the horseshoeing trade at an early age in Pine Hill, where his father Rudy had started a blacksmith business. Moving to Brunnerville and eventually settling permanently in Lexington, Morris quickly became a highly skilled blacksmith in his own right for over 60 years. As his business grew, he began to serve additional customers from neighboring counties. (Courtesy of the author's collection.)

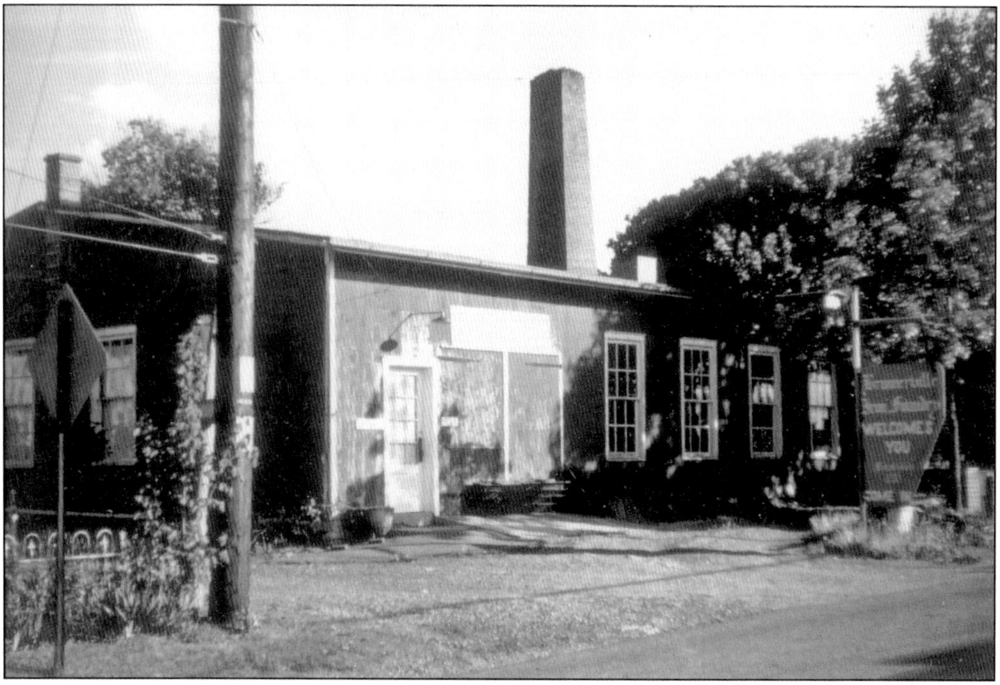

In 1850, Peter Brunner opened a blacksmith and wainwright shop at this location in what is now Brunnerville, adding a machine shop five years later. After finding success in these fields, he added a foundry to the business. In 1898, while Aaron Wissler was owner, the foundry was damaged by fire. It was immediately rebuilt, and within 90 days it was back to business as usual. (Courtesy of Tom Hackman.)

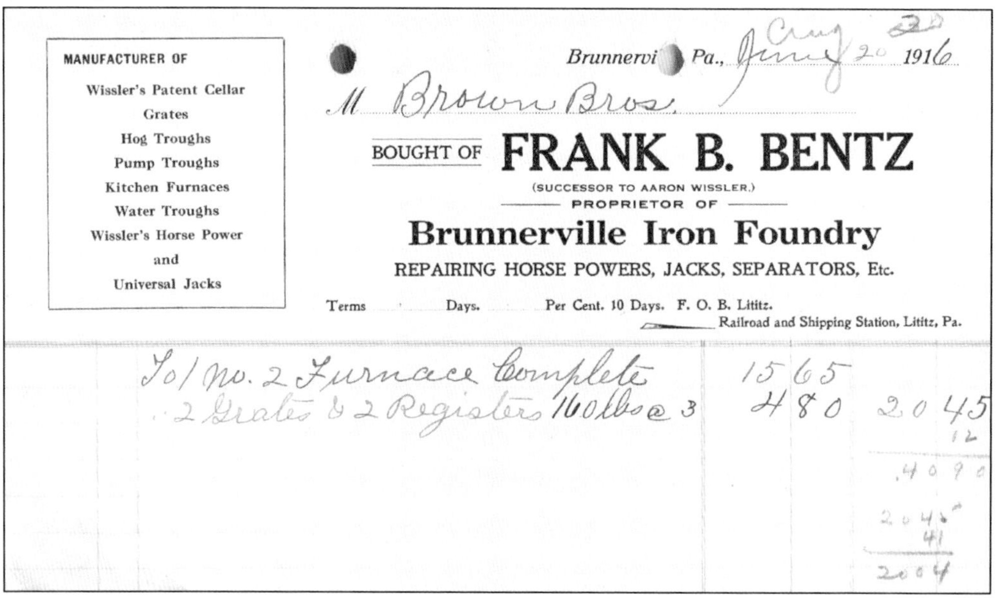

MANUFACTURER OF
Wissler's Patent Cellar Grates
Hog Troughs
Pump Troughs
Kitchen Furnaces
Water Troughs
Wissler's Horse Power
and
Universal Jacks

Brunnervi Pa., Aug 20 1916

M Brown Bros.

BOUGHT OF **FRANK B. BENTZ**

(SUCCESSOR TO AARON WISSLER.)
PROPRIETOR OF
Brunnerville Iron Foundry
REPAIRING HORSE POWERS, JACKS, SEPARATORS, Etc.

Terms Days. Per Cent. 10 Days. F. O. B. Lititz.
Railroad and Shipping Station, Lititz, Pa.

To 1 No. 2 Furnace Complete 15 65
2 Grates & 2 Registers 160 lbs @ 3 4 80 20 45

When Wissler died in 1905, Frank Bentz purchased the foundry. Bentz was a farmer before purchasing the foundry and would often use his own horses to deliver the finished products to his many customers throughout Lancaster County. When Bentz died in 1930, his grandson F. Earl Landis purchased the business. (Courtesy of the author's collection.)

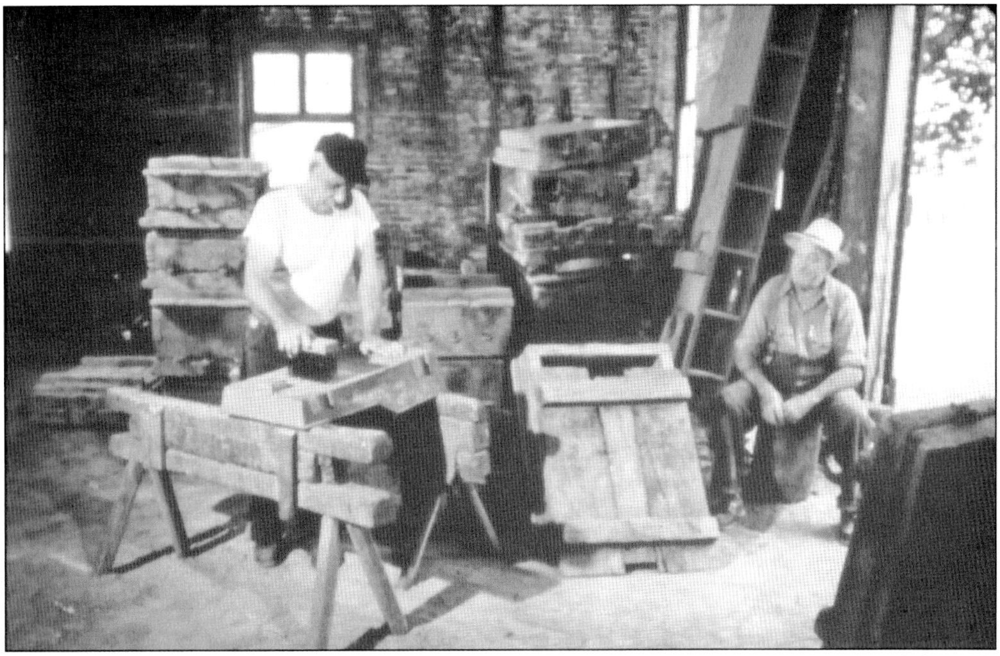

Once the casting for an iron product was removed from a mold, it had to be ground and cleaned, as shown here. This procedure was done to smooth out rough spots on the product. In a sales catalog published by Earl Landis, a No. 3 trough measuring 3.5 feet long by 20.5 inches wide cost $12. (Courtesy of the author's collection; photograph by Mel Horst.)

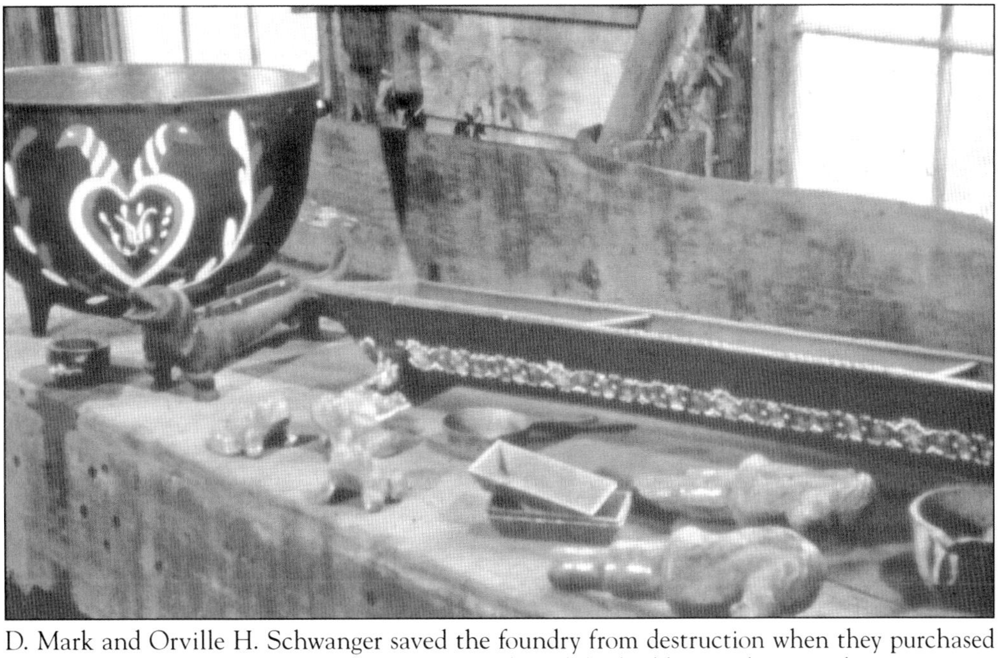

D. Mark and Orville H. Schwanger saved the foundry from destruction when they purchased it in 1962. These brothers saw the historical value of the building and operated it as a tourist attraction. Pennsylvania Dutch products, such as bullfrog doorstops, dog-shaped boot scrapers, horse head hitching posts, and other iron products, were made during this time. (Courtesy of the author's collection; photograph by Mel Horst.)

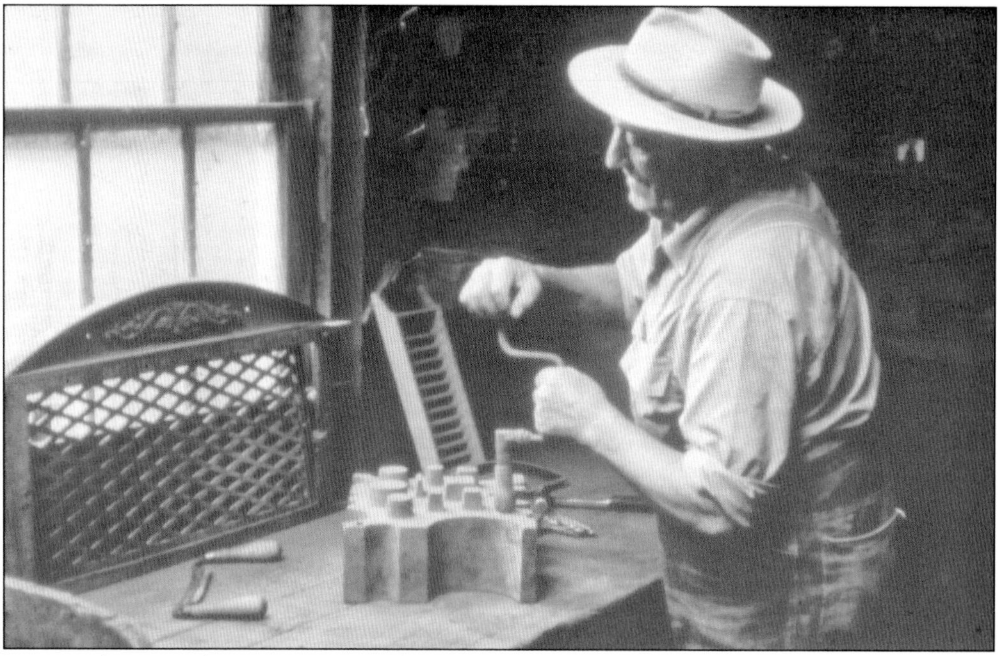

In 1969, the Pennsylvania Historic and Museum Commission announced a proposal to purchase the property with Project 70 funds. Project 70 was passed into law on June 22, 1964, as a means for the state to issue bonds for the purchase of public parks, recreation areas, and other historical purposes. The intent was to save the Brunnerville Foundry from demolition. Unfortunately, the money was needed elsewhere to maintain existing Project 70 efforts, thus the purchase never went through. The foundry was eventually torn down, which saw the end of the iron industry in the township. Throughout its many years of existence, the foundry employed people ranging in ages from 13 to 82, as seen below. (Above, courtesy of the author's collection, photograph by Mel Horst; below, courtesy of the Robert "Sketch" Mearig collection.)

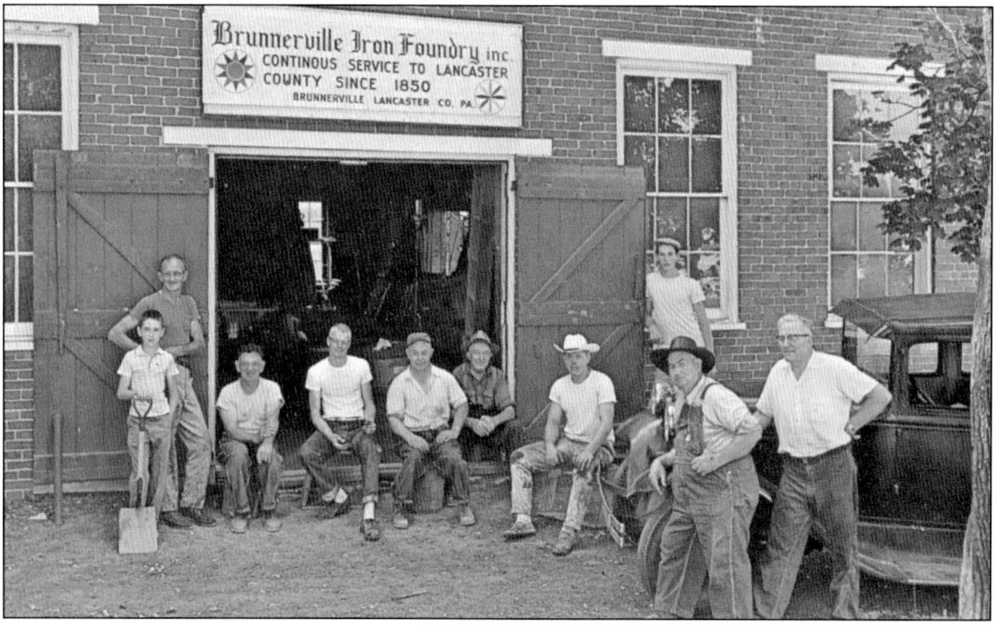

Five

Hotels and Taverns

For hundreds of years, hotels and taverns throughout the township played an important part in the area's economic growth. Acting as the central hub of activity in the community, the early taverns of Warwick Township were places where local residents and travelers could stop and rest for the night, get a nourishing meal, catch up on the town's gossip, or even drink away a hard day's work. Jacob Huber's Tavern, located on East Newport Road, served as an example as one of these early inns. In other cases, the local tavern was a gathering place where the citizens of the community could pay their taxes. When built, these taverns were usually placed at the edge or a crossroad of a town, so the traveler was able to make it their last stop before leaving or the first place they saw and stopped at before entering a new town. Oftentimes, water troughs were placed in front of the tavern to water thirsty horses, and stables were located in back of the building to lodge horses—and sometimes poor travelers for the night. As business declined and more modern restaurants and bars were established, these inns and taverns gradually disappeared. Today, most of these buildings located throughout the township have been demolished, renovated, or converted for use as private homes or apartment buildings.

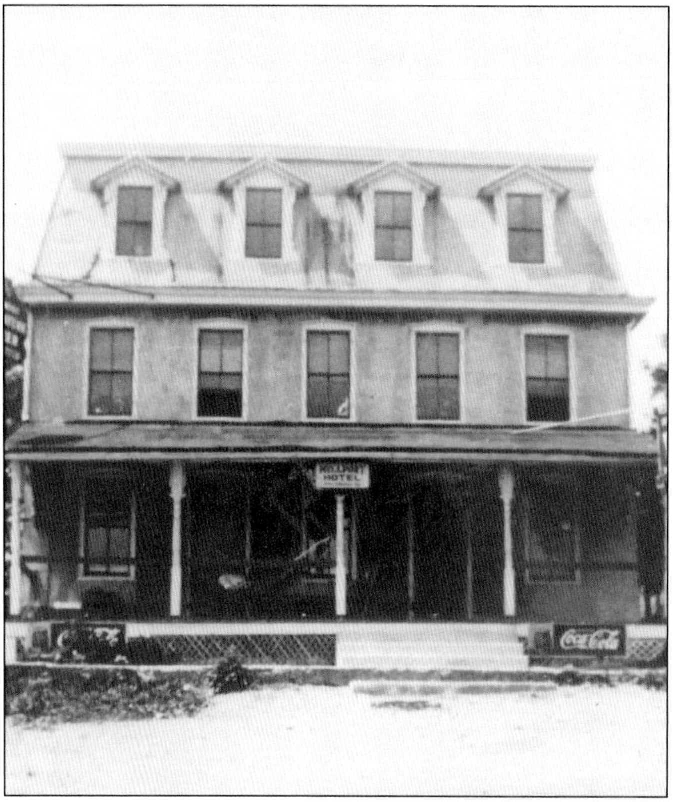

Dating back to 1864, the Millport Hotel (often referred to as the Disston Hotel), was owned and operated by Aldus H. Hackman who can be seen on the hammock. After selling the hotel in 1944, he and his wife operated Hackman's Bar, which was located at 2036 Main Street in Rothsville. Later, the bar and restaurant transferred ownership and was renamed Jim and Shirley's. (Courtesy of Tom Hackman.)

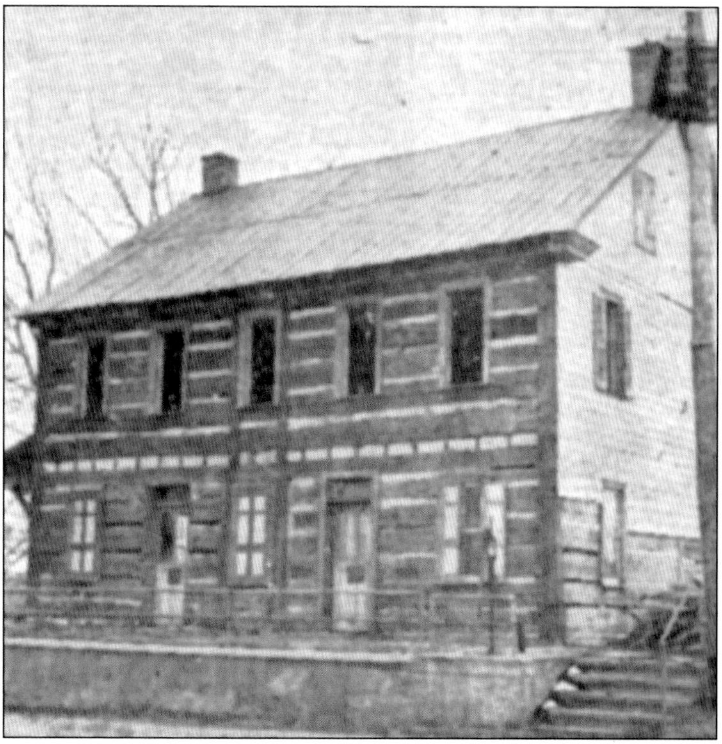

The Kissel Hill Hotel began as early as 1789 and continued up until the late 1940s. It was torn down about 1952 in order to straighten a curve in Route 501. It was extremely well built, with logs that measured a foot thick. These logs were exposed when the white clapboard exterior of the building was stripped away as the hotel was being readied for demolition. (Courtesy of Lancaster Newspapers.)

During its early inception, this location was known as the Kissel Hill Inn. In 1864, this hotel (below) was known as the New Haven Hotel and Store, with A. W. Shober acting as merchant and owner. In 1865, it was referred to as Shober's Tavern. By 1913, John H. Bausman ran the hotel. In 1952, the hotel site boasted at auction nine rooms containing a total of 13 acres and 82 perches of land. Also on the property that year was a large barn and shed. Herbert Beck, Lititz historian, noted that this area attracted many purple martin birds to its location. (Right, courtesy of Landis Valley Farm Museum; below, courtesy of Lancaster Newspapers.)

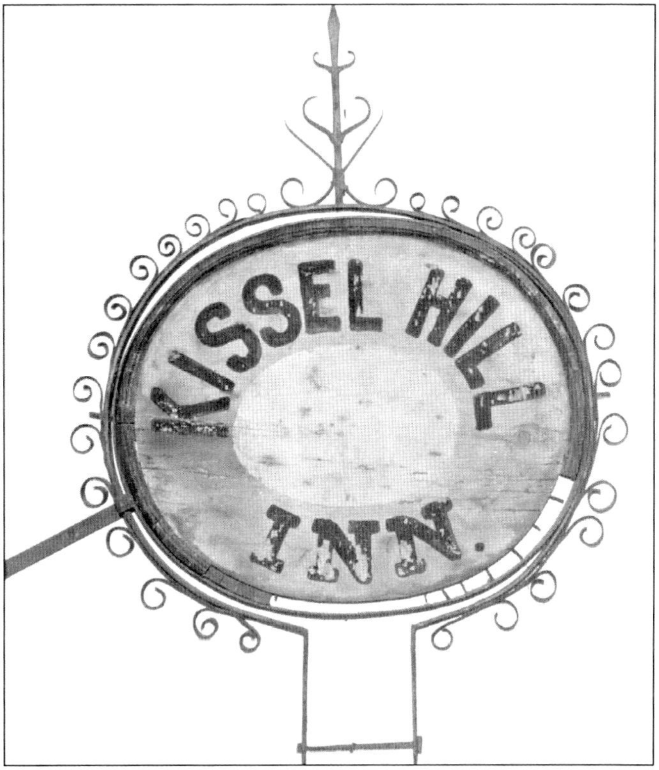

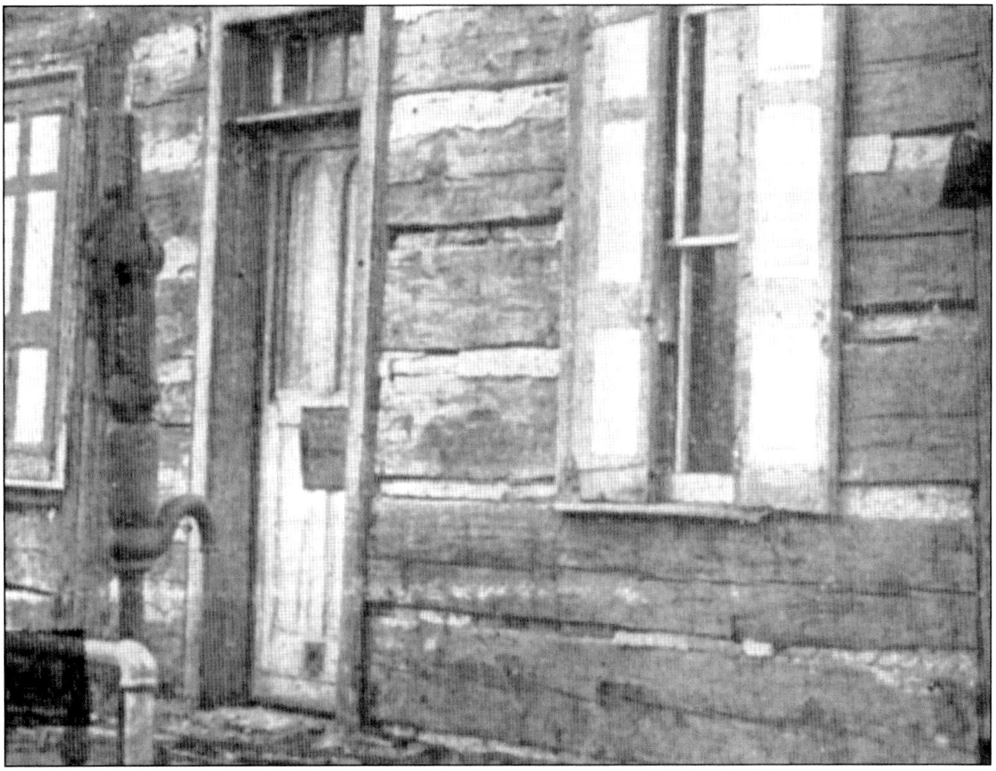

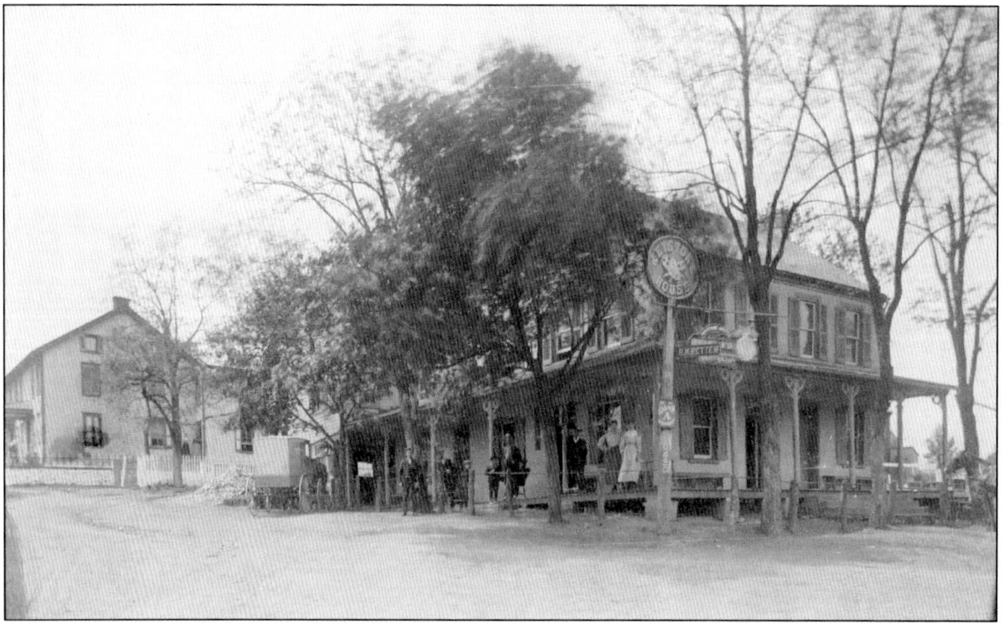

The Keystone House or Hotel located at 2034 Main Street in Rothsville, dates back to at least 1864, with S. N. Klausner serving as proprietor. That same year, Samuel Hallacher purchased the hotel and remained the owner until 1899, when J. S. Hallacher purchased the establishment. (Courtesy of the Robert "Sketch" Mearig collection.)

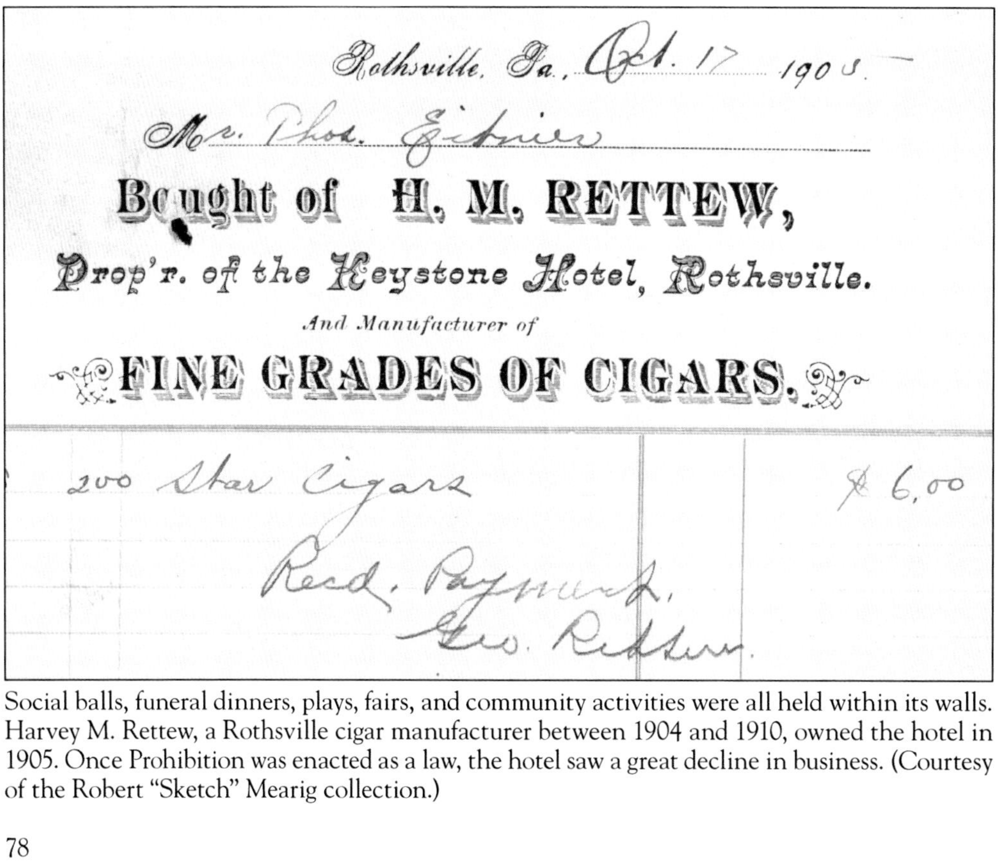

Rothsville, Pa., Oct. 17 1905.

Mr. Thos. Eitnier

Bought of H. M. RETTEW,

Prop'r. of the Keystone Hotel, Rothsville.

And Manufacturer of

FINE GRADES OF CIGARS.

200 Star Cigars $6.00

Recd. Payment.
Geo. Rettew.

Social balls, funeral dinners, plays, fairs, and community activities were all held within its walls. Harvey M. Rettew, a Rothsville cigar manufacturer between 1904 and 1910, owned the hotel in 1905. Once Prohibition was enacted as a law, the hotel saw a great decline in business. (Courtesy of the Robert "Sketch" Mearig collection.)

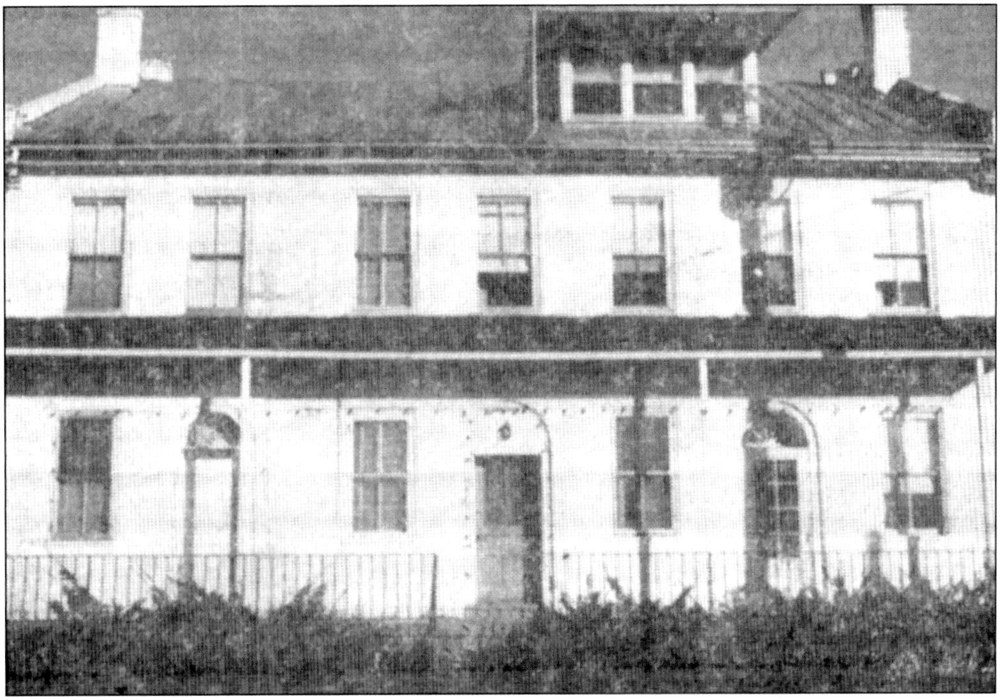

The Rome Hotel was most likely the township's earliest hotel, dating back to 1730. The original road leading to Clay, built in 1728, was the first road that went north through the township, and it started at this hotel. In 1864, this establishment was known as Buser's Hotel. This establishment did a thriving business until the Moravian town of Lititz also began overnight accommodations. (Courtesy of the Robert "Sketch" Mearig collection.)

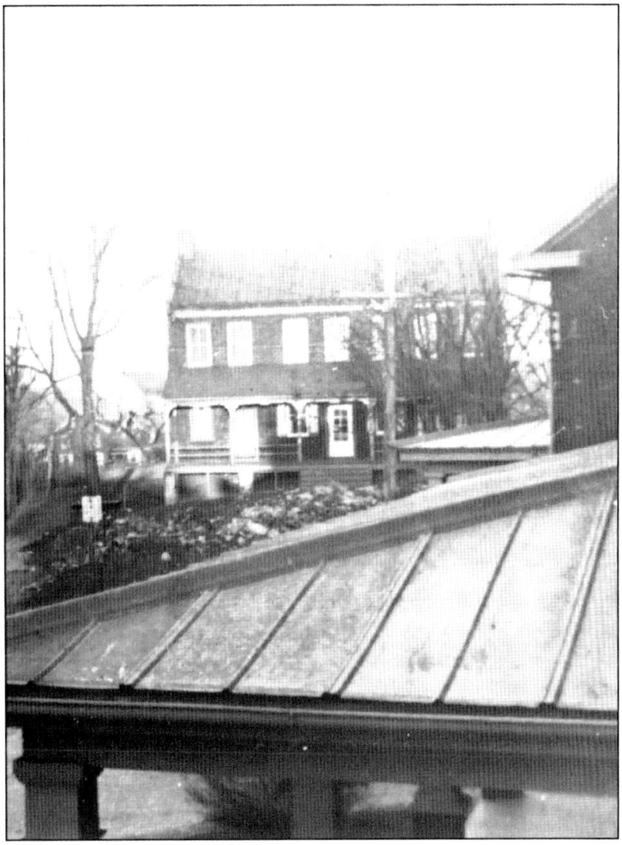

In later years, the hotel had a reputation for serving minors to help add to its income, and in 1910, owner Christian Imhoff got into trouble with the law for serving liquor to a Native American minor. As business declined, the hotel was converted into an apartment building, eventually being torn down. (Courtesy of the Robert "Sketch" Mearig collection.)

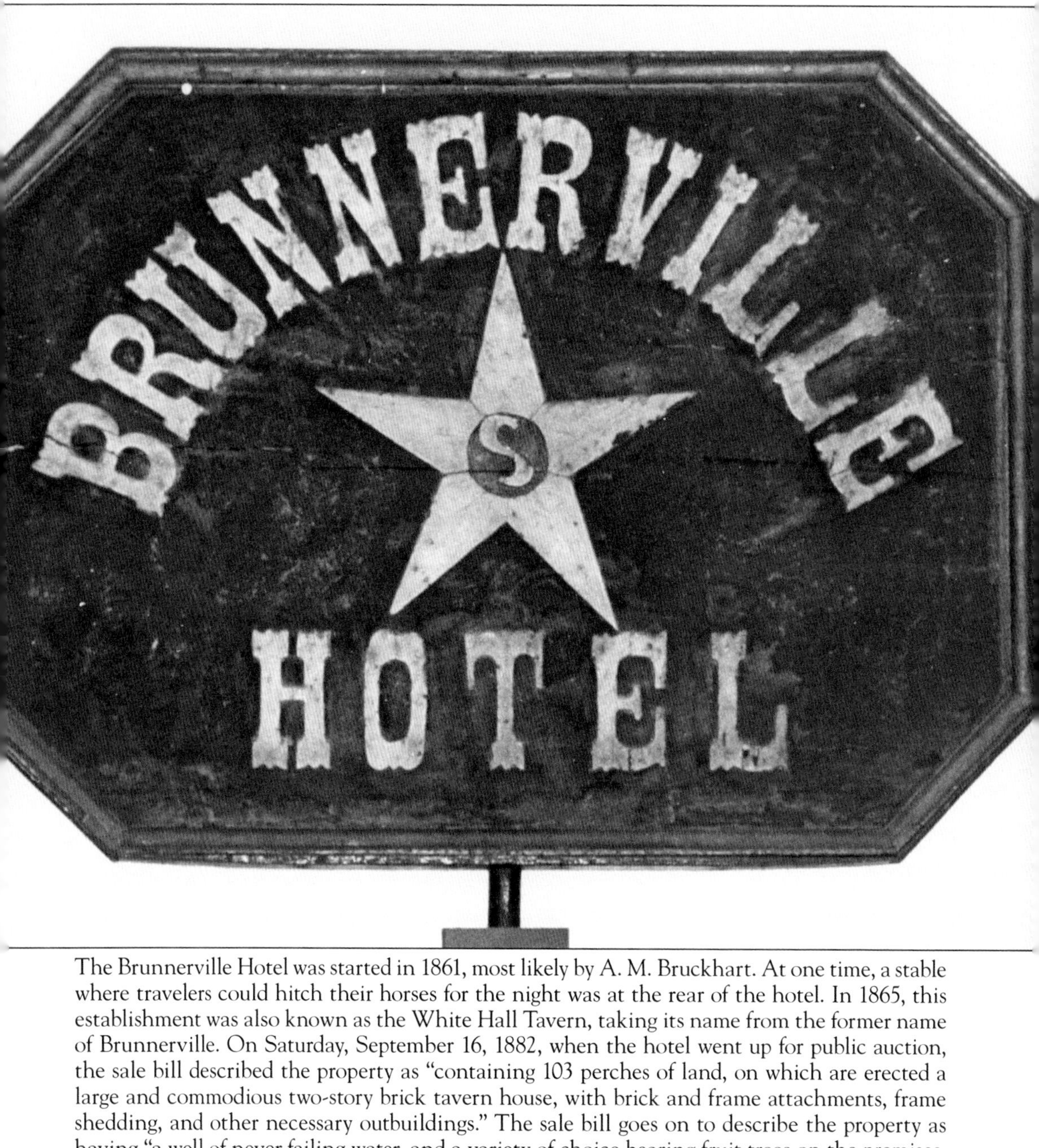

The Brunnerville Hotel was started in 1861, most likely by A. M. Bruckhart. At one time, a stable where travelers could hitch their horses for the night was at the rear of the hotel. In 1865, this establishment was also known as the White Hall Tavern, taking its name from the former name of Brunnerville. On Saturday, September 16, 1882, when the hotel went up for public auction, the sale bill described the property as "containing 103 perches of land, on which are erected a large and commodious two-story brick tavern house, with brick and frame attachments, frame shedding, and other necessary outbuildings." The sale bill goes on to describe the property as having "a well of never-failing water, and a variety of choice bearing fruit trees on the premises. The property is well fenced and in good shape." (Courtesy of Landis Valley Farm Museum.)

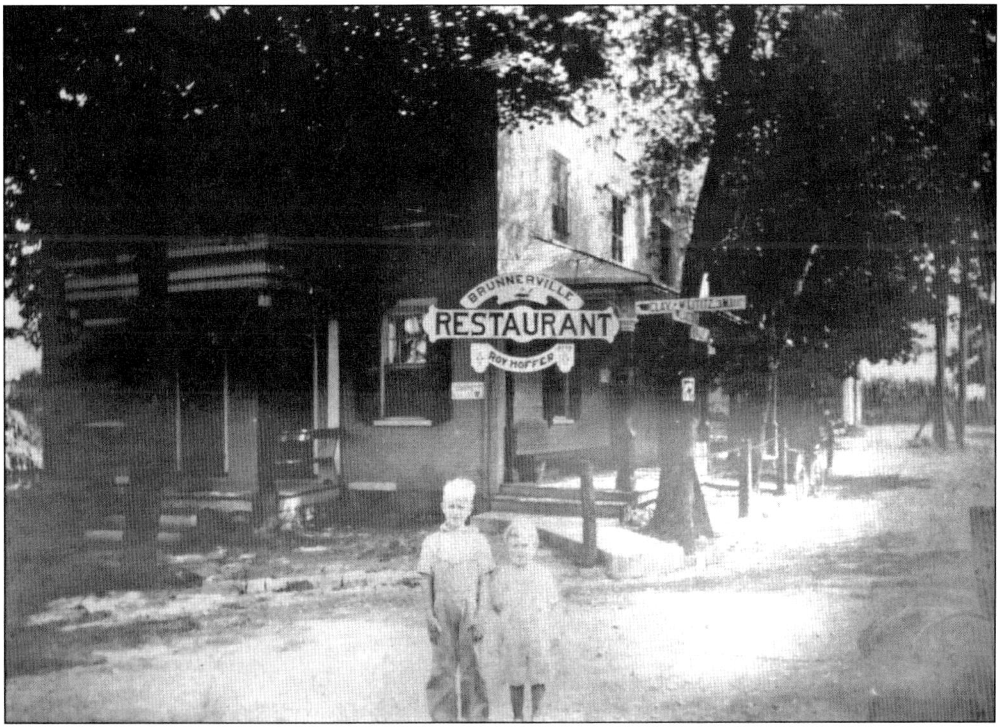

From 1920 to 1933, taverns across the United States felt the pinch of Prohibition. Roy Hoffer owned this hotel during Prohibition and decided to change the name to the Brunnerville Restaurant. Although it is unclear whether Hoffer sold liquor during Prohibition, after the ban was lifted, the name changed back to the Brunnerville Hotel. Pictured are Hoffer's two sons, Wilbur (left) and Richard (right). (Courtesy of Tom Hackman.)

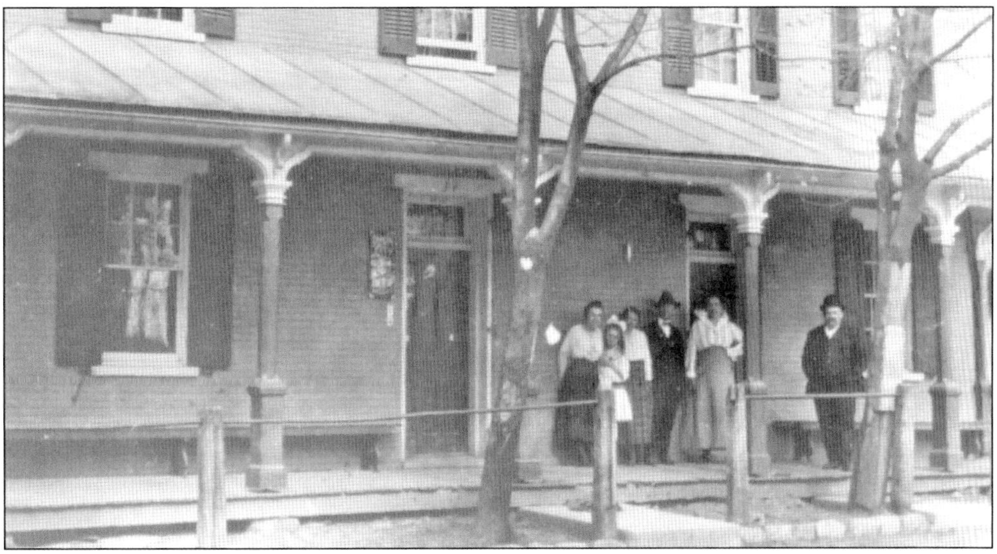

At the crossroads in Brunnerville, this establishment still greets and satisfies patrons with delicious food, satisfying beverages, and a beautiful outside deck. Upstairs rooms that once boarded travelers are no longer for rent. Pictured at far right is Levi K. Gockley, who owned the hotel in 1916, and some unidentified friends. (Courtesy of Tom Hackman.)

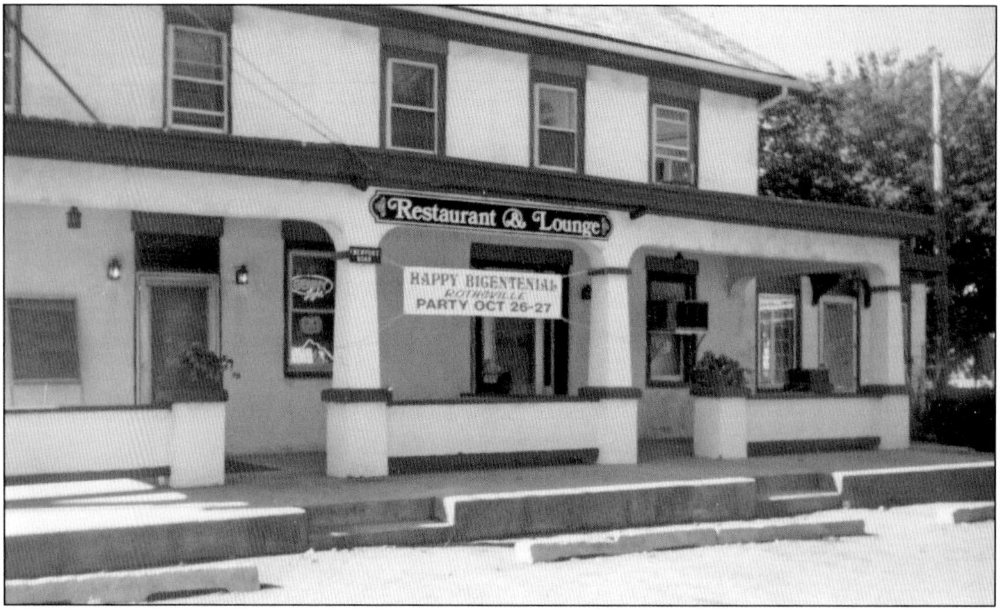

The current White Swan Hotel was built in 1790 by Phillip Roth, who named it Roth's Tavern. The property was advertised for public auction on February 15, 1850, listed as containing "71 acres, about 18 acres thereof is woodland and the remainder is divided into convenient fields, under good fences, and in a high state of cultivation." John Lowry purchased it in 1875, renaming it the Rothsville Hotel. In 1884, ownership changed to Susan Young Habecker and her husband, George Young. It was during their ownership that the race track located behind the tavern began operations. By 1909, it was owned by Barton and Emma Kieffer, who renamed it the Swan Hotel. About 1940, Fannie Miller became owner and changed the name to the current White Swan. (Both, courtesy of Sharyn Deater.)

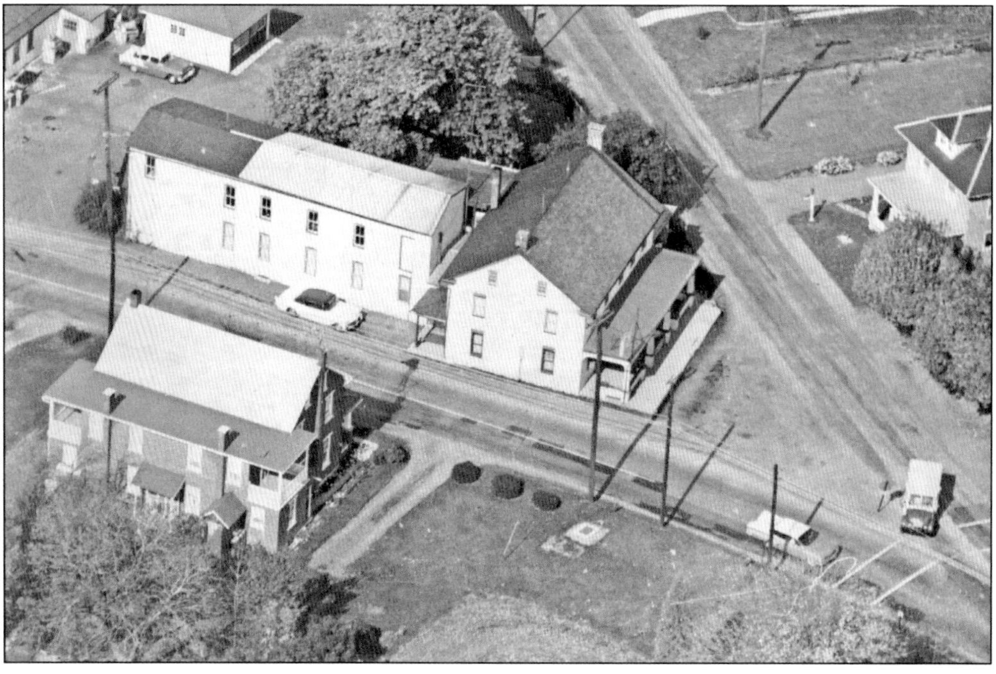

Six

Schools and Churches

As families grew within the township, a need was felt to educate both the adults and the children in the ways of both heavenly faith and scholarly education. Small church services, which in many cases were organized in neighborhood homes, began to grow as a need was realized to build community churches. For the first time, many families and neighbors could come together and all worship under the same roof. Throughout the years, these churches were expanded as members were added to the congregations. Public education started much in the same way, as small one-room schoolhouses were built in every community within Warwick Township. Parents would often pay teacher's wages by the day, plus supplies. If a student was deemed poor, the cost of education was paid by the County of Lancaster. Eager students in these early schools were taught the German language, grammar, and in many cases, passages from the Bible.

Some of the larger areas within the township, like Rothsville and Lexington, had two primary schools to fulfill the needs of their population's children. The need for larger schools became evident, and as they were built, the one-room schools were demolished or sold to be converted to private residences. For example, once the Lookout School in Pine Hill ceased, Amos Metzler purchased it and reassembled it at 225 East Lexington Road at the location of the former Lexington Union School. The two buildings were combined to create a two-family home, which eventually became a private residence. It still stands today.

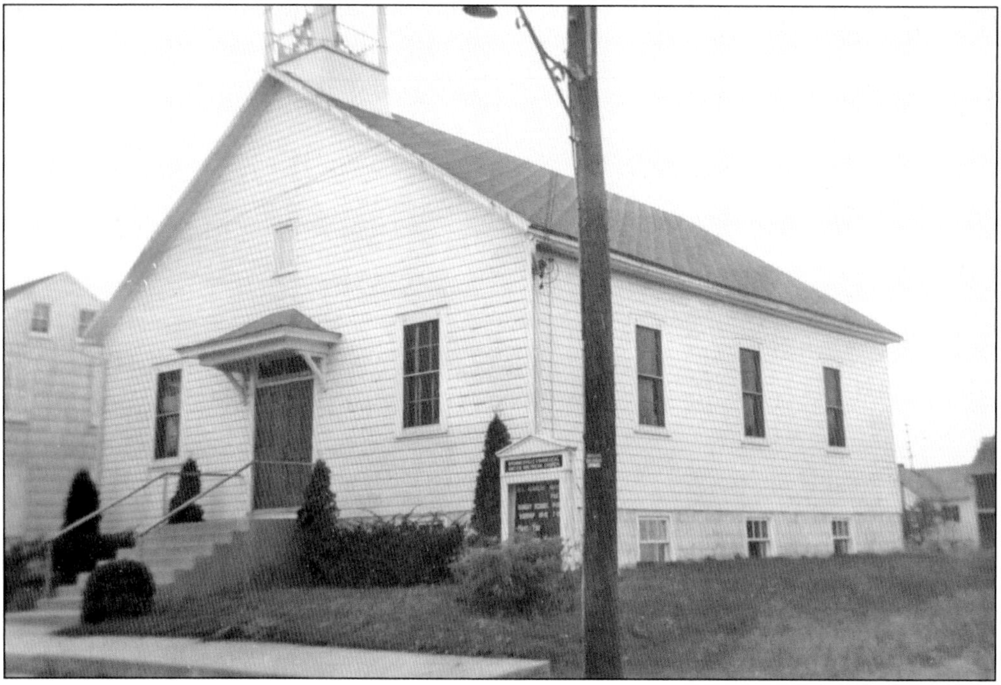

This church had its origins with Sunday school classes meeting at the original Brunnerville brick schoolhouse in 1866 and John B. Wissler serving as the first superintendent. By 1869, a charter was drawn up and land was purchased, with a church being erected along the short street in the village. The construction of the church was completed in 1870. (Courtesy of the Robert "Sketch" Mearig collection.)

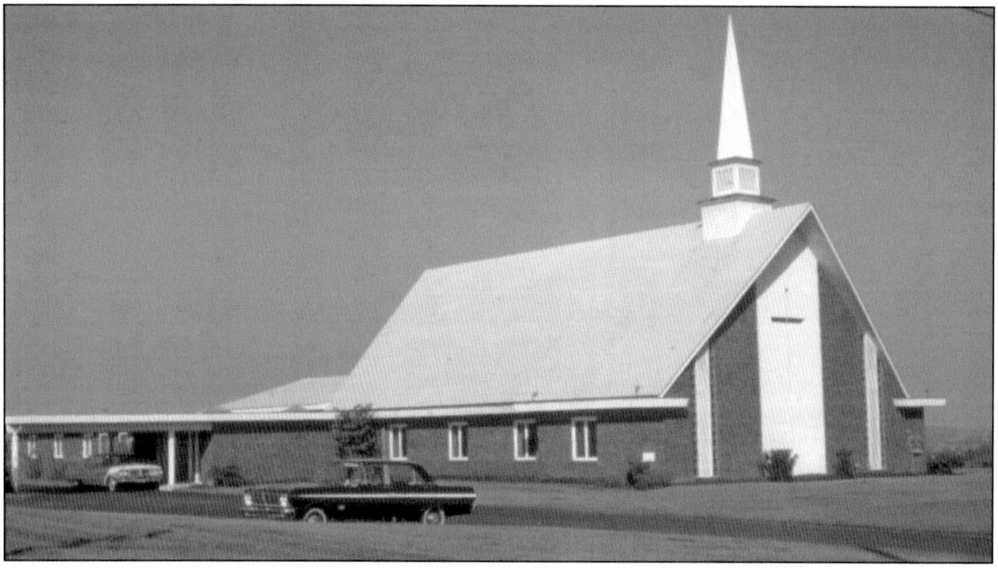

On October 12, 1873, the organization was known as the Brunnerville Union Sunday school. The school's reorganization was on May 8, 1881, and it was renamed the United Brethren in Christ Sunday School. By the 1960s, the congregation was in need of property for a bigger church. In 1966, land was purchased at 517 Pine Hill Road, and a much larger and modern church was constructed. (Courtesy of Tom Hackman.)

Beginning in 1840 with Lutheran families living in the Millport and Rothsville areas coming together to worship in their homes, a church was finally constructed on this site in Rothsville in 1848. Seeing a growing need to expand, the original church was dismantled in 1899, and a new church was constructed on the same site. The Jerusalem Evangelical Lutheran Church is pictured at right. (Courtesy of Sharyn Deater.)

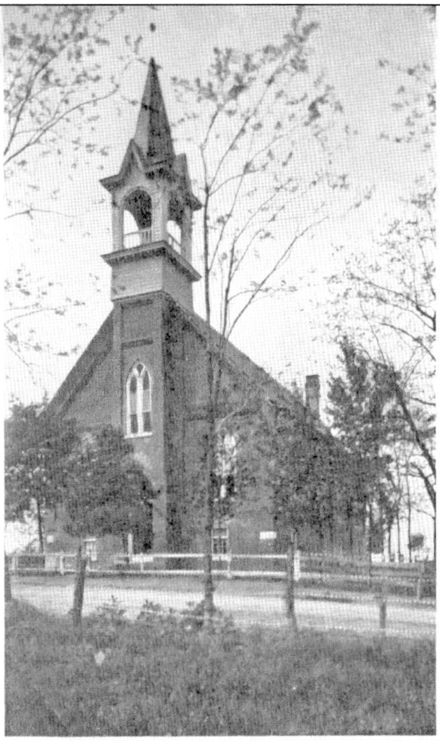

Lutheran Church, Rothsville, Pa.

G. G. LANDIS, PUBLISHER

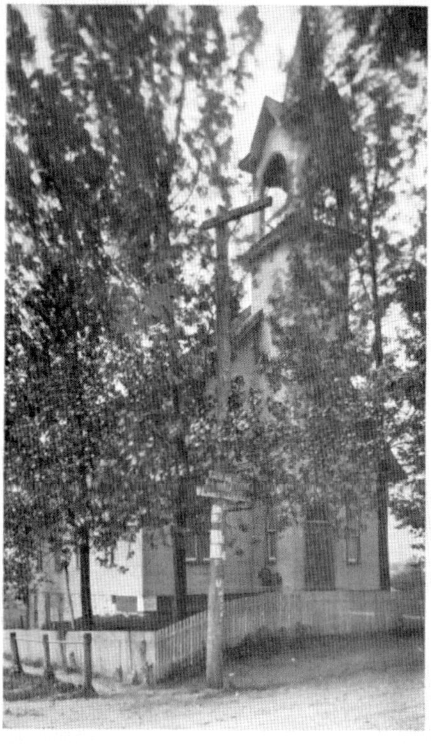

United Evangelical Church, Rothsville, Pa.

St. Paul's Evangelical Congregational Church was formed in 1894, with the cornerstone being laid during that same year. Dedication services were held the next year. In 1944, during one of the area's worst storms, lightning struck the church and damaged the steeple, which eventually was replaced. By 1961, renovations to the facility had cost $22,000, with T. D. Bellis serving as pastor during this time. (Courtesy of the Robert "Sketch" Mearig collection.)

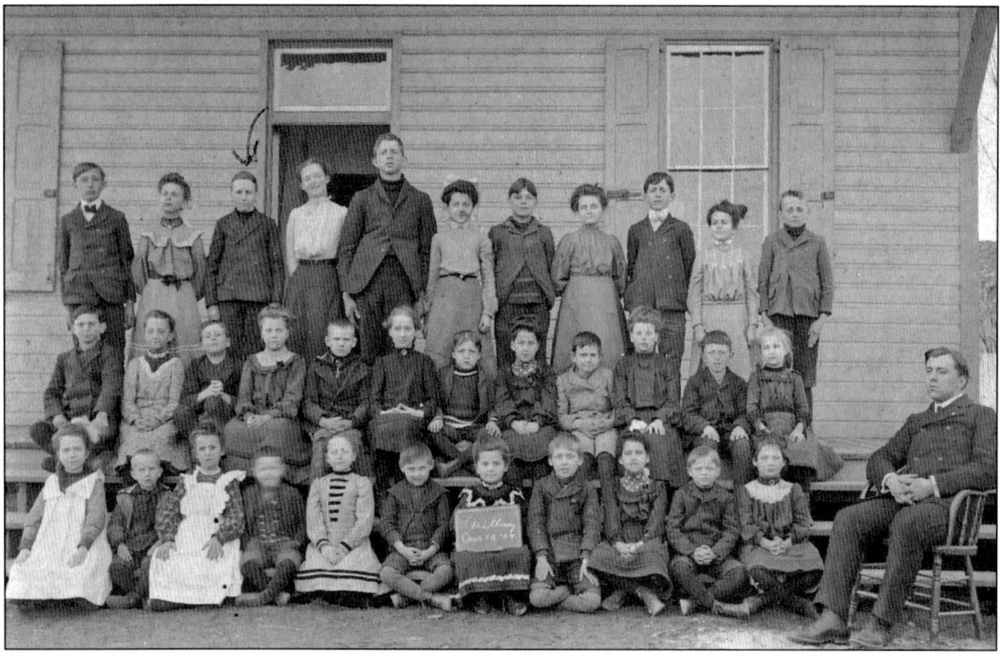

In this image dated March 30, 1904, grades first through eighth at the Millway School pose. All grades were taught by teacher Chester Hoffman in the same classroom. During the school year of 1891, E. R. Shirk served as teacher, with H. E. Siagenhaup serving as teacher in 1892. (Courtesy of the Lititz Historical Foundation.)

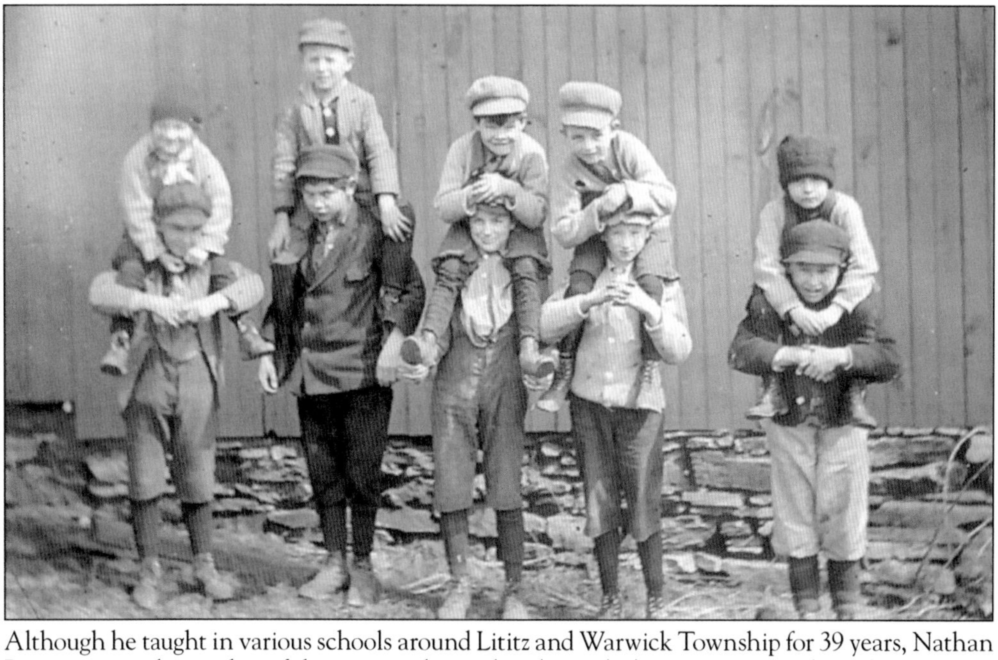

Although he taught in various schools around Lititz and Warwick Township for 39 years, Nathan Reist was not the teacher of these young boys when he took their picture standing alongside the Millway School. During his time as a teacher, Reist would bring plant specimens, arrowheads, and other objects that he had found into his classroom for his students to study. (Courtesy of private collection.)

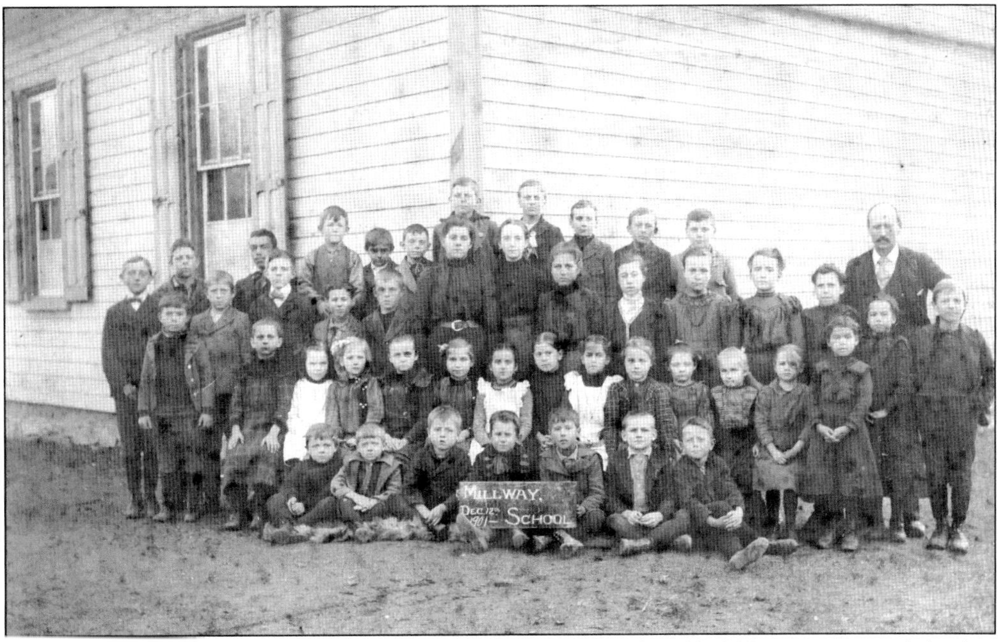

The pupils of the Millway School are shown here on December 12, 1901. The original deed to this school traces back to December 31, 1892, with $250 paid by the Warwick School District for 80 perches (half an acre) of land. The school district eventually sold the property at public sale to John Reitz on April 1, 1924, for $870. (Courtesy of John David Wissler.)

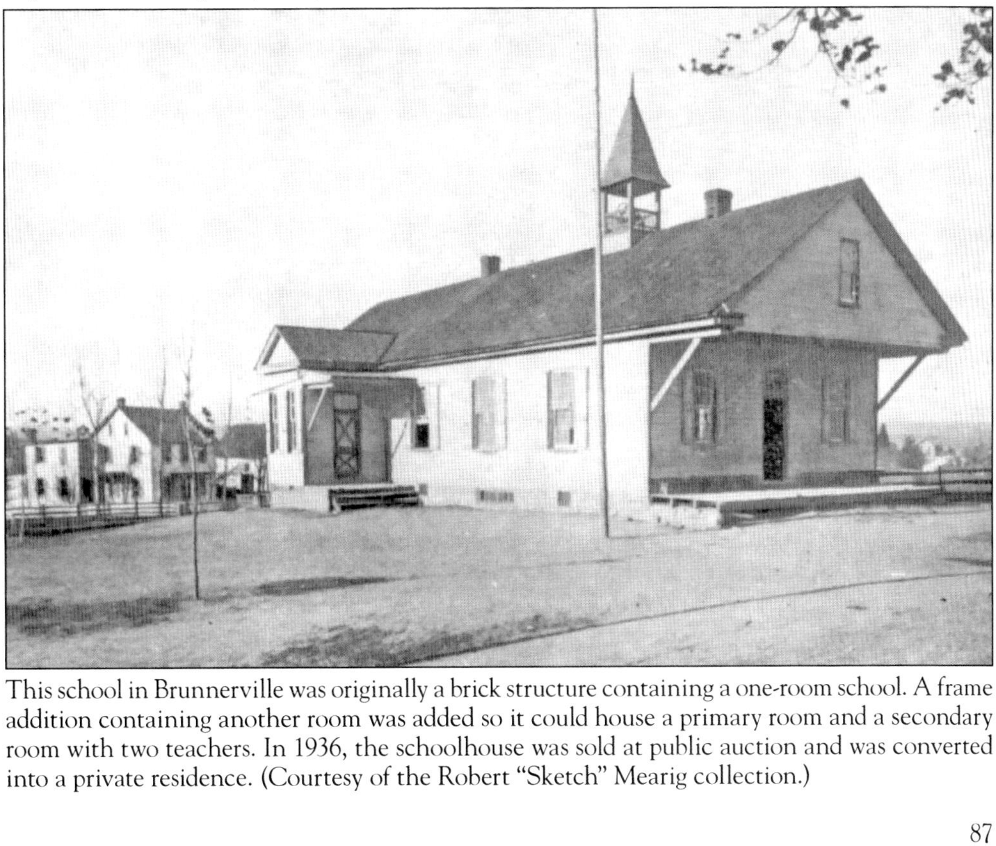

This school in Brunnerville was originally a brick structure containing a one-room school. A frame addition containing another room was added so it could house a primary room and a secondary room with two teachers. In 1936, the schoolhouse was sold at public auction and was converted into a private residence. (Courtesy of the Robert "Sketch" Mearig collection.)

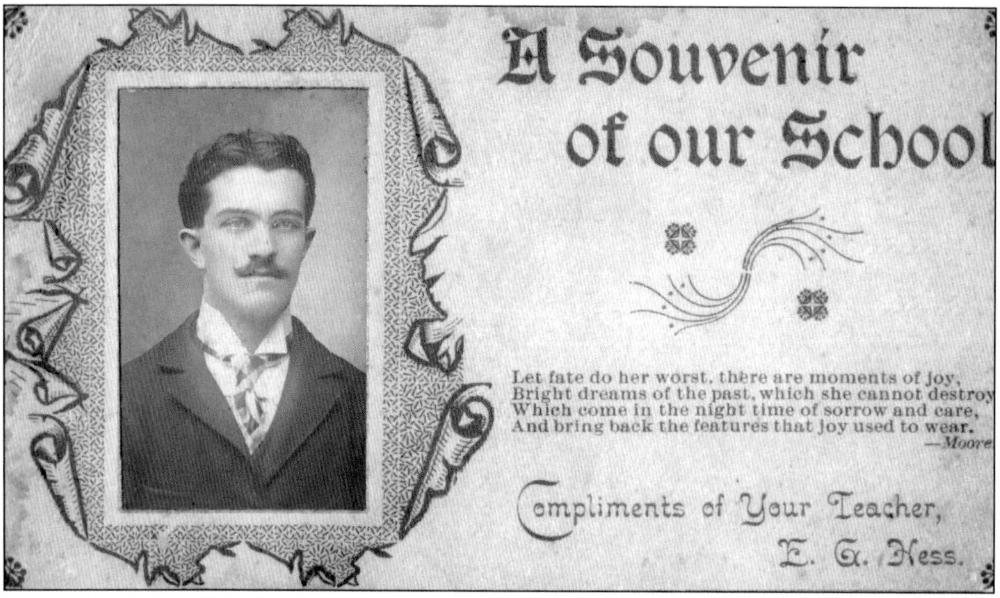

During the 1898–1899 school year, E. G. Hess taught at Buch's School, which was located at 525 West Orange Street in the township. On the back of this card, all of the names of the pupils who attended that year were listed, along with the name of S. W. Buch, who acted as the school's president. (Courtesy of the Robert "Sketch" Mearig collection.)

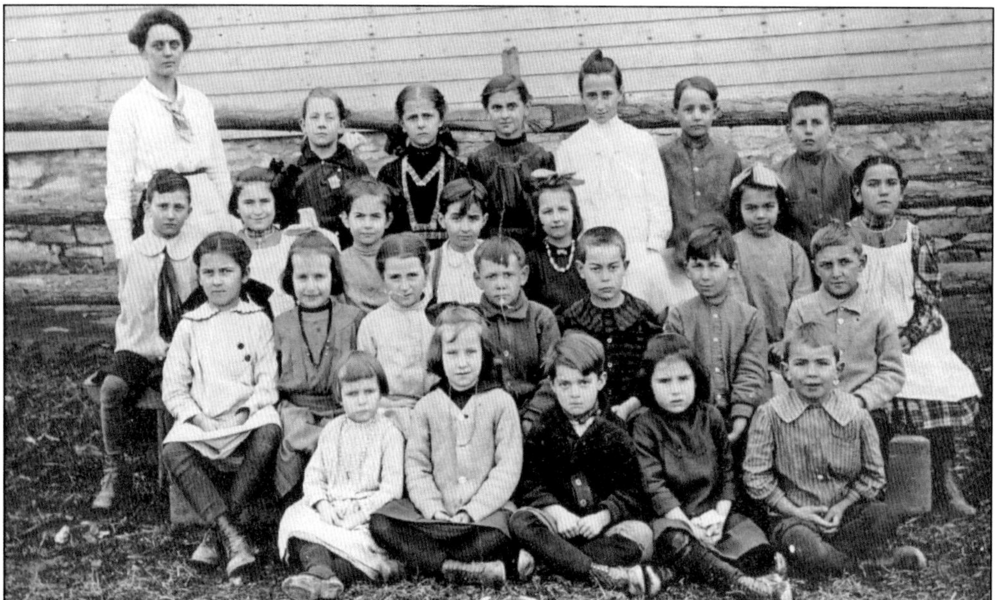

The Brunnerville School students of 1915 posed for this picture, taken by Reidenbach Photography of Lititz. The students are, from left to right, (first row) Mabel Earhart, Esther Irvin, Clyde Hoffer, ? Leslie, and Earl Reist; (second row) ? Buch, Erla Hess, Ida Kauffman, Jacob Hackman, Milton Landis, ? Fryberger, and William Hunt; (third row) Morris Eckert, ? Pfautz, Mildred Carpenter, Elmer Hershey, Mirium Geyer, ? Fryberger, and ? Pfautz; (fourth row) Pauline Hess (teacher), Esta Flory, Esta Habecker, Gertrude Hoffer, Olive Kauffman, ? Stoner, and Harry Buchter. (Courtesy of Tom Hackman.)

When the original Brunnerville School was in operation in the early 1900s, it was divided into two sections: grades one through four (primary) and grades five through eight (secondary). Gertrude Dietrich (left) taught secondary while Pauline Hess (right) taught primary. Additional teachers from this school included Emma Habecker, Francis Lefever, Mary Smith, and Carrie Hammond. (Courtesy of Tom Hackman.)

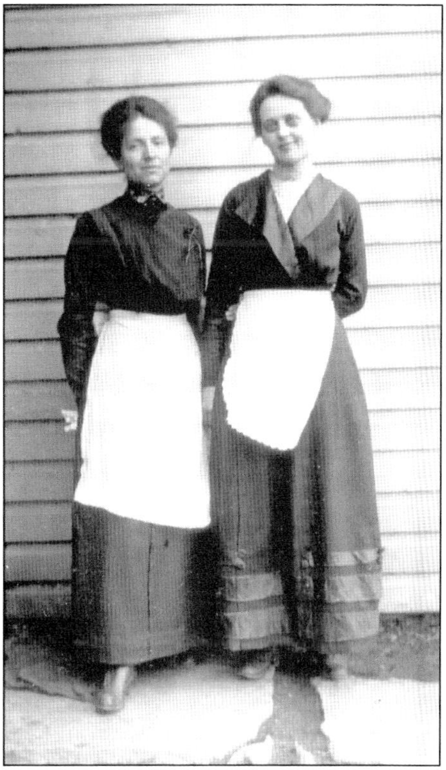

Nathan Reist captured yet another great school memory when he took this photograph inside the Brunnerville School. Perhaps this was a graduation ceremony of some kind at the end of the school year. The school also had its share of male teachers, with H. R. Gibble serving during the year of 1892, and J. M. Reighter serving during the 1894 school year. (Courtesy of private collection.)

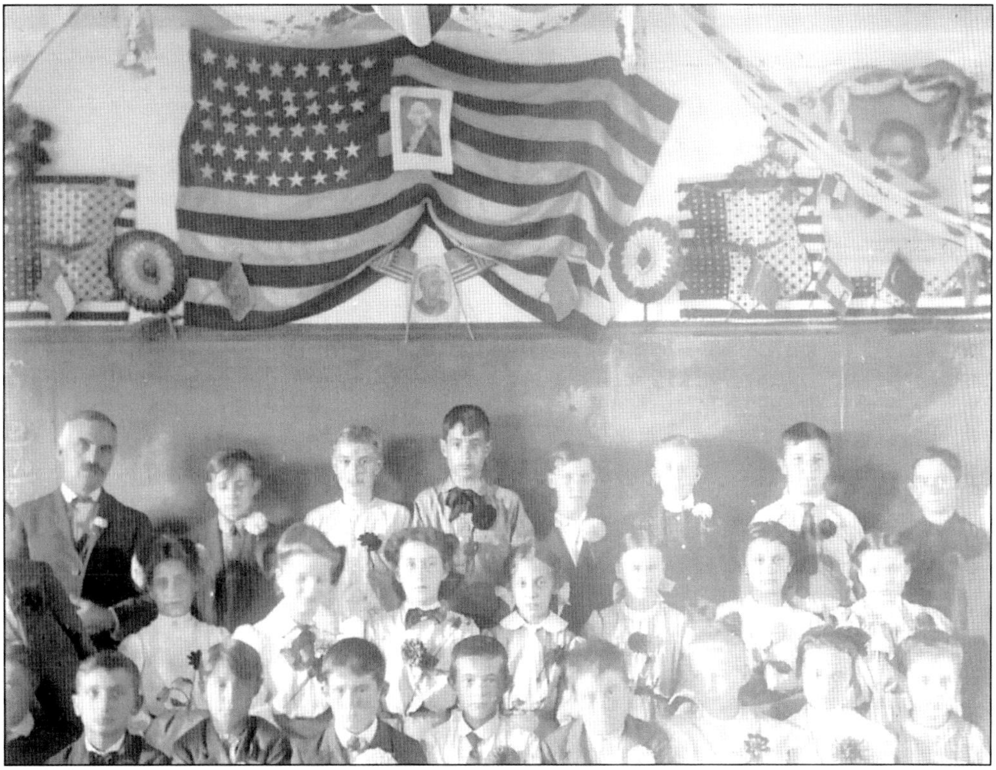

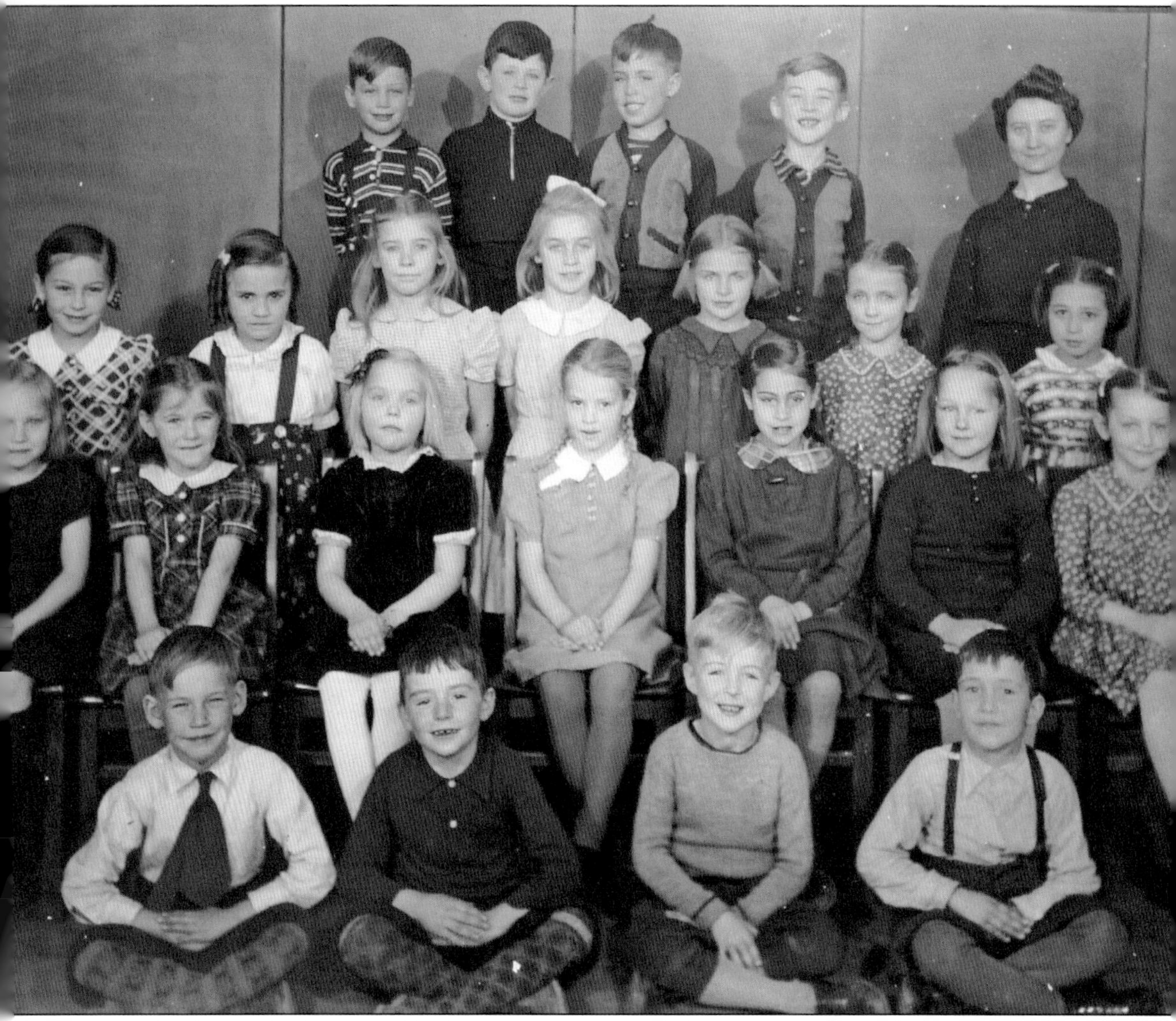

It was by sheer luck that this old photograph was stumbled upon recently at a local antique flea market in Lancaster County. Seen here is a student class picture of first and second grades taken inside John Beck Elementary School in 1941. Originally a five-grade school when built in 1936, this school has seen several expansions throughout the years. Currently, it houses 31 classrooms, all containing cable television and Internet access. The library has also expanded over the years and currently has 12 computer stations. Education throughout the years in Brunnerville has certainly come a long way. Ralph Keith, a former student at the original Brunnerville School, purchased the old two-room school for a sum of $1,050 at public sale the same year that John Beck Elementary was opened. (Courtesy of the author's collection.)

For many years, the Pleasant View School at 811 Furnace Hills Pike was one of two schools located in Lexington. In 1937, it was sold at public sale and converted into a residence. Sometime between 1943 and 1948, the building was moved east about 30 feet to allow Route 501 to be relocated, lowered, and widened to accommodate the heavier flow of traffic. (Courtesy of Doris McCreary.)

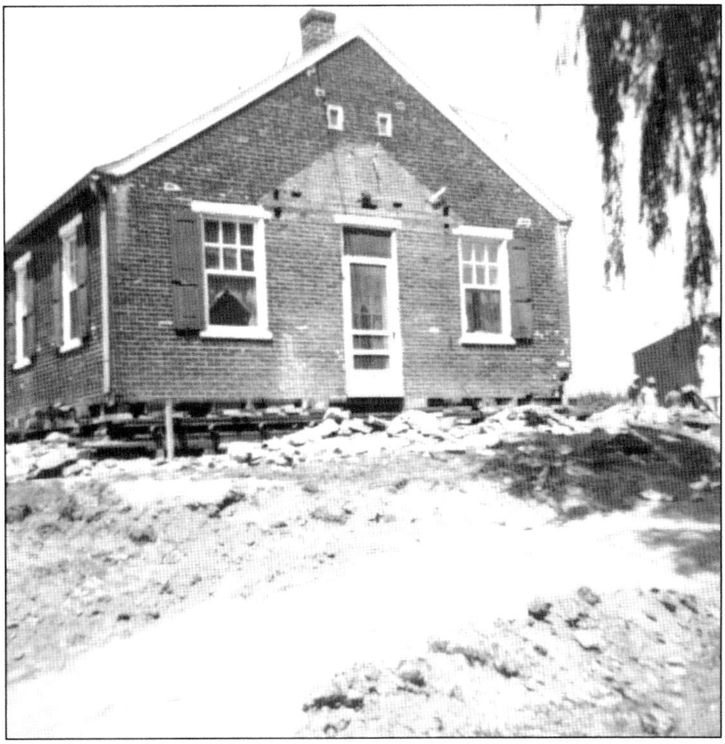

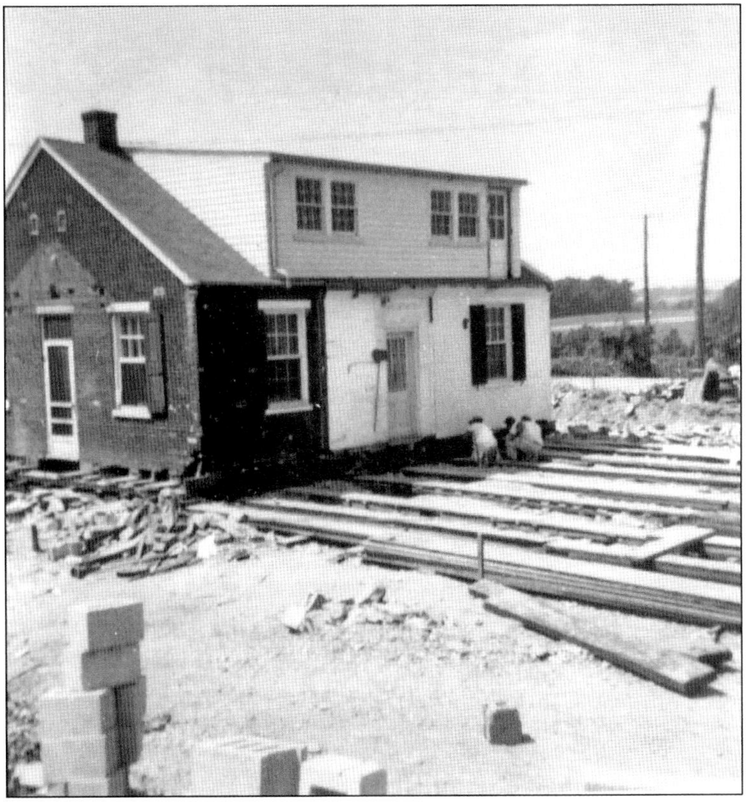

Moving the schoolhouse no doubt took many hours of skillful and painstaking planning. Various men helped with this task, all working together in unison to keep the structure and integrity of the dwelling intact during the tedious move. The building still stands today as a private residence. (Courtesy of Doris McCreary.)

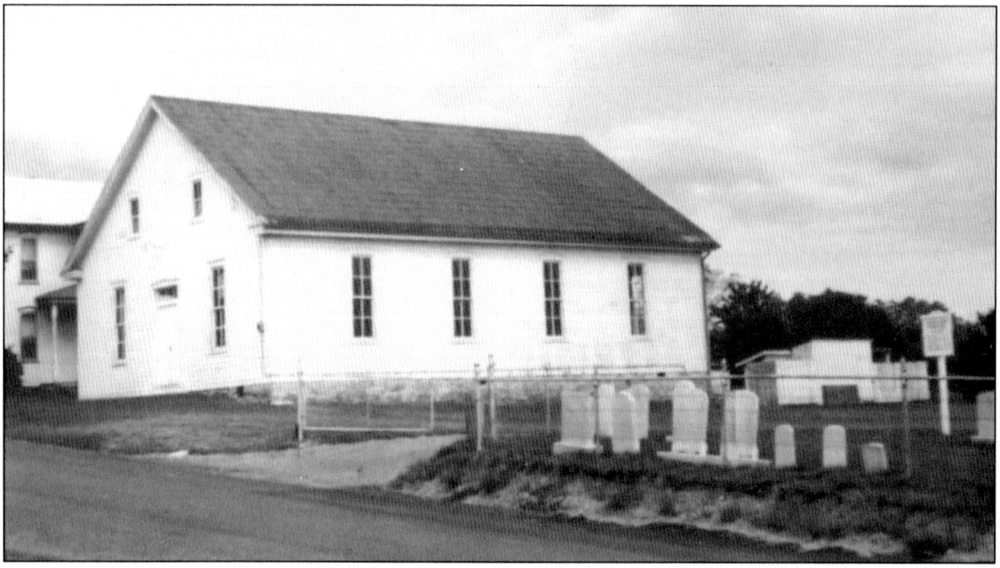

Using land donated by Elias Grube, the New Zion Children in Christ Church (also known as the Rothsville United Zion Church) was constructed in 1890. James Heitler of Rothsville served as the first minister. Located on the northwest corner of Twin Brook Drive in Rothsville, the congregation eventually dwindled in size with church services ceasing by 1967. Soon thereafter, the building was razed. (Courtesy of Sharyn Deater.)

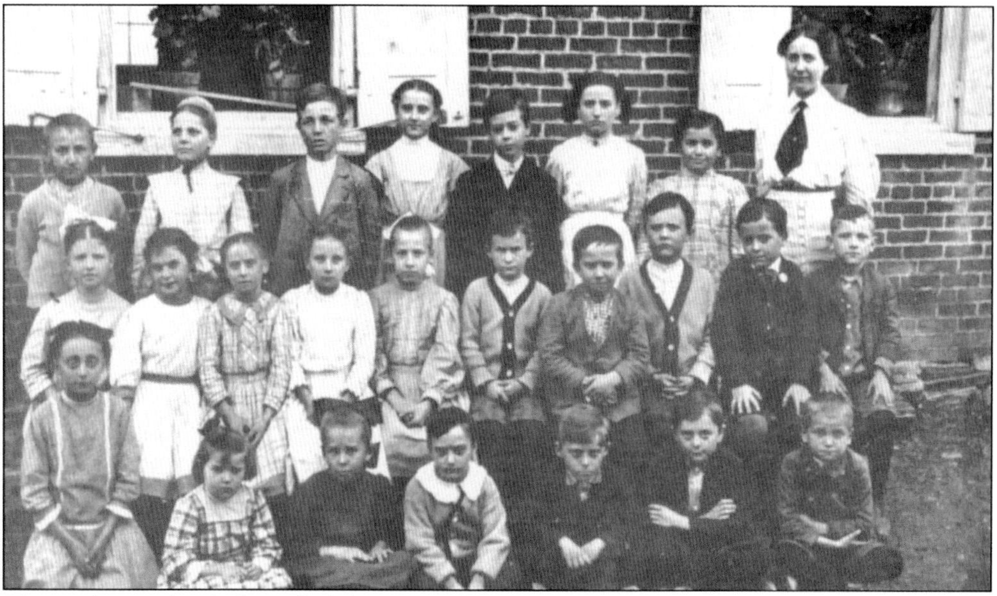

The Lookout School, also called the Pine Hill School, was, as the name suggests, located in Pine Hill. Here is the class from about 1910 with Edna Eckman serving as teacher. The students are, from left to right, (first row) Rachel Groff, Earla Miller, Mary Hollinger, Clarence Levan, Paul Groff, Norman Groff, and Grant Miller; (second row) Florence Miller, Lizzie Spangler, Carrie Groff, Lucy Hackman, Marie Shank, Earl Haldeman, Frank Frederick, Ralph Haldeman, Freeman Becker, and John Hackman; (third row) John Horning, Mabel Metzler, Samuel Greenly, Esther Groff, Cullen Carpenter, Maude Spangler, and Jennie Lorah. (Courtesy of the Robert "Sketch" Mearig collection.)

Salem Lutheran Church of Kissel Hill had its beginnings with the cornerstone laying on June 1, 1823, after a one-acre lot was purchased for $60. The total cost of constructing the building after all labor and materials were added up came to the sum of $2,060.22. The Lutheran and Reformed congregations in the Kissel Hill area now had a place of worship. (Courtesy of Polly Garner.)

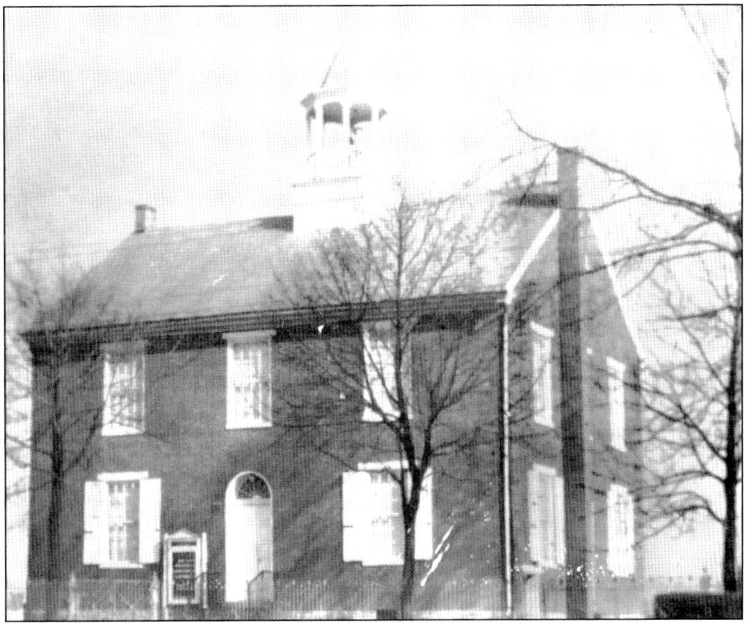

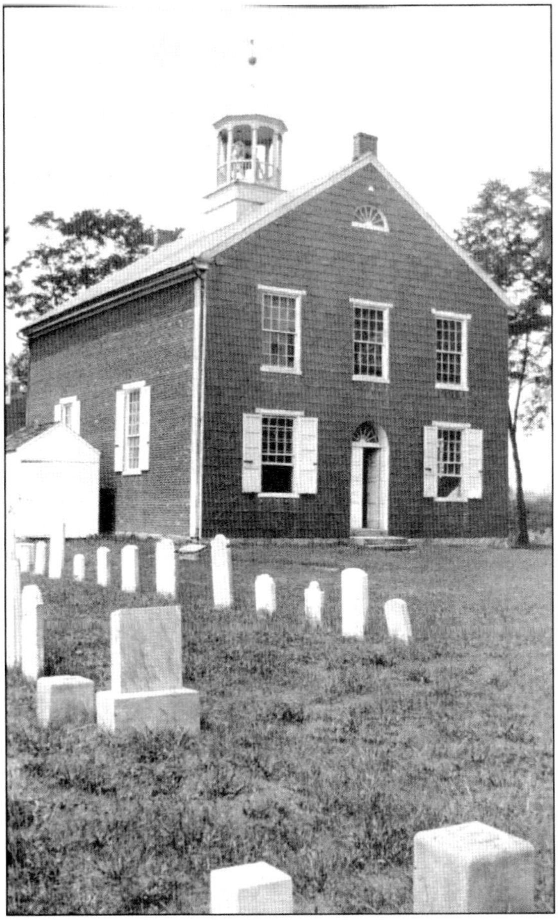

The first minister of the Lutheran congregation was William Bates, who served from 1824 to 1839. The first minister of the Reformed congregation was Daniel Hertz, serving from 1823 to 1831. The cemetery behind the church was called the Churchyard in the beginning. In an early church register, it was written that William Nixon and Christian Young were the first people buried in the Churchyard in 1824. (Courtesy of Polly Garner.)

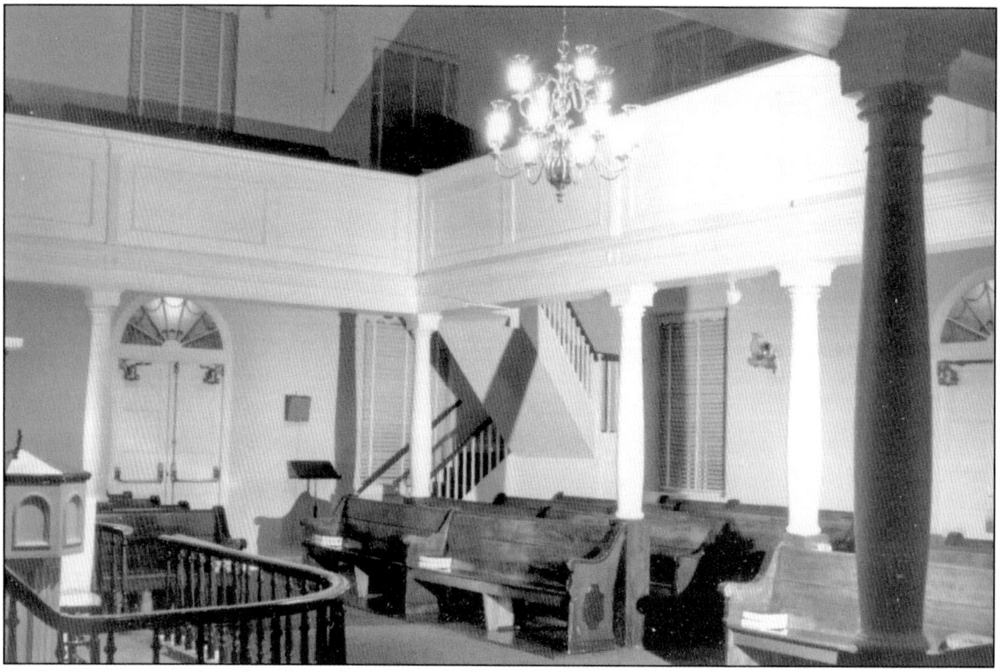

In the beginning, the church had a wine glass–shaped pulpit, which could be reached by a spiral staircase. Sermons were preached from this lofty perch until 1872, when it was modernized. In November and December 1921, lights were installed inside the church and used for the first time for that year's Christmas service. In 1915, the original organ was replaced with a new one. (Courtesy of Polly Garner.)

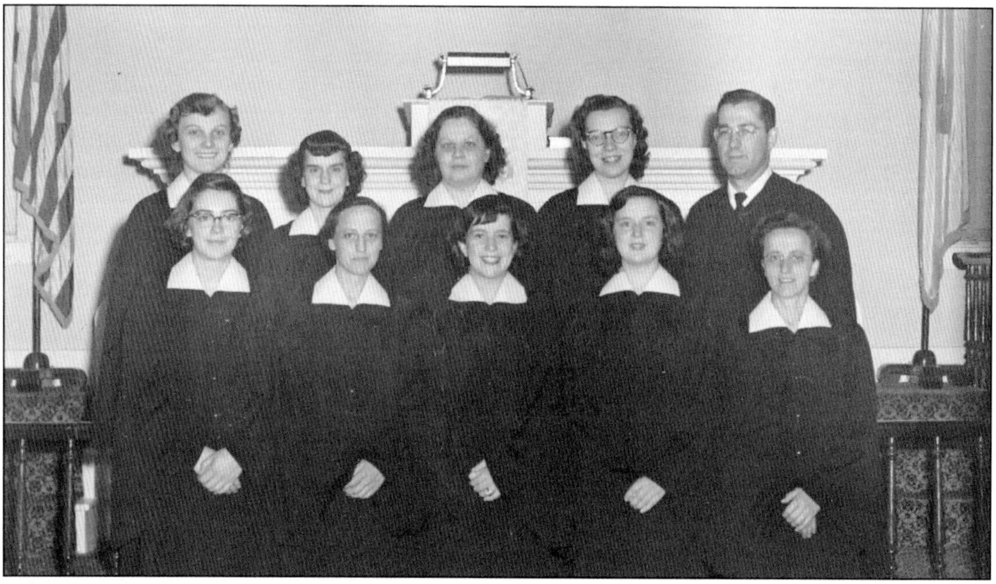

Salem has members with good singing voices who volunteer their time as members of the church's choir. This image, taken between 1950 and 1955, shows, from left to right, (first row) Joan Habecker, Florence Stauffer, Shirley Gehman, Gerry Gehman, and Beulah Stauffer; (second row) Fay Garner, Polly Gehman, May Stauffer, Bernitia Ember, and Rev. Paul Whitmoyer. Whitmoyer served with the church between 1950 and 1955. (Courtesy of Polly Garner.)

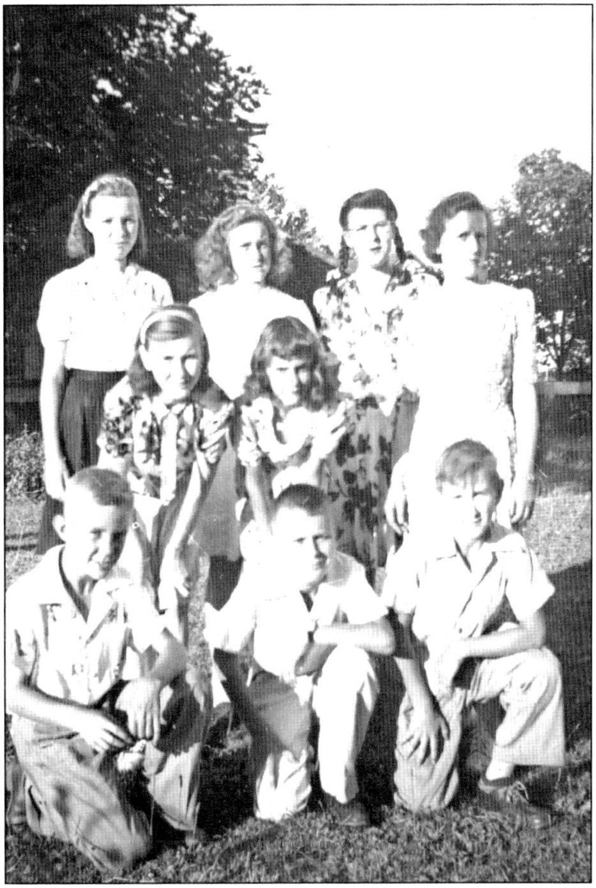

In 1960, there was an expansion to the church building when a cornerstone was laid for a Sunday school building. In 1945, members of the Sunday school class were, from left to right, (first row) Sonny Hoffman, Bobby Garner, and Fred Kopp; (second row) Joyce Kopp, Polly Gehman, and teacher Ella Stauffer; (third Row) Bernitia Ember, Fay Stauffer, and Shirley Buchter. (Courtesy of Polly Garner.)

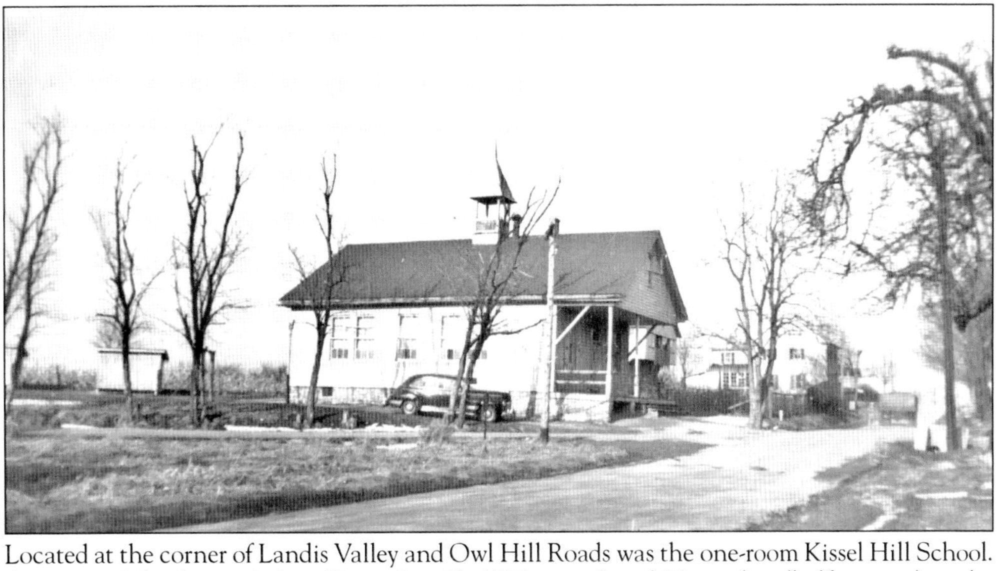

Located at the corner of Landis Valley and Owl Hill Roads was the one-room Kissel Hill School. An original deed recorded on December 22, 1893, transferred 80 perches (half an acre) to the school district from Ambrose Mahlschnee and his wife, Annie. This photograph was taken in the early 1940s. (Courtesy of Martha Xakellis; photograph from Eva Behmer Myers.)

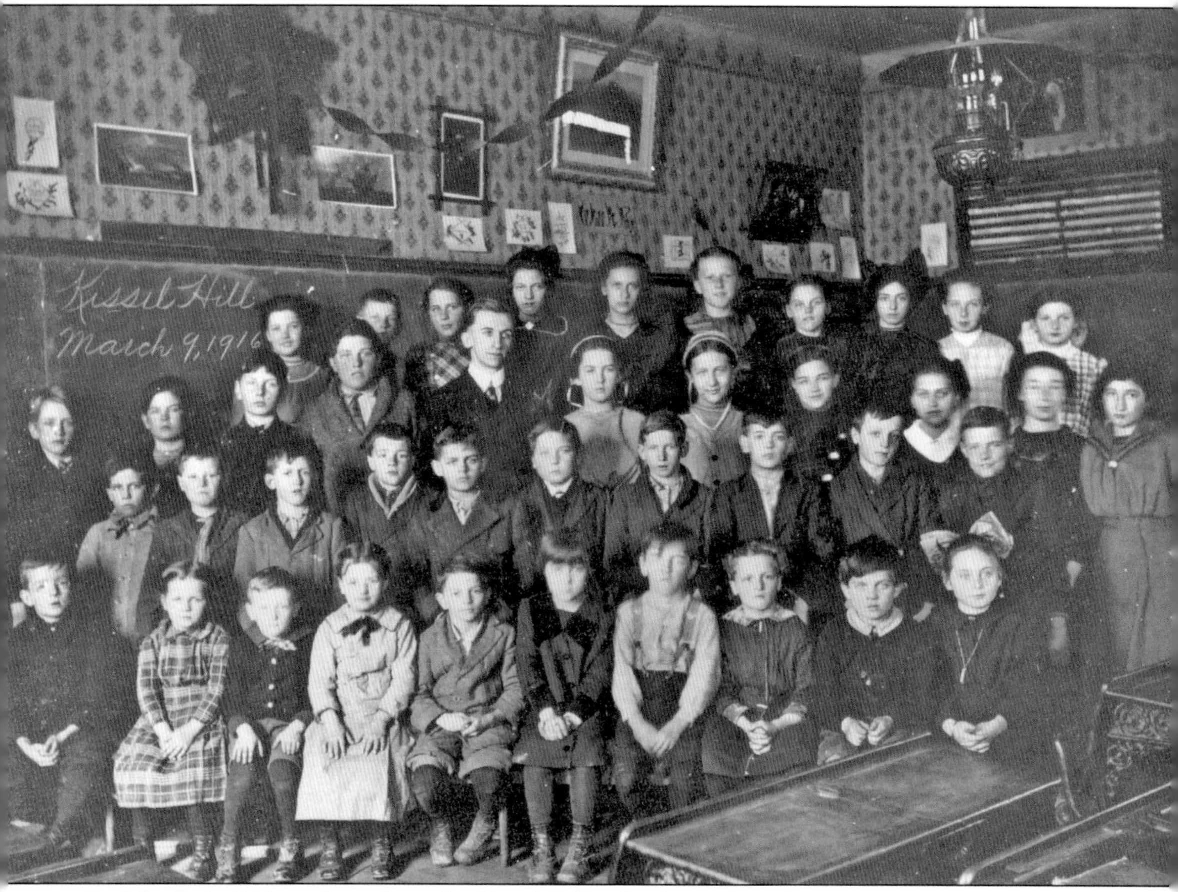

On March 9, 1916, students from the Kissel Hill School are, from left to right, (first row) Paul Wertz, Anna Stauffer, Paul Rupp, Bertha Sensenich, Raymond Witmer, Alma Webber, Henry Young, Ella Stauffer, Paul Meiskey, and Kathryn Heitsher; (second row) Roy Stauffer, Bryan Grube, Chester Frey, Martin Sensenich, John Habecker, Earl Steffy, Theodore Frey, Chester Habecker, Ralph Stauffer, and Harry Sensenich; (third row) Elmer Hess, Wayne Young, Nelson Freidly, Harry Steffy, H. E. Studenroth (teacher), Ella Young, Ella Mae Mellinger, Hettie Sensenich, Esther Frederick, Elizabeth Webber, and Mary Frey; (fourth row) Nettie Young, Wayne Grube, Grace Snyder, Sarah Shaeffer, Luella Webber, Florince Grube, Esther Frey, Ella Mae Shriener, Alma Freidly, and Emma Freidly. (Courtesy of Polly Garner.)

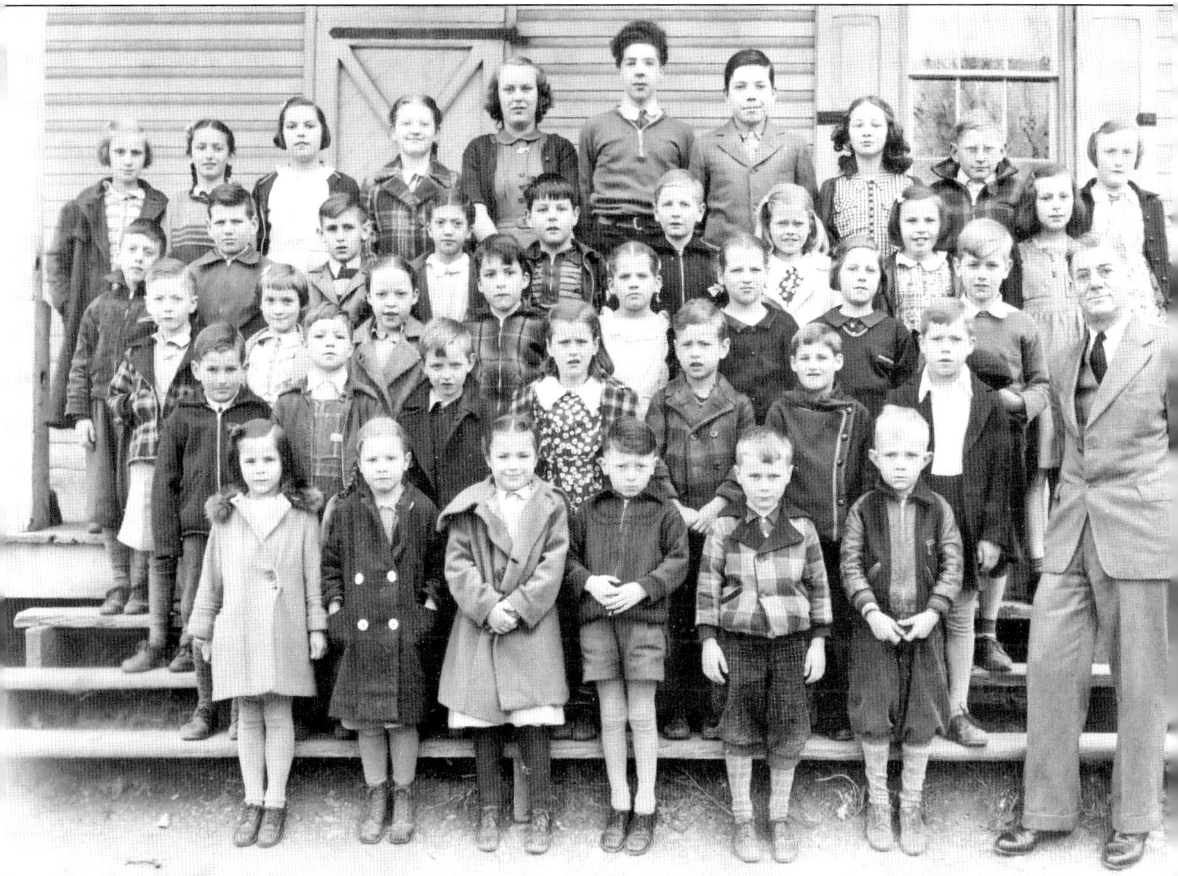

Teacher Hiram Minnich is posing with his Kissel Hill students in the 1938–1939 school year. With many of the students wearing their coats, it is evident that this photograph was taken on a cold or windy day. From left to right are (first row) Annabell Singer, Mary Sensenig, Dorcas Weaver, unidentified , Bob Garner, and Charles Hoffman; (second row) Robert Stauffer, Elias Grube, ? Tome, Nancy Grube, Rick Farrell, Carl Snyder, and Bob Steffy; (third row) Chet Habecker, Fay Stauffer, Laura Weaver, John Troutman, Ruth Stauffer, Rhoda Stauffer, Thelma Haines, and Donald Fisher; (fourth row) Carl Snavely, Roy Stauffer, Carl Singer, Fern Fahnestock, Jim Brenner, Harold Grube, Jean Grube, Judy Troutman, and Shirley Buchter; (fifth row) Elizabeth Hess, Flora Lindeman, Betty Haines, Romaine Habecker, Lois Buchter, Billy Packard, Ralph Haines, Jane Hollinger, Russell Hess, and June Stauffer. (Courtesy of Polly Garner).

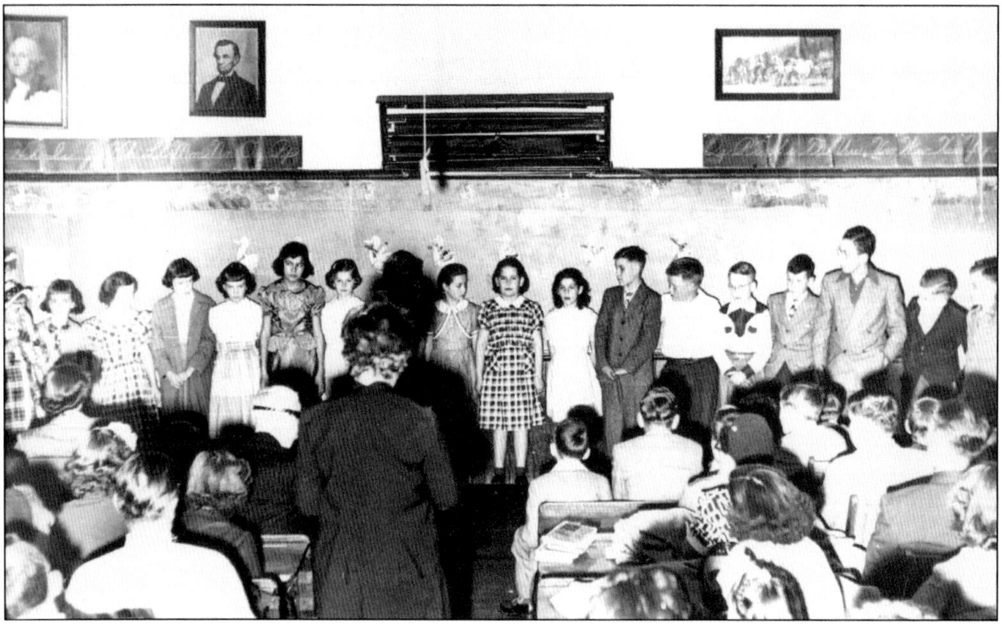

The spelling bee was a special day in the one-room Kissel Hill School when this undated photograph was taken. This was a chance for the teachers to show off their best spellers in front of the parents and friends of the students and provided a social event for the area. A prize, usually a special book, would be awarded to the top speller. (Courtesy of Polly Garner.)

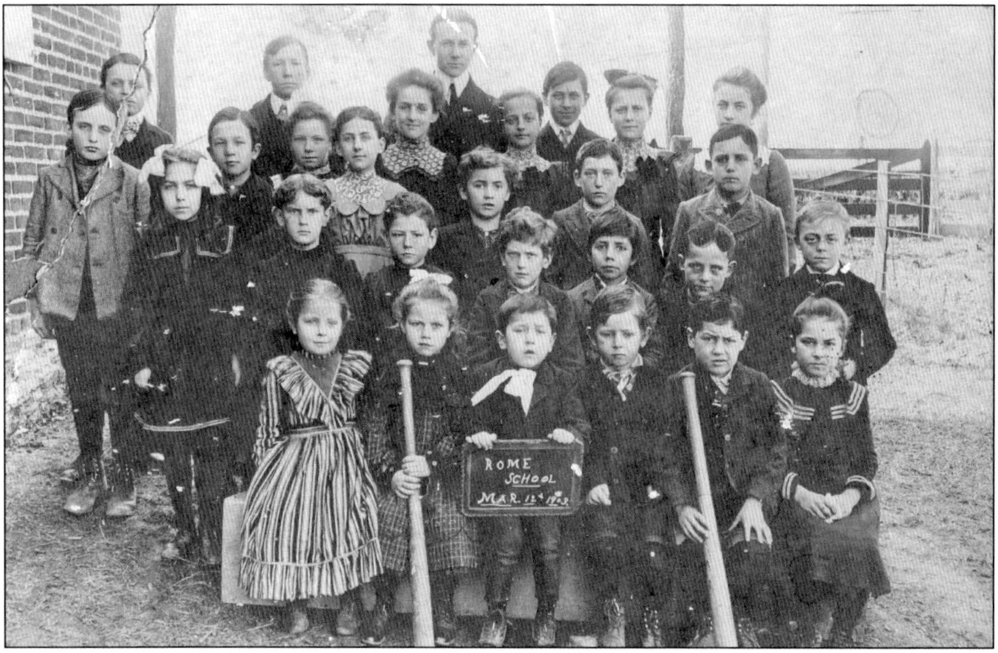

Ready for a game of baseball with bats in hand, these students of the Rome School posed for this picture on March 12, 1903. The students and teacher in this image are unidentified. However, it is confirmed that Lou S. Yetter taught school here during 1879, with Cyrus R. Gibble teaching by 1885. Lizzie R. Gibble was listed as the teacher in 1892. (Courtesy of the Lititz Historical Foundation.)

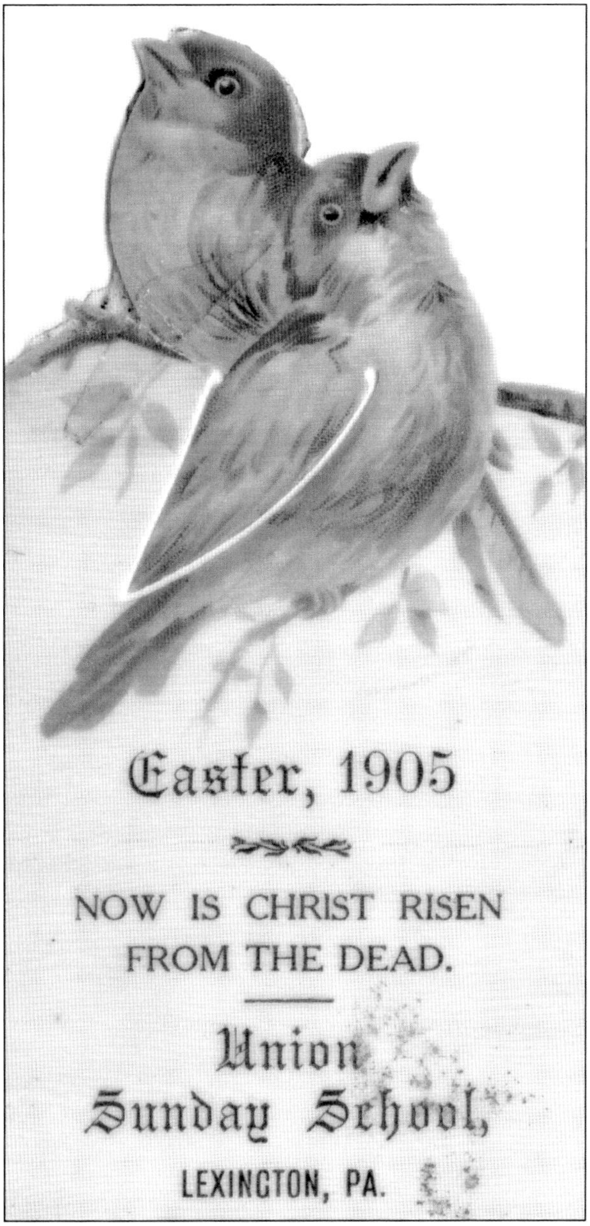

Although this seems like an unassuming bookmark, it is indeed very special, with an interesting story behind it. This originated from the Lexington Union Sunday School, a small, non-denominational meetinghouse that once stood on the southwest corner of Union House and Lexington Roads in Lexington. Originally constructed in 1836, the meetinghouse was used for many spelling bees, meetings, and community activities. In 1947, after a fire caused by a gas lamp destroyed most of its contents, it was decided that the structure would not be rebuilt due to safety concerns. Money raised by the sale of the salvageable items would be used for something that would be of use to the Lexington area. It was decided that a reservoir would be built to provide an adequate water supply for the benefit of the residents in the case of another fire in the village. The underground reservoir with the cement lid aboveground serves as the only reminder of where this meetinghouse once stood. (Courtesy of the Lititz Historical Foundation.)

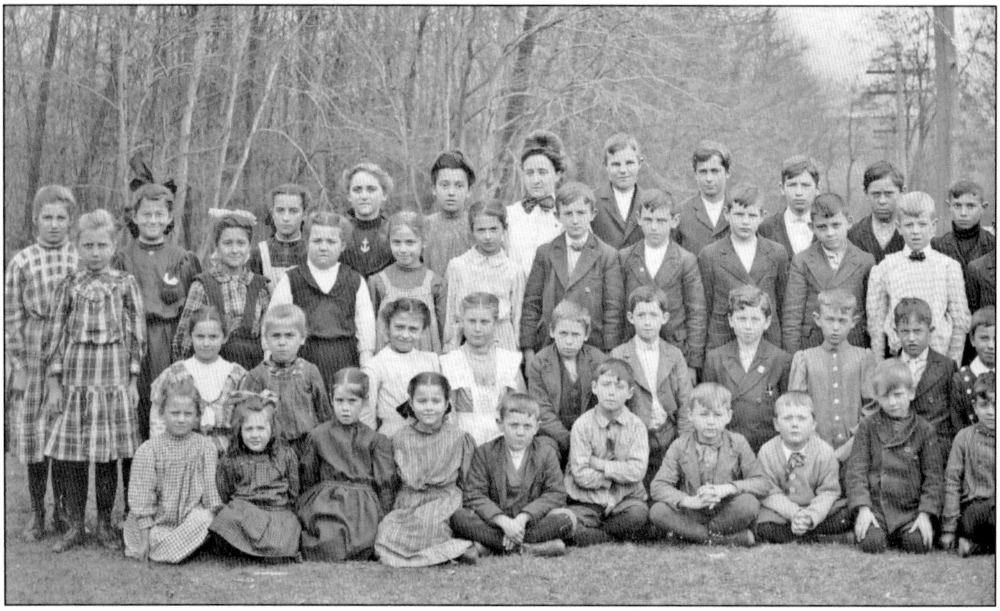

Students of Rothsville had their first formal education in October 1833 at Bentzes schoolhouse, taught by educator Phillip Kraatz. By 1848, the Rabbit Hill Schoolhouse, which was located at 1716 Old Rothsville Road, served as the school building. Constructed of brick, this schoolhouse seated about 50 pupils. This was in operation until 1882, when it was replaced by Rothsville's new Lower Rothsville School. Pictured are some children who attended these early schools. The Lower Rothsville School, located at 1726 Old Rothsville Road, included eight grades of education until the Rothsville Central School was built in 1895. The upper grades then went to the new school, alleviating the crowding at the old school. The new facility was the first wood-frame one-room schoolhouse in Rothsville. In 1910, it closed after the Warwick Township High School was constructed. (Both, courtesy of Sharon Deater.)

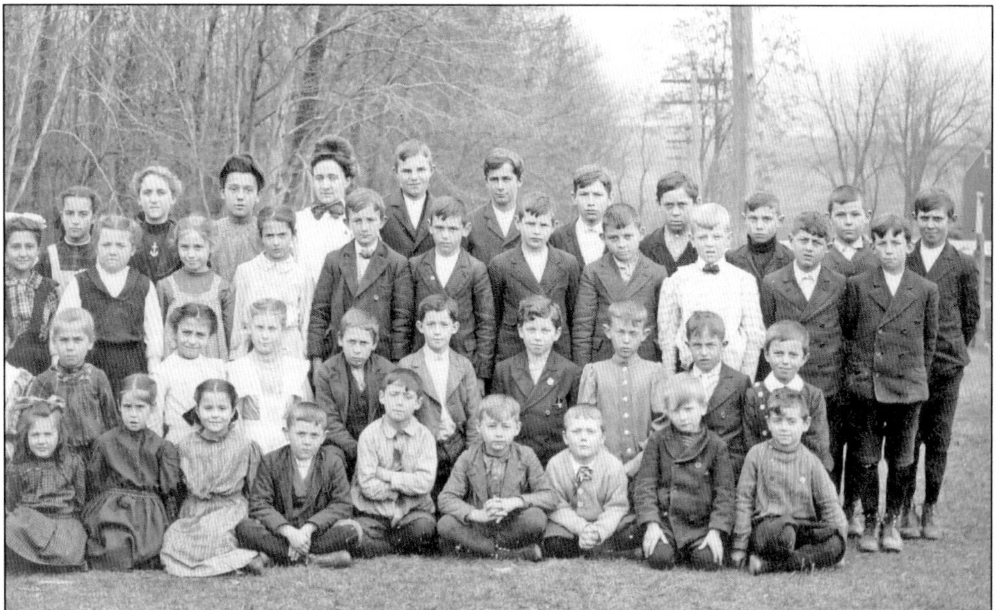

The Warwick Township High School, known as Rothsville High School, was built in 1910, with dedication ceremonies taking place November 12 of that same year. Students of all grades attended school here. There was a primary room, secondary room, and a three-year high school. For the first time, students of all ages who lived in the Rothsville area had one school to attend. (Courtesy of the Robert "Sketch" Mearig collection.)

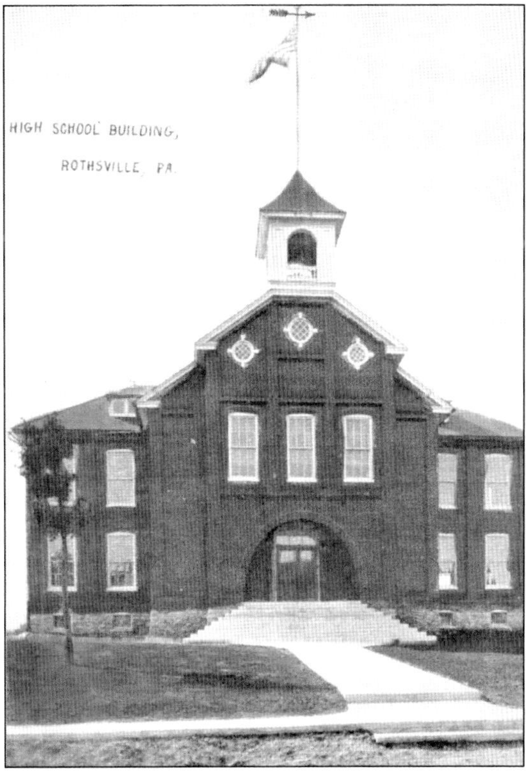

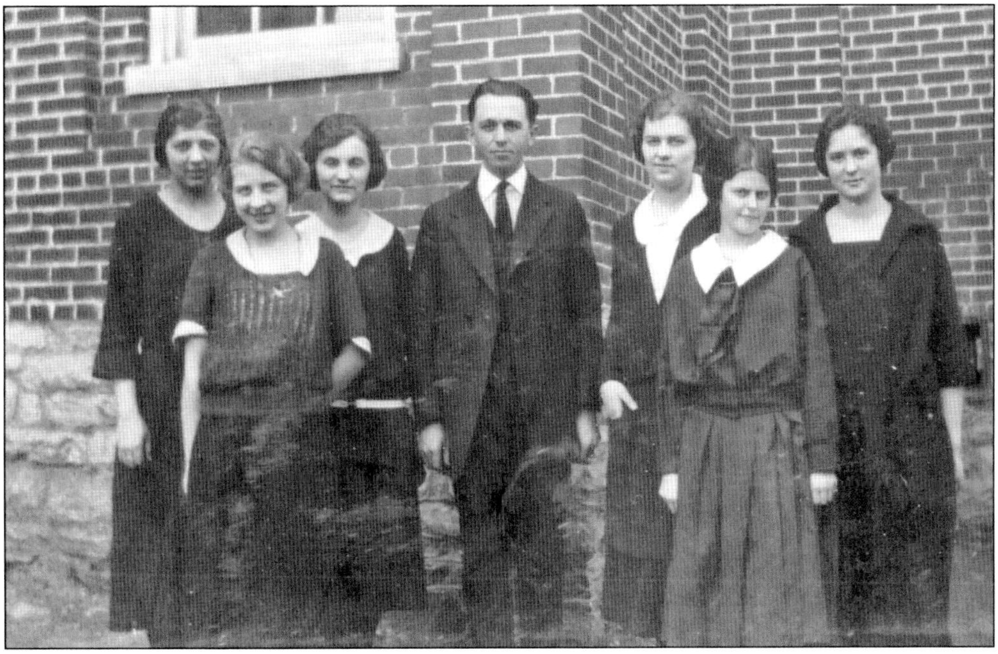

By 1917, the student body had grown to 47 pupils, with J. Harvey Rodgers serving as principal. Several unidentified teachers are seen here in this picture taken about 1930. The first instructors to teach in this new school were Mamie Kofroth, Iva Martin, and Joseph Mohn. (Courtesy of Sharyn Deater.)

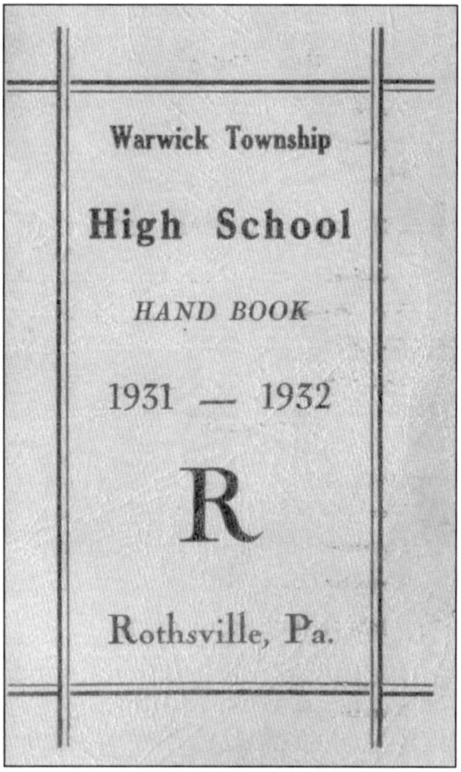

Included in this handbook from the 1931–1932 school year at Rothsville High School were rules and regulations of clubs, which books were to be read by certain grades, and various pep rally cheers. One of the cheers for the school that year was "Red and black, red and black; these're the colors we must back! Sis Boom Bah! Sis Boom Bah! Rothsville High School, Rah! Rah! Rah!" (Courtesy of the author's collection.)

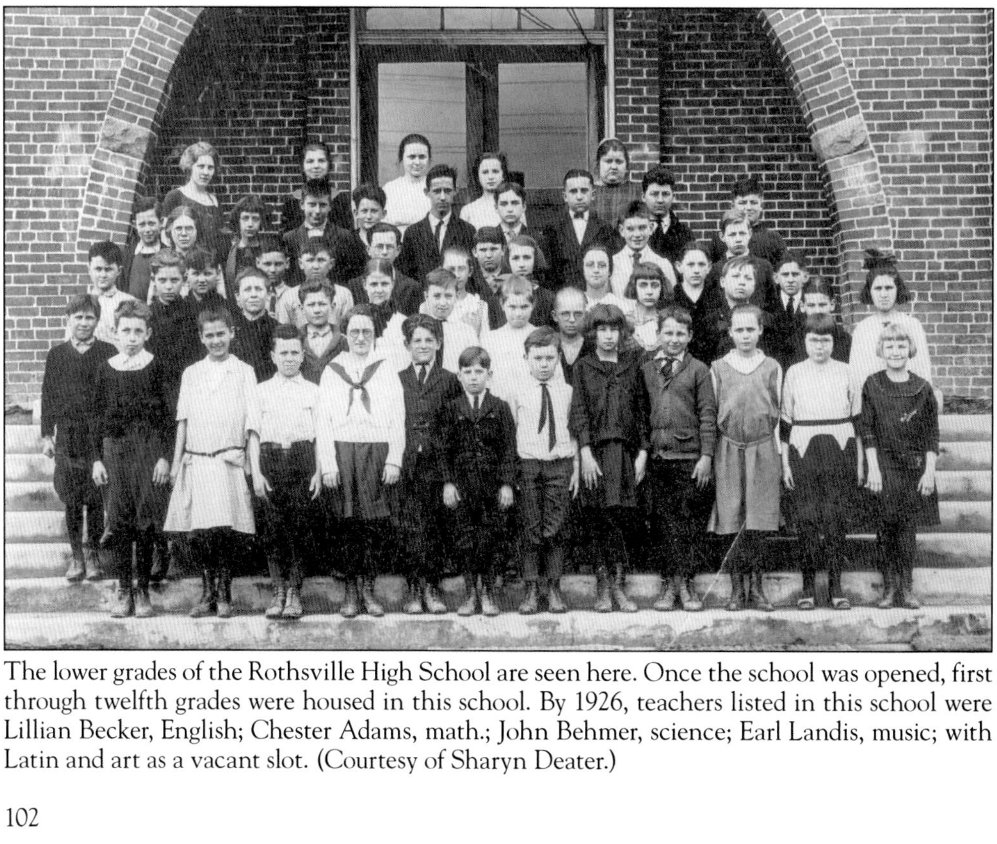

The lower grades of the Rothsville High School are seen here. Once the school was opened, first through twelfth grades were housed in this school. By 1926, teachers listed in this school were Lillian Becker, English; Chester Adams, math.; John Behmer, science; Earl Landis, music; with Latin and art as a vacant slot. (Courtesy of Sharyn Deater.)

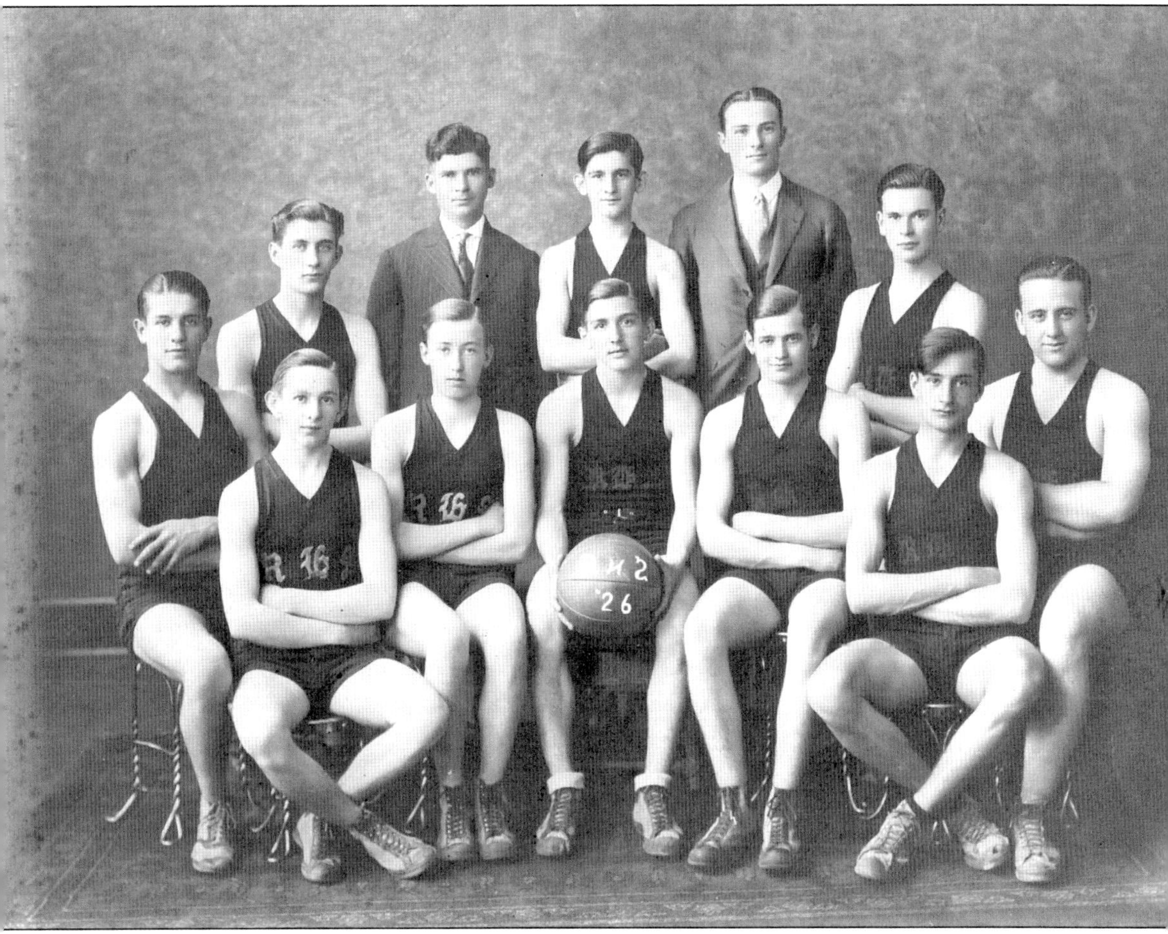

The Rothsville High School basketball team of 1926 is pictured here, ready to take on opposing teams such as Marietta, Lititz, Parkesburg, Quarryville, Downingtown, Hershey, Manheim, and Camp Hill. In 1919, a girls' basketball team was started, with principal J. Harvey Rodgers serving as team manager and L. Leoti Mumma as team captain. In the bottom row, second from left, is Raymond Deater, who died tragically in an automobile accident in 1928 when he was 18. While traveling near the boundary line between Lebanon and Lancaster Counties, the car he was driving went out of control while speeding around a curve at the bottom of a hill. The other two young men that he was traveling with (Chester W. Bowman and Samuel H. Birkenbine) also lost their lives in this terrible accident. (Courtesy of Sharyn Deater.)

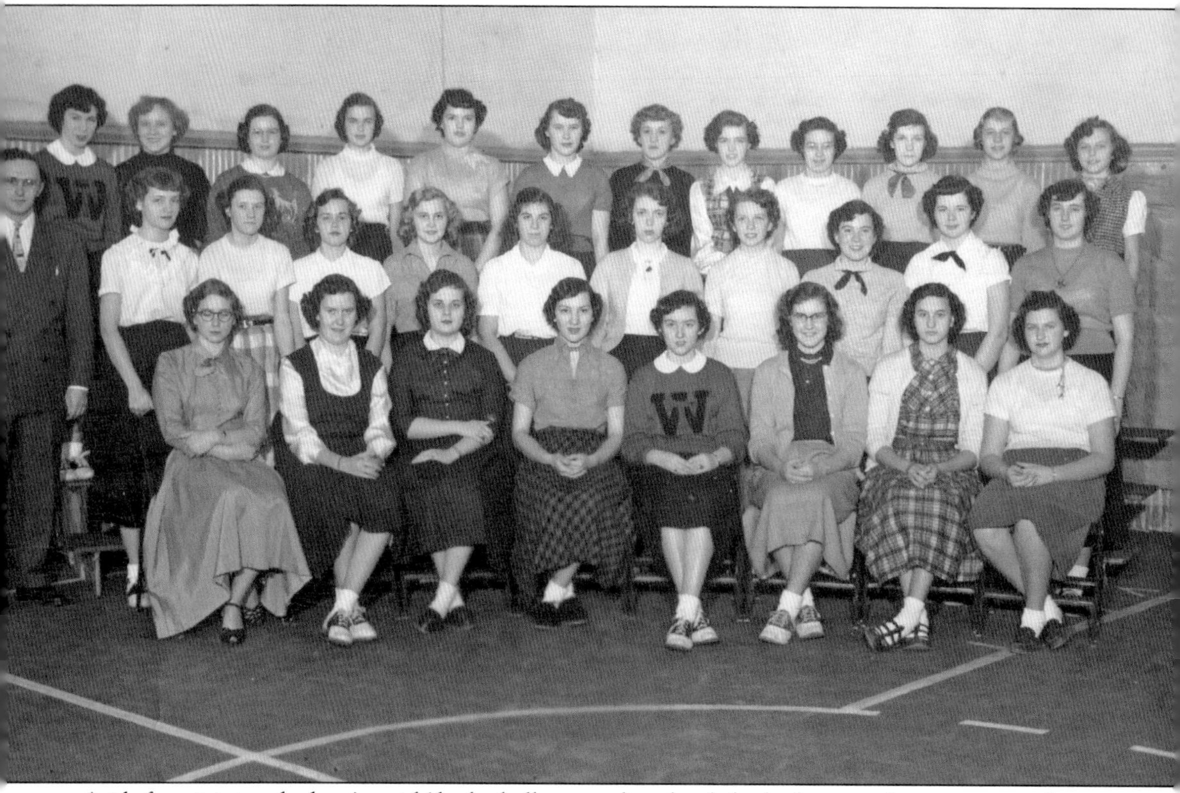

Aside from joining the boys' or girls' basketball teams, the school also had many other extracurricular activities that students could join. Those activities included glee club, the school newspaper committee, track, science club, dramatics, or the women's archery club. In 1931, this club was called the Indian Arrow Club and was composed of 10 sophomore girls, with their motto being "Learn to shoot, and shoot to learn." By 1920, the school also had a club called the Clio Literary Society, where students could debate teams from other schools. Young minds were challenged to think on their feet or with prepared notes during this competition. The senior play was also a popular activity, and friends and family members attended these special events at the school. This group picture, although unidentified, was most likely one of these various clubs mentioned. (Courtesy of the Lititz Historical Foundation.)

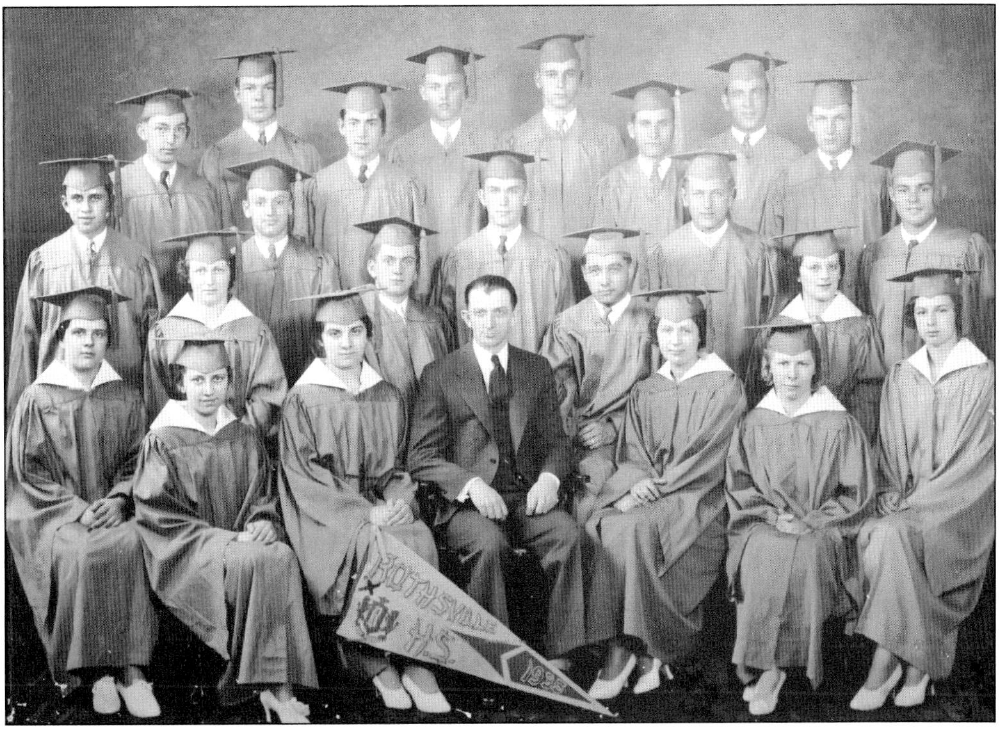

Here are the members of Rothsville High School's graduating class of 1935. Alphabetically they are: Raymond Bucher, Henry Burkholder, Jacob Bushong, Warren Bushong, Willis Carvel, Helen Erb, Howard Erb, Russell Erb, James Hess, Arthur Hyle, Amos Martin, Mary Mentzer, Anne Minnich, Kathryn Mummert, Elva Oberholtzer, Coretta Rettew, Edward Jerome Vogeler (class president), Harold Young, Wanda Snyder, Aaron Stoner, Virgina Sturgis, with the rest unidentified. (Courtesy of the author's collection.)

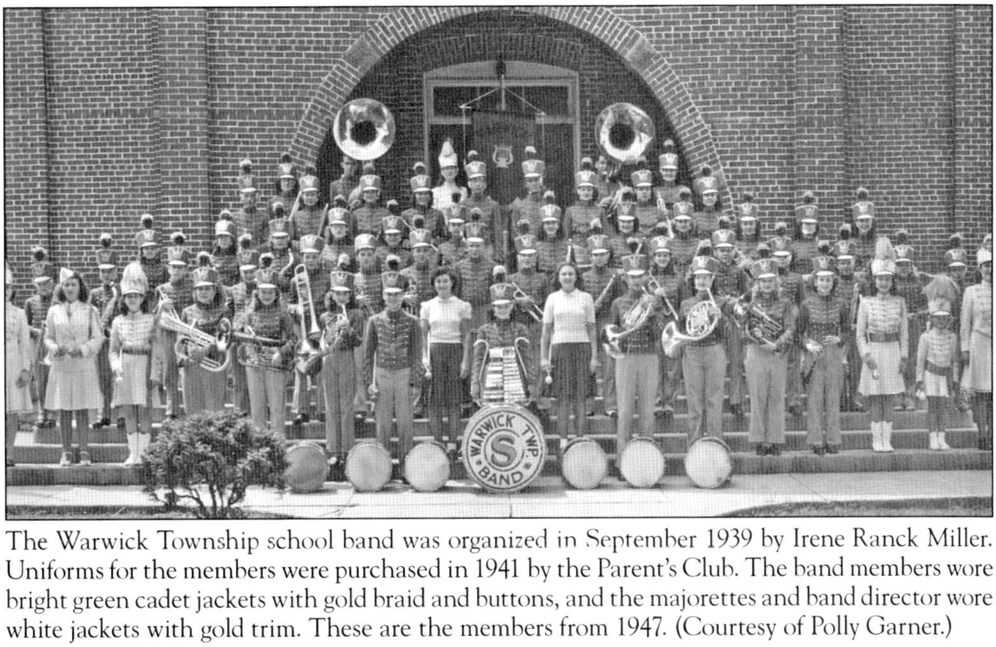

The Warwick Township school band was organized in September 1939 by Irene Ranck Miller. Uniforms for the members were purchased in 1941 by the Parent's Club. The band members wore bright green cadet jackets with gold braid and buttons, and the majorettes and band director wore white jackets with gold trim. These are the members from 1947. (Courtesy of Polly Garner.)

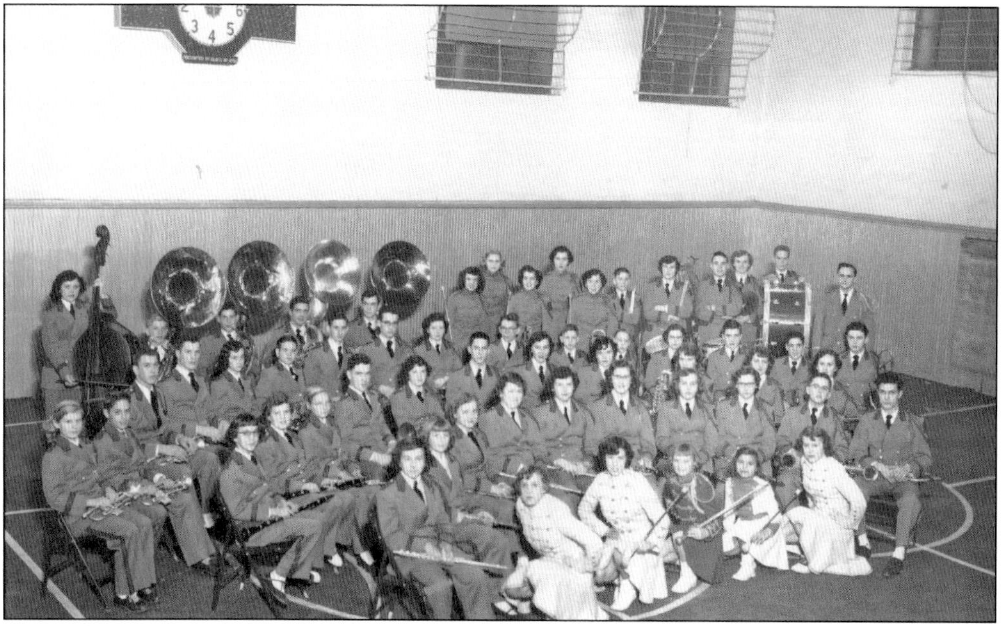

Pictured is the 1951–1952 band. In 1944, Irene Ranck Miller left the school district and moved to Alabama, with Evelyn Ling assuming directorship for only one year. Marvin Detambel then took over her duties as band director and added a larger horn section. Before the school year started in 1946, Miller returned to her old role, and Detambel took over the duties of supervisor of vocal music. (Courtesy of the Lititz Historical Foundation.)

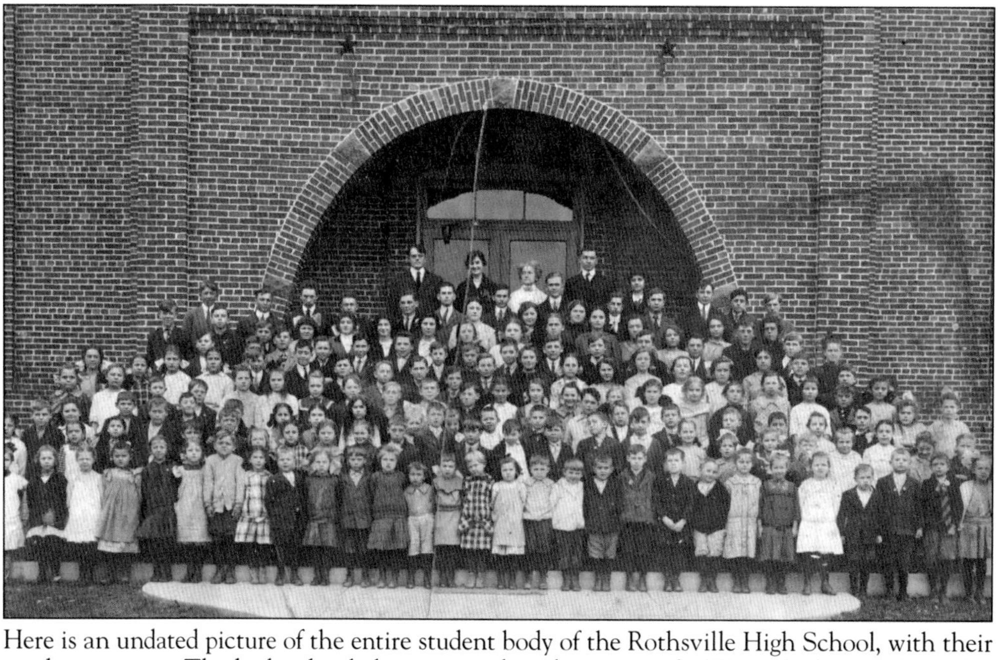

Here is an undated picture of the entire student body of the Rothsville High School, with their teachers present. The high school classes ceased in the spring of 1956, with the new Warwick High School built in Lititz and eventually dedicated on March 24, 1957. The Rothsville School then became an elementary facility housing six grades, which were eventually reduced to three grades. (Courtesy of the Robert "Sketch" Mearig collection.)

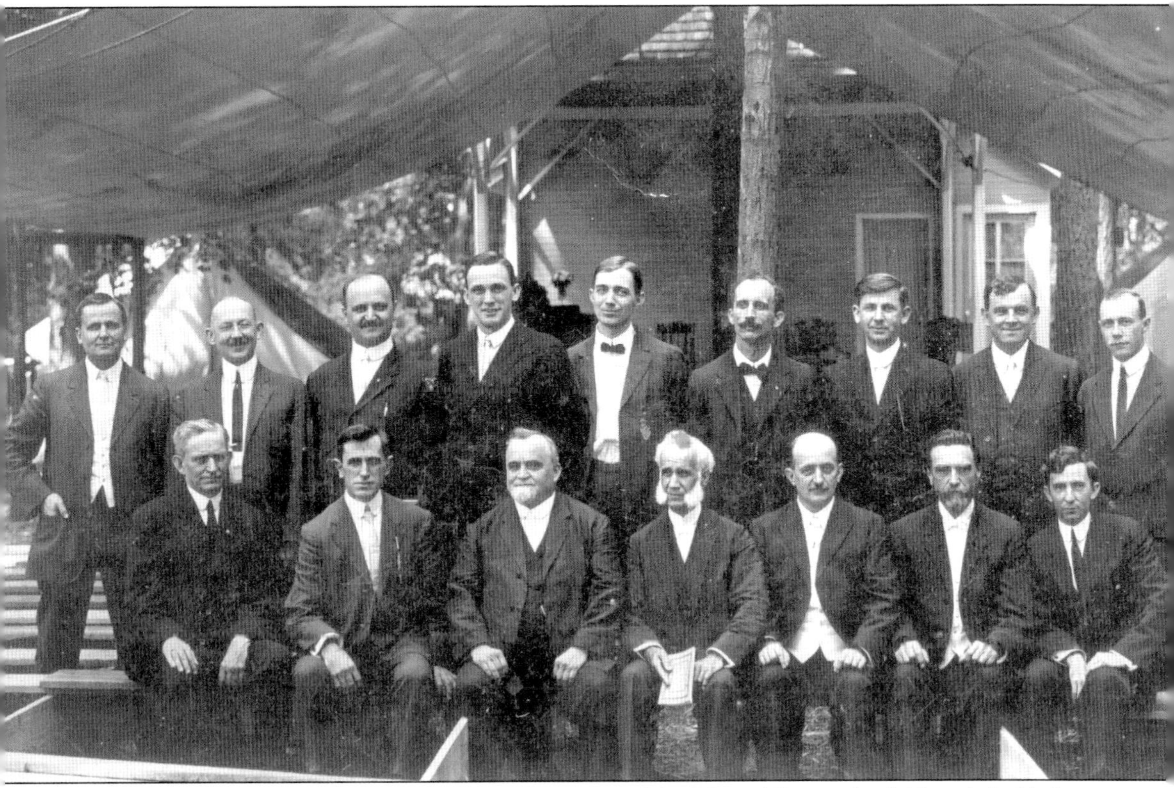

Between 1894 and 1916, religious camp meetings of the United Evangelical Church held their meetings in Millway. This area proved to be a very popular and gorgeous location for these meetings, as persons in attendance could walk throughout the countryside of the Millway area being touched by God's presence when not attending a service. This rural area proved to be a pleasant place to stop and appreciate the gorgeous landscape. The meetings were sponsored by the Harrisburg District of the United Evangelical Church, which is known today as the Evangelical Congregational Church. Seen here is a group of these ministers from a 1911 camp meeting. From left to right, the ministers are (first row) N. A. Barr, H. J. Kline, F. E. Erdman, J. M. Renker, H. S. Kreidler, W. H. Hartzler, and N. N. Lower; (second row) C. W. Heffner, H. M. Jones, P. T. Brocious, J. A. Heck, G. L. Gensmer, J. S. Harper, J. F. Gross, C. D. Huber, and B. E. Coleman. (Courtesy of Ronald Reedy.)

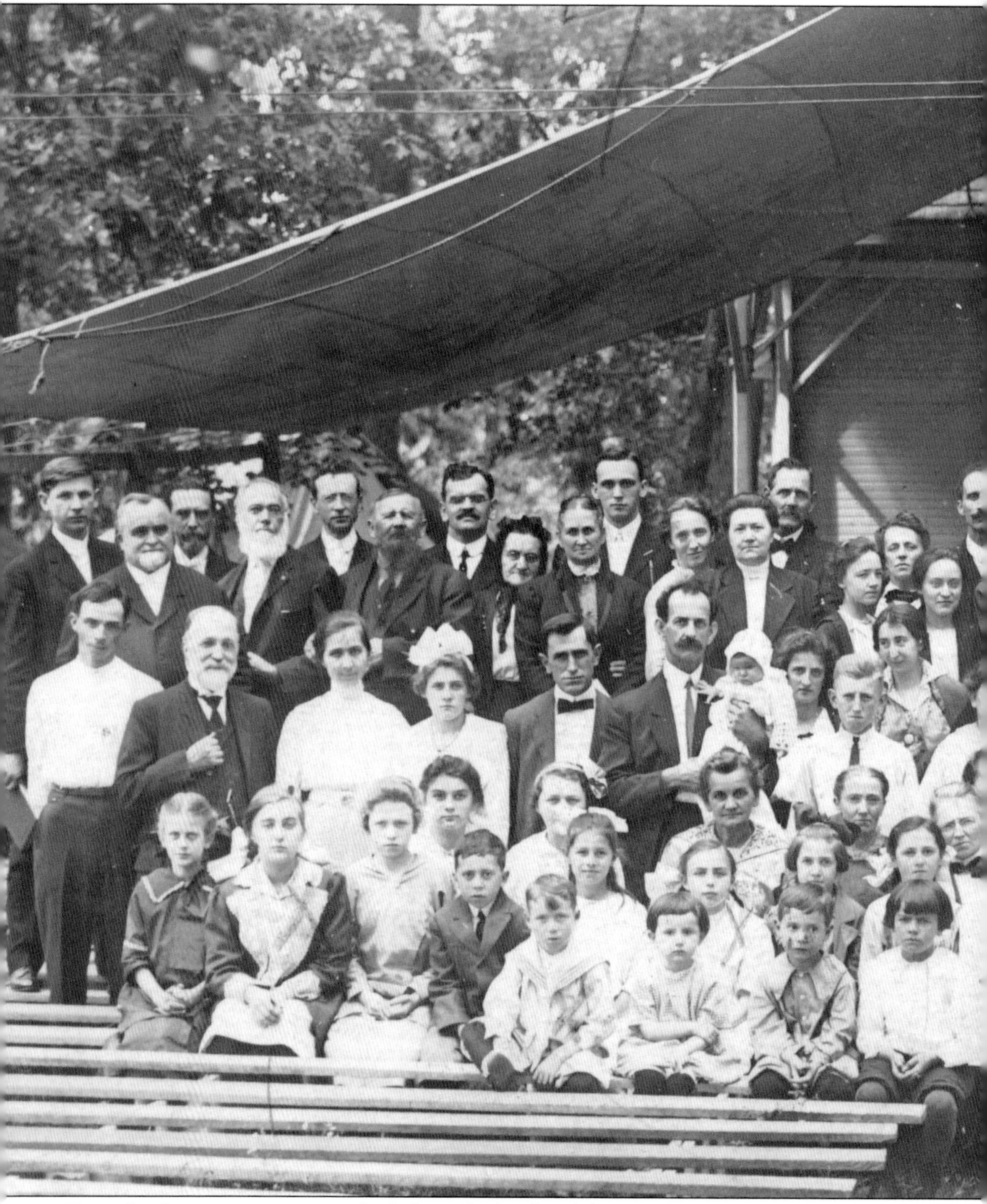

Tents for the meetings were pitched along the banks of the Cocalico Creek with 4,000 in attendance in 1897. In 1903, the turnout at the meeting was greatly affected by intense heat and heavy rains. On Wednesday, July 26, 1911, the United Evangelical Church of the Harrisburg District opened their annual camp at John Wolf's Grove in Millway along the Reading Rail

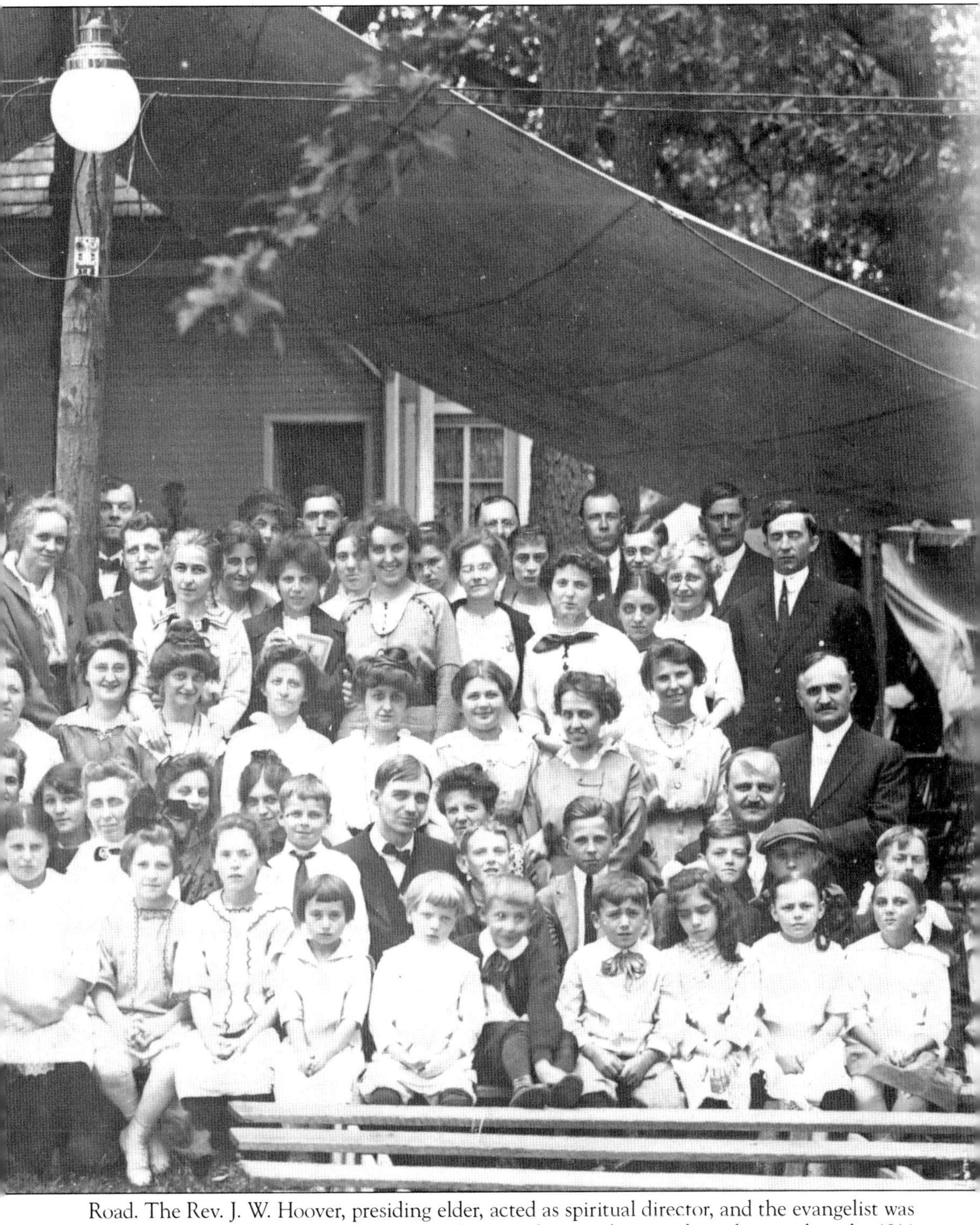

Road. The Rev. J. W. Hoover, presiding elder, acted as spiritual director, and the evangelist was Rev. W. H. Hartzler of Myerstown. Shown here is a large gathering of people attending the 1914 meeting. (Courtesy of Ronald Reedy.)

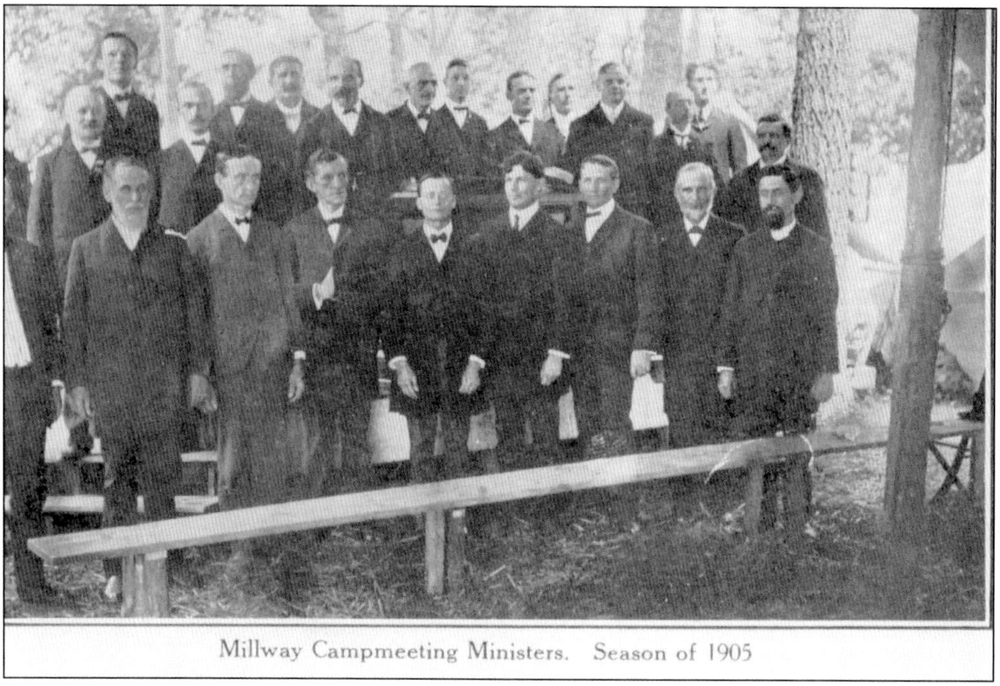

During the camp meeting season of 1905, these gentlemen served as ministers. Three years later, the attendees of the 1908 camp meeting had the distinct pleasure in hearing Bishop W. F. Heil preach. Also present that day was the corresponding secretary of the Missionary and Church Societies, the Rev. B. H. Niebel. (Courtesy of the Robert "Sketch" Mearig collection.)

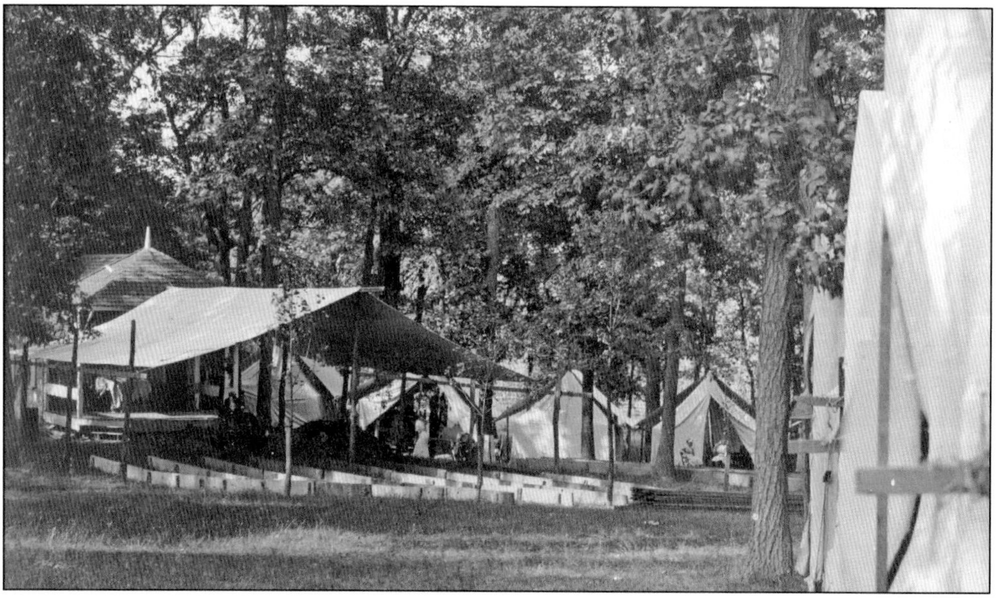

Summer evangelistic meetings were attended by entire families. They would come from near and far to hear the gospel preached and be converted by the word of God. Throughout the early 1900s, two- and sometimes three-week-long meetings were held, with converts baptized in the nearby creek. On Saturday July 29, 1911, and continuing until August 14, the American Salvation Army held its annual camp meeting in Millway. (Courtesy of Ronald Reedy.)

Seven

THE ELEMENTS

From one end of the temperature spectrum to the other, the elements of hot and cold have proven both successful and devastating to companies and neighborhoods of Warwick Township. Whether it was the use of hot iron in the Brunnerville Iron Foundry or ice manufacturing plants selling their large blocks of ice for use in their customer's homes to preserve food, all have played a unique part in the township's history. Heavy winds and tornadoes have also affected the area, bringing with them devastation and damage. For children, a heavy snowfall often meant a day off from school, allowing them to play in the beautiful winter wonderland for hours. For the adults, it meant braving the elements on the treacherous roads to get to work or to shovel snow so they could leave for work. Various fire companies within the township evolved and continue to save lives and fight massive fires. These brave volunteers place their lives on the line everyday and hold fire prevention programs for the community. The photographs in the following chapter not only explore how recreation is experienced during the winter and summer months, but also how the extreme heat or cold played a vital part in the township's prosperity throughout the years.

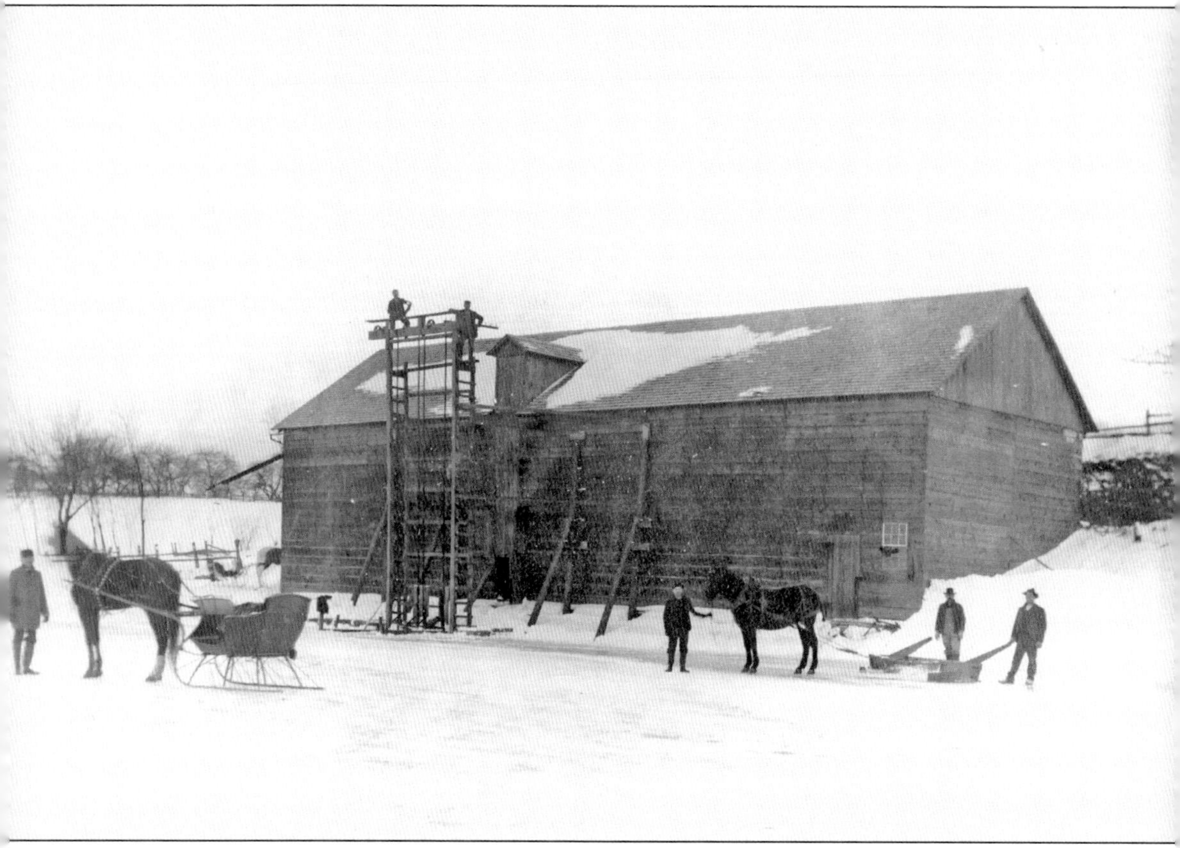

In the days before commercial refrigeration, ice had to be harvested from frozen dams and ponds such as the one pictured here. Levi H. Yerger operated a very successful ice dam in Brunnerville in the early part of the 20th century. The business was located along Brunnerville Road just before it crosses Newport Road heading toward Lititz. As the weather became colder, ice would form on the still water of the dam. When it was thick enough, the employees harvested the ice using horses that pulled saws across the surface of the ice to cut it into blocks. The ice was then hoisted into the storage building using the shaft as seen in this picture. While in storage, the ice was packed between layers of sawdust, which would help to keep it cool and preserve its temperature. (Courtesy of the Robert "Sketch" Mearig collection.)

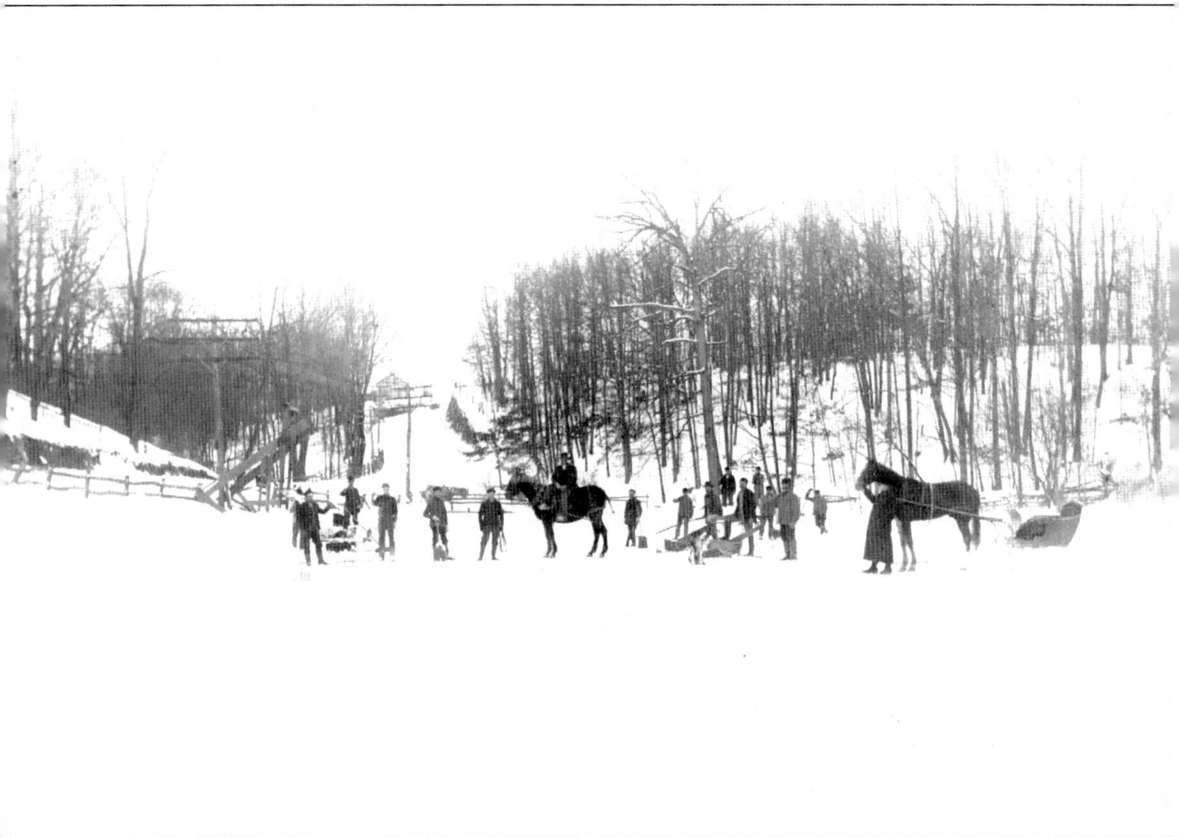

The dam at Yerger's Spring Lake Ice Dam measured approximately 15 feet in height. When the ice was delivered to a customer's home, the deliveryman would put the block of ice into the top compartment of the family's icebox. The ice would cool the air, and as the air sank down through the next part of the icebox, it would keep the food cool to slow down the spoiling process. Ice became such a popular item in homes all across America that daily deliveries—especially in warm weather—were as common as other household necessities. Dams like these sprang up all over the United States, creating many jobs. Workers often slipped and fell on the ice, badly injuring themselves. Several years later, modern refrigeration techniques were introduced, eliminating the need for an iceman to make deliveries. (Courtesy of the Robert "Sketch" Mearig collection.)

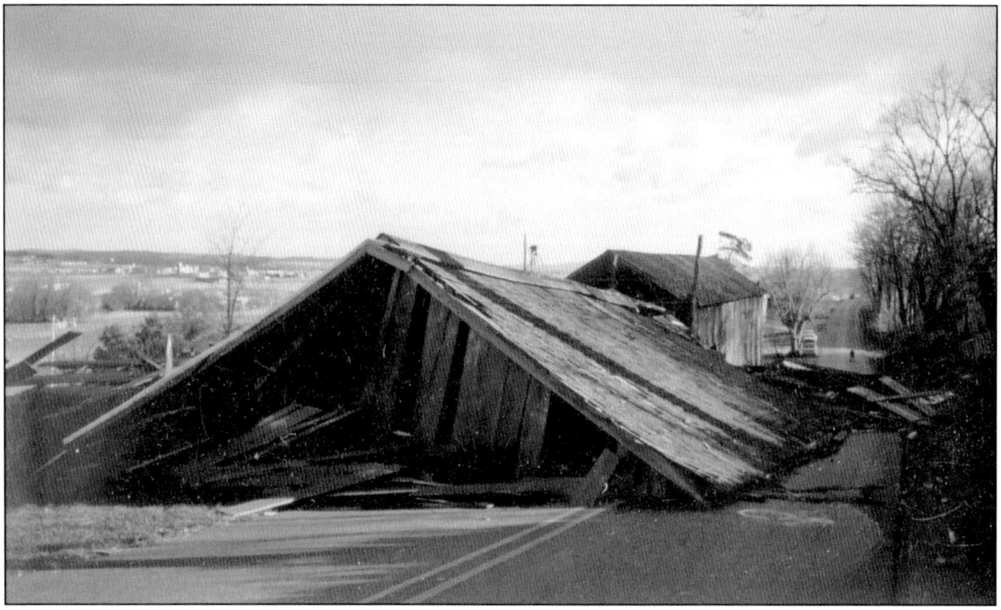

On the historic Siegrist property along Pierson Road near Owl Hill, this building was once one of the largest, longest tobacco sheds in Lancaster County. In 1946, part of the shed blew down in a heavy windstorm. In 1989, the rest of the shed, seen here, was blown out onto the road and caused traffic to be rerouted. (Courtesy of Wayne Siegrist.)

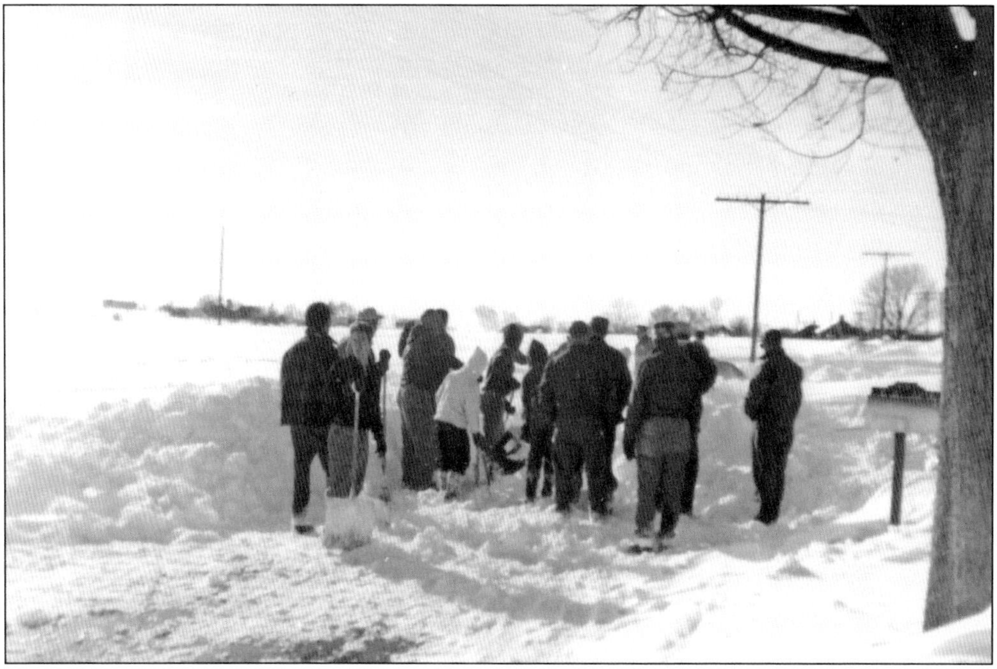

In 1958, a very strong snowstorm passed through, with many residents losing power for three days. The people of Brunnerville gathered and began to shovel their nearby roads. They worked toward Midway and eventually made it to Lexington. The shoveling had to be an exhausting job, but people helping people is what helps give Warwick Township its wonderful charm. (Courtesy of Mary Roth.)

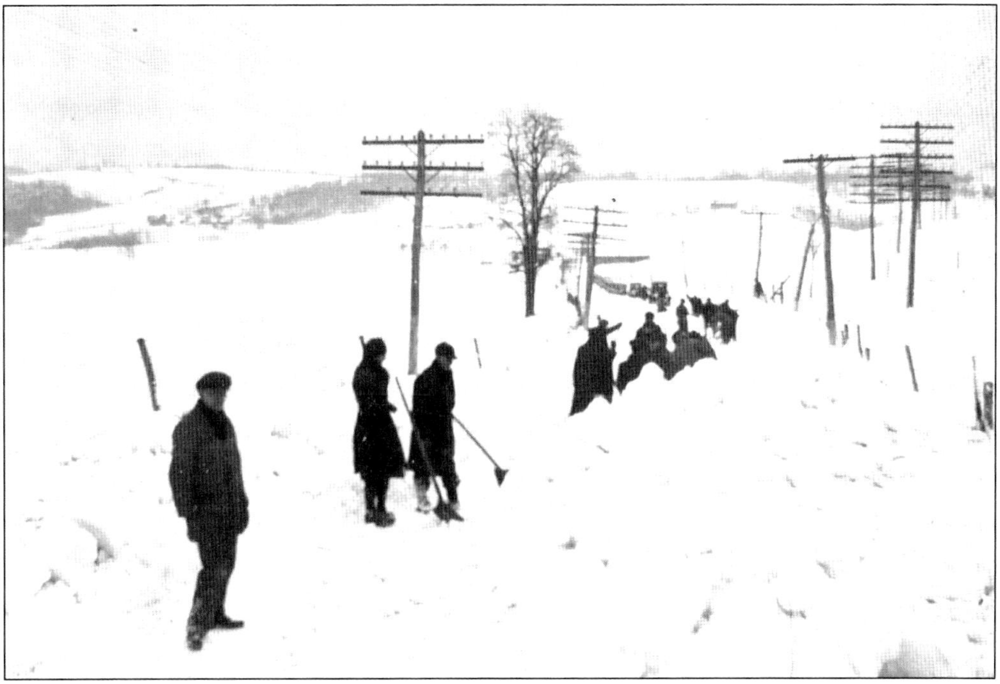

Similar events took place in Rothsville (above) and again in Brunnerville (below) many years ago during heavy snowstorms. Without the use of mechanical snow plows, the people of these areas gathered together and began to shovel along nearby roads, helping to free their neighbors. This undertaking was not easy and at times could be dangerous. Although dressed for the very cold weather, the residents involved in these efforts were no doubt very cold and very tired after shoveling for the many hours it took. What a chore it must have been to negotiate the snowdrifts upon making their way back home on foot through the snowy, slippery conditions. (Both, courtesy of Sharyn Deater.)

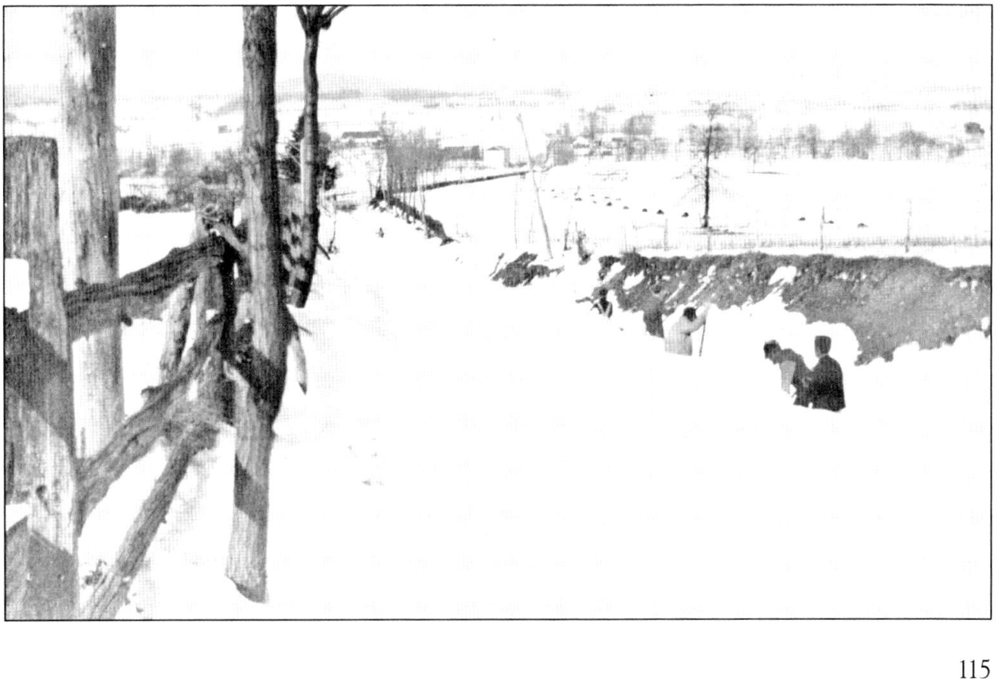

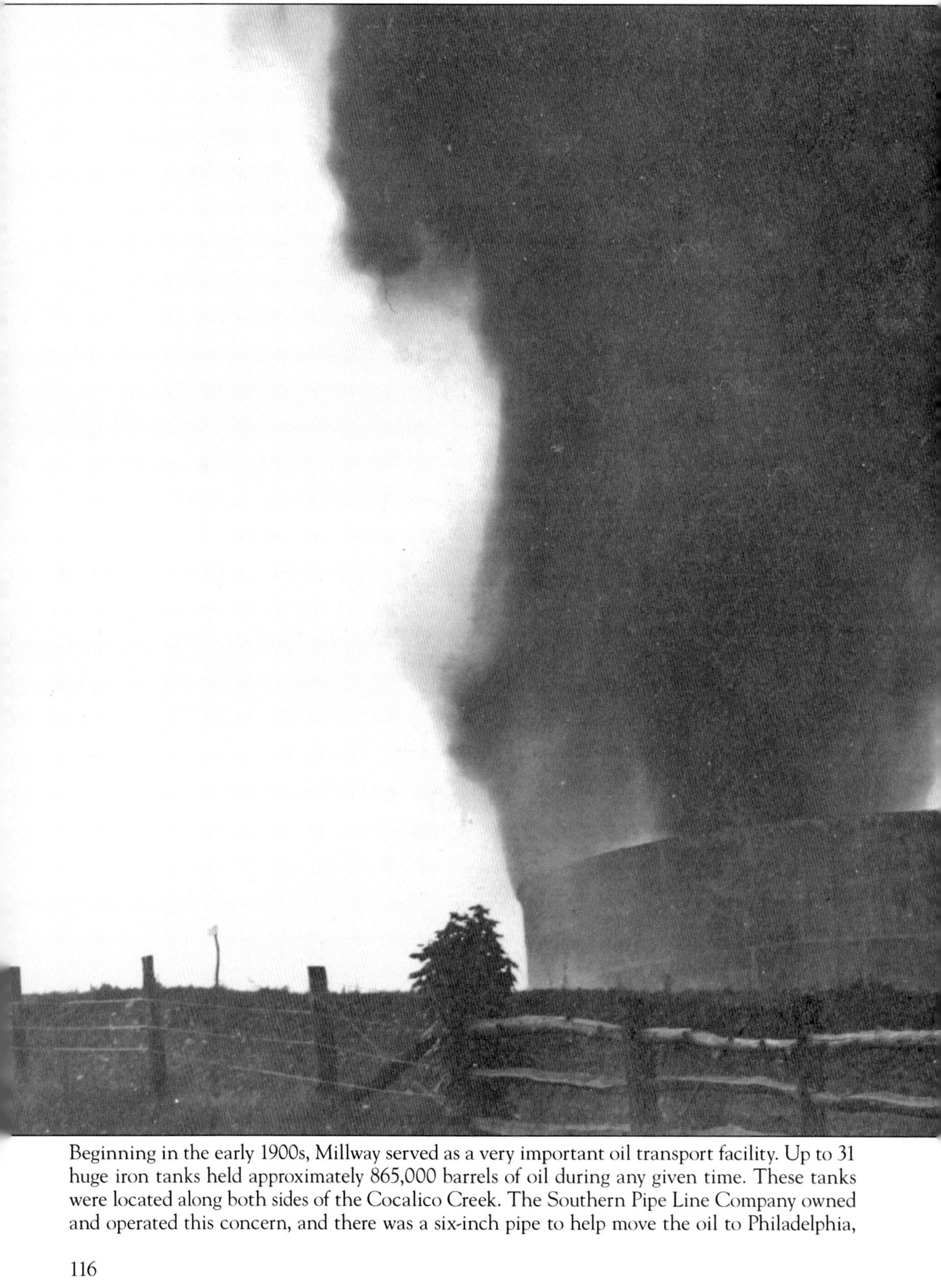

Beginning in the early 1900s, Millway served as a very important oil transport facility. Up to 31 huge iron tanks held approximately 865,000 barrels of oil during any given time. These tanks were located along both sides of the Cocalico Creek. The Southern Pipe Line Company owned and operated this concern, and there was a six-inch pipe to help move the oil to Philadelphia,

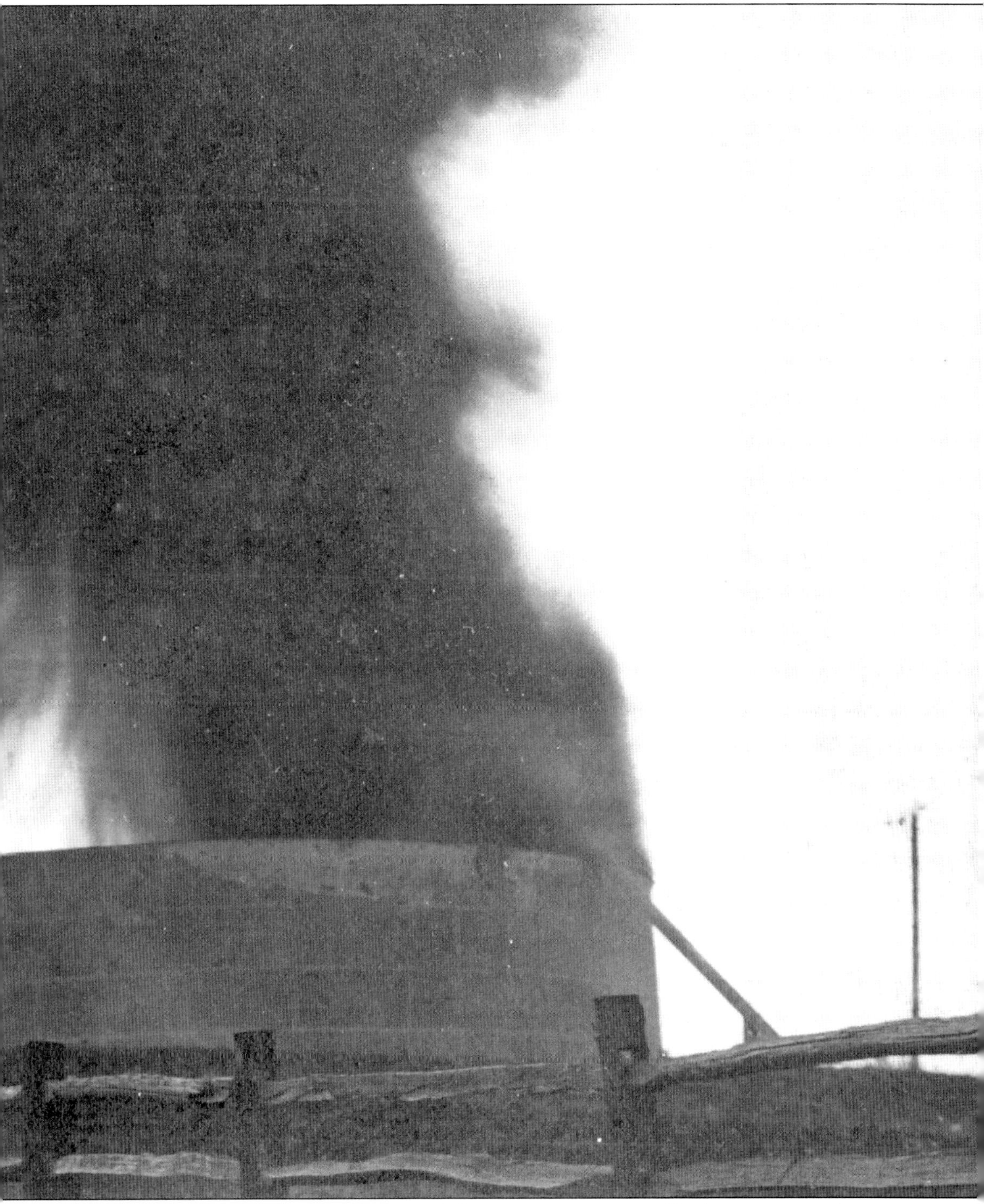

Baltimore, and Bayview, New York. In 1913, with its vast system of boilers, pumps, and engines, it was referred to as "A marvel of mechanical efficiency." This operation ceased in the 1950s, when serious leaks spread pollution all the way to the nearby town of Mount Joy. (Courtesy of John David Wissler.)

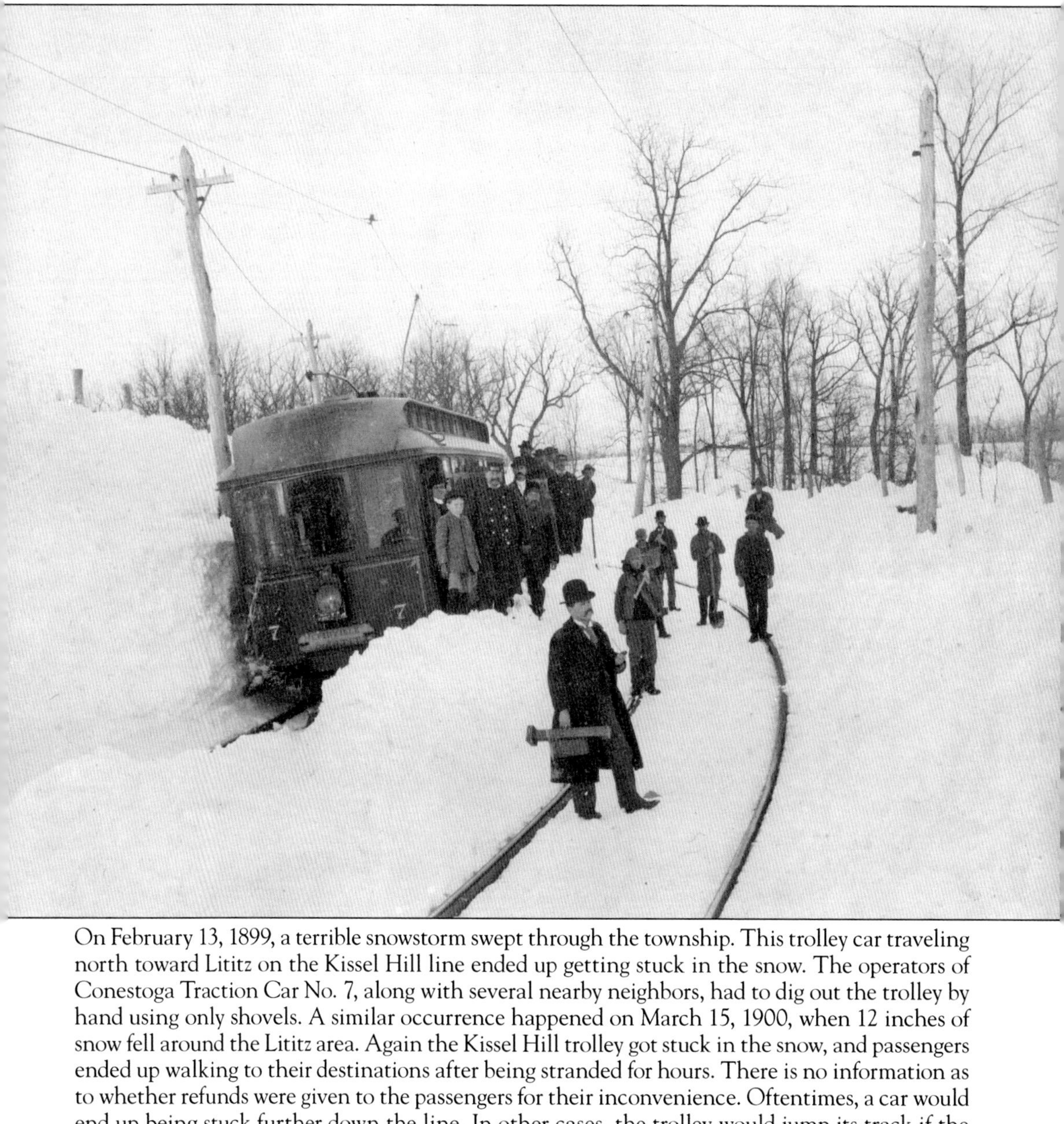

On February 13, 1899, a terrible snowstorm swept through the township. This trolley car traveling north toward Lititz on the Kissel Hill line ended up getting stuck in the snow. The operators of Conestoga Traction Car No. 7, along with several nearby neighbors, had to dig out the trolley by hand using only shovels. A similar occurrence happened on March 15, 1900, when 12 inches of snow fell around the Lititz area. Again the Kissel Hill trolley got stuck in the snow, and passengers ended up walking to their destinations after being stranded for hours. There is no information as to whether refunds were given to the passengers for their inconvenience. Oftentimes, a car would end up being stuck further down the line. In other cases, the trolley would jump its track if the snow was too intense. (Courtesy of the Robert "Sketch" Mearig collection.)

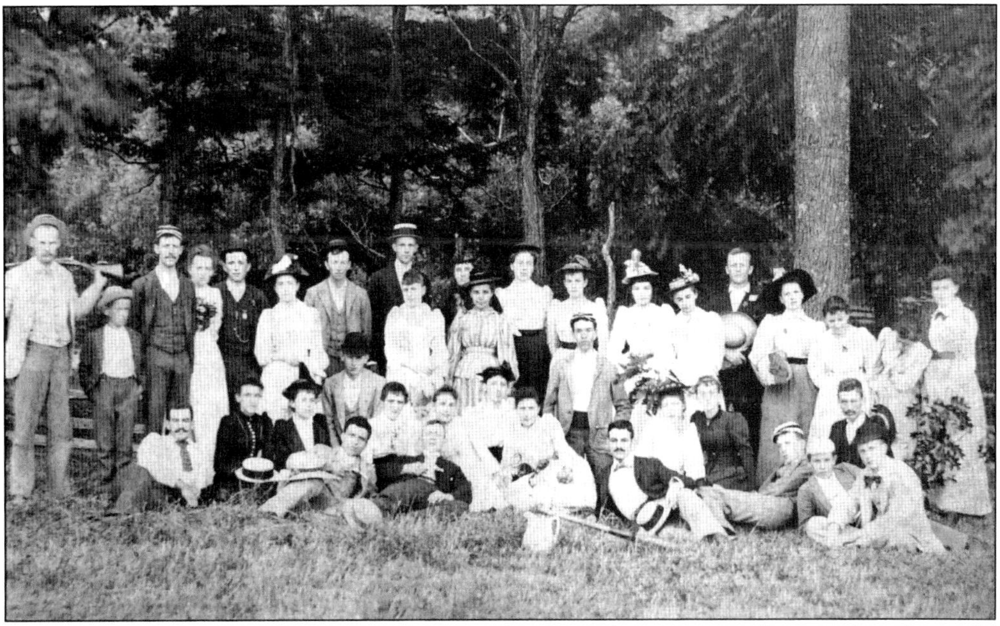

On July 5, 1892, this large group of people posed to have their picture taken. With its beautiful creek and country pastures, Millway made a wonderful setting for this gathering on a warm summer day. Pitchers that might have held lemonade can be seen. Several men are holding rifles, giving a sense that small game hunting or target practice took place that day. (Courtesy of the Robert "Sketch" Mearig collection.)

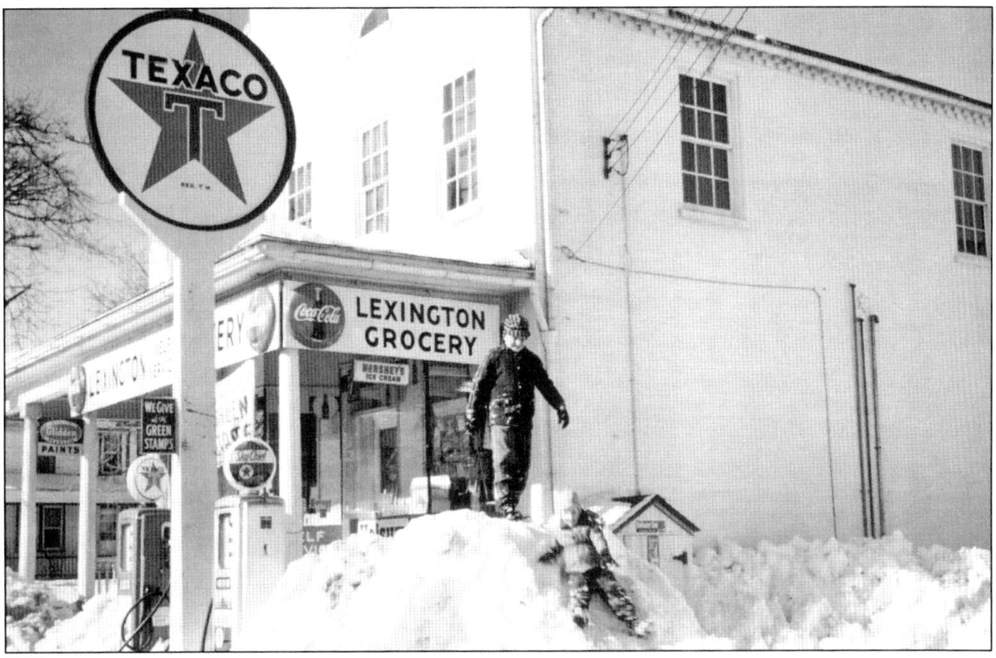

In 1959, two of the Donmoyer brothers used this pile of snow as a makeshift slide. Bob Donmoyer can be seen standing on top of the pile, with his younger brother Brian sliding down. The small storage shed to their left served as a place for oilcan storage for their parents' store. (Courtesy of the Donmoyer family.)

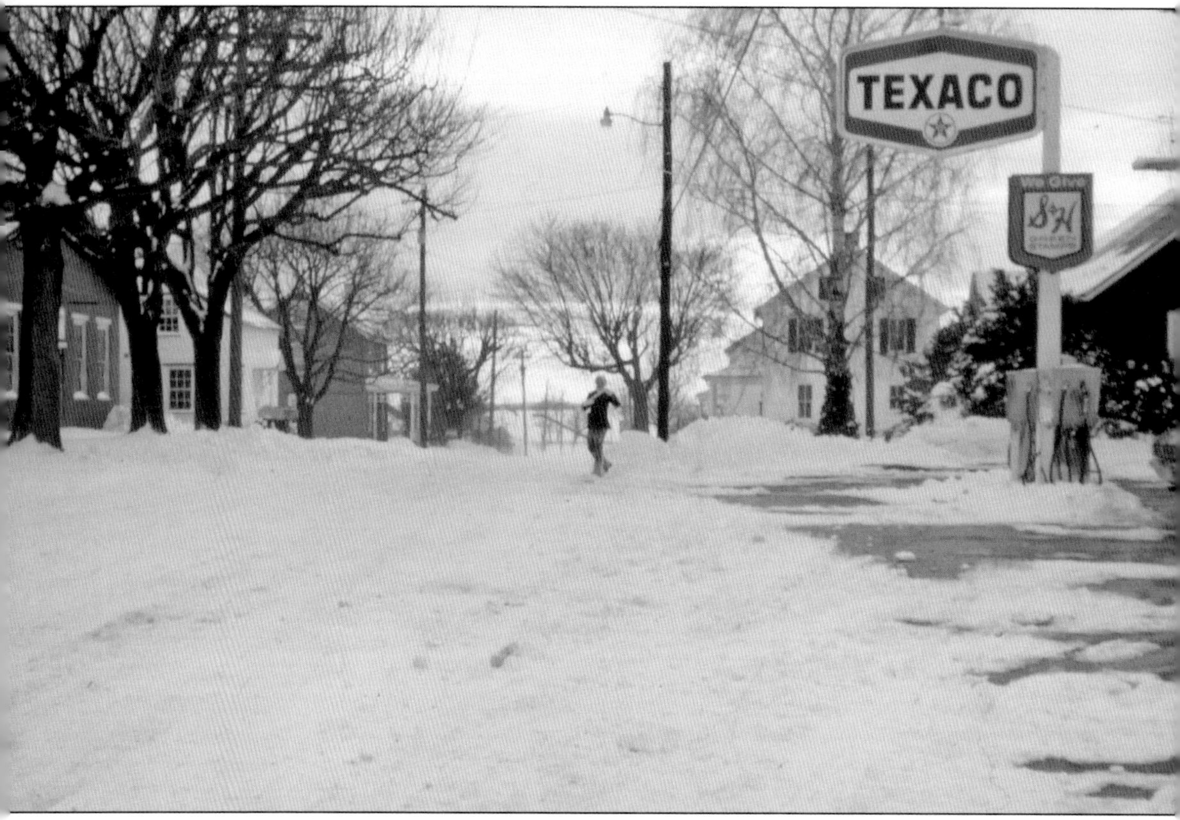

In this 1970s image, the gasoline pumps at Bruce Wike's Brunnerville Garage can be seen on the right, with the Brunnerville Foundry located on the left. On a cold winter's day, this person braved the elements and shoveled the service station's parking lot to make a clear space for any customer who needed to bring their car in for last minute snow tire installation. After the Mearig brothers purchased the service station from Wike and relocated it across the street, the older building served as a used car lot and beer-making supplies store during different times. Currently it serves as Adair's Brunnerville Carpet Shop, owned by Michael Adair. The Brunnerville Post Office was also housed in this building for a number of years, moving across the street when the Mearigs built their new service station. (Courtesy of Tom Hackman.)

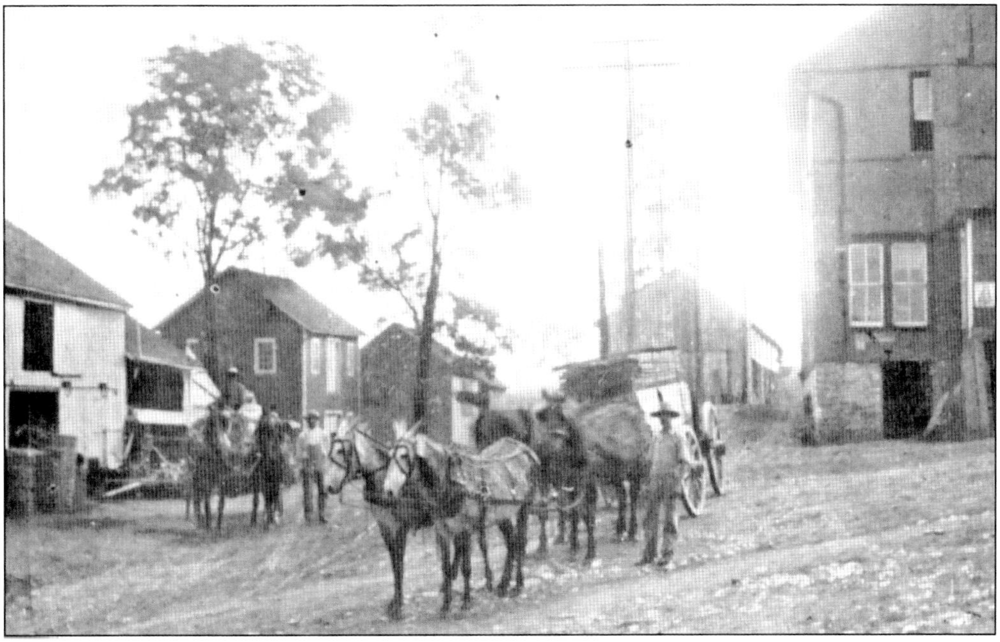

On Monday, May 13, 1907, around noon on a windy day, a spark from a passing freight train ignited the shingled roof of Moore and Reitz's coal and lumberyard building in Millway. In minutes, the entire building was engulfed in flames. The residents immediately noticed the blaze, and a bucket brigade was soon created in an effort to put out the fire. The devastating inferno quickly spread to the property's grain elevator, fertilizer building, wagon shed, and implement building. Ashes from the fire spread across Millway, covering over a mile in diameter. (Above, courtesy of the Robert "Sketch" Mearig collection; below, courtesy of Richard Reitz.)

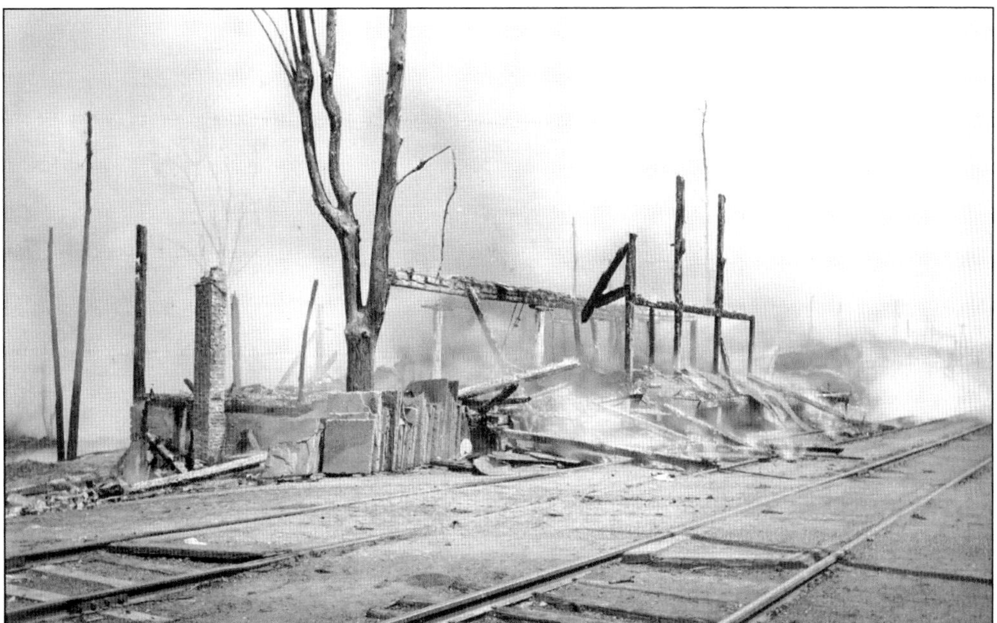

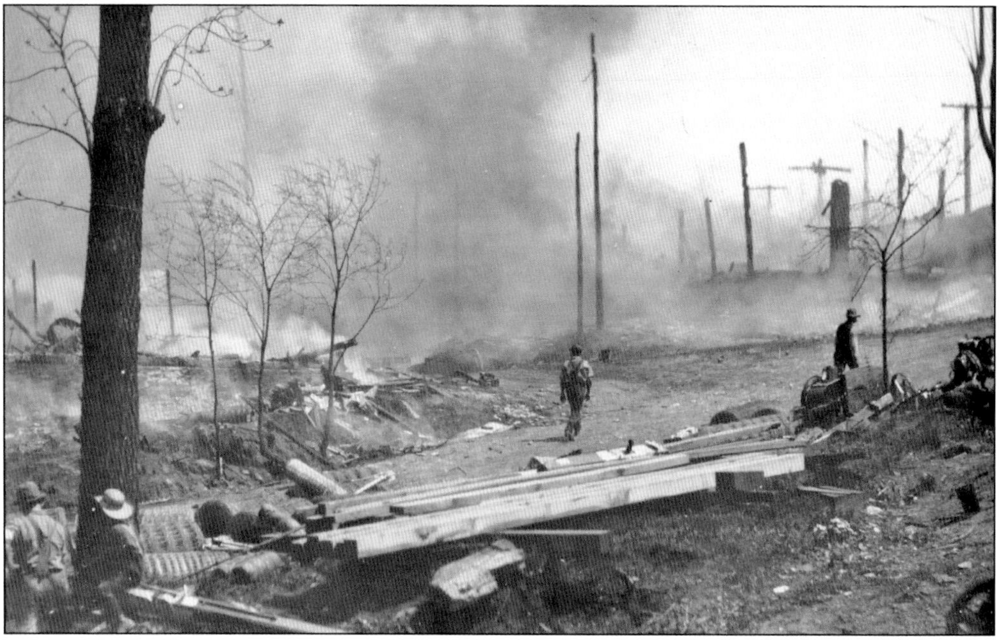

A total of two acres of property and buildings were lost in the blaze, with the charred remains of the buildings still smoldering well into the next day. The fire was declared one of the largest in Lancaster County of that era. The mill was rebuilt that same year, with many Millway residents working long hours to hurry along the completion. In the fall of the following year, Elam S. Moore sold his stake in the business, and the businesses name was changed to J. H. Reitz Coal and Lumberyard. Once rebuilt, the business flourished more than ever. (Both, courtesy of John David Wissler.)

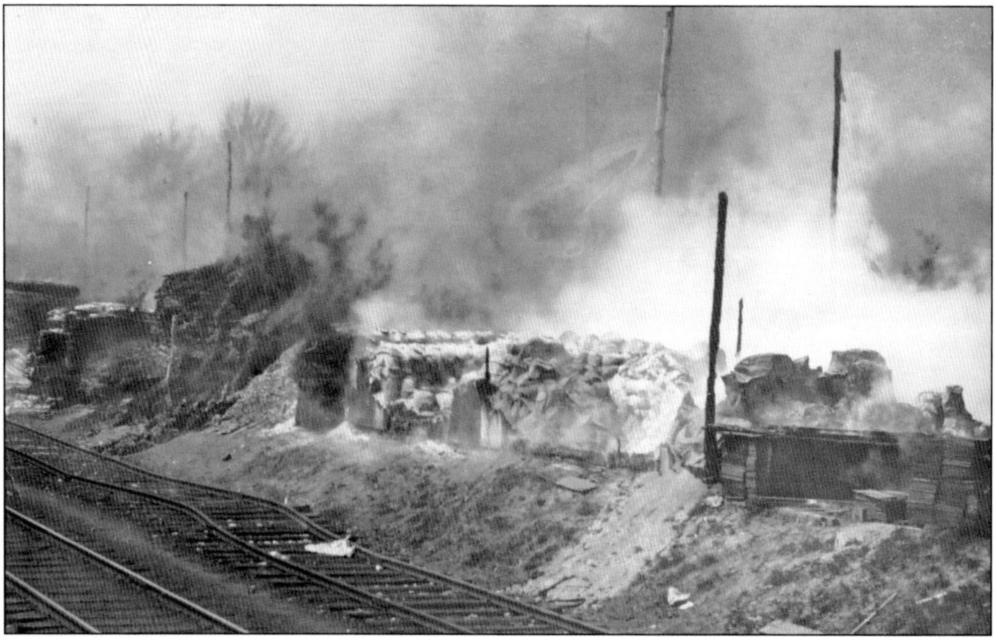

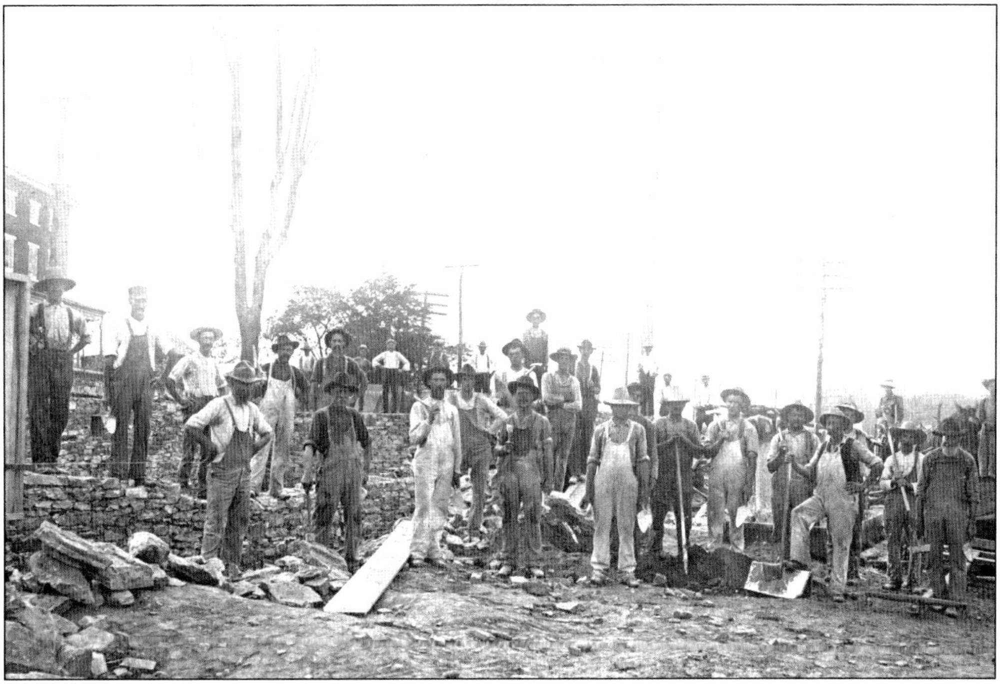

In late October 1909, the Moore and Reitz Company brought a lawsuit against the Reading and Columbia Railroad to recover damages. They alleged that there was no spark arrester installed on the locomotives engine, which most likely would have prevented the fire two years earlier. They sued for $15,000 in an effort to recover the loss of the contents of their warehouse. (Courtesy of John David Wissler.)

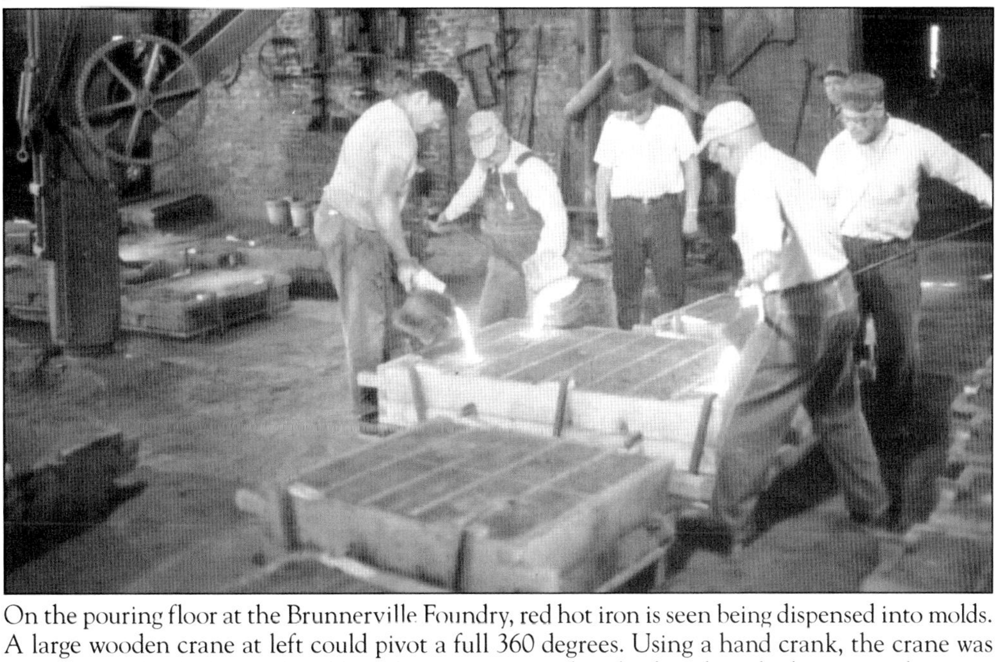

On the pouring floor at the Brunnerville Foundry, red hot iron is seen being dispensed into molds. A large wooden crane at left could pivot a full 360 degrees. Using a hand crank, the crane was used to lift a load of several molds and patterns created at the foundry, which were too heavy to be lifted by hand. (Courtesy of the author's collection; photograph by Mel Horst.)

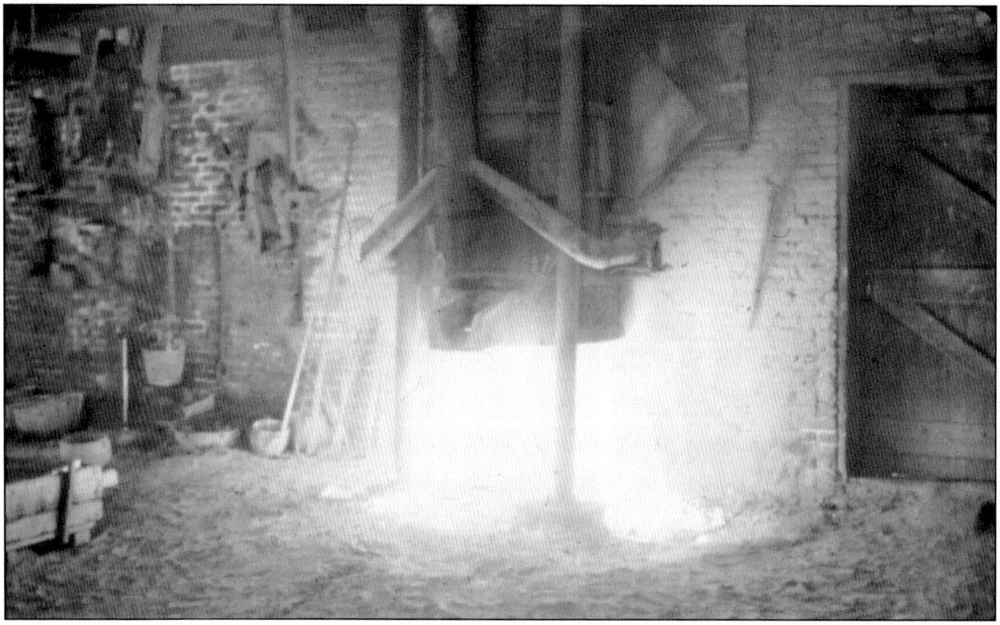

The foundry's cupola is seen here dumping unused iron. The cupola furnace was manufactured on four iron legs. After use, it was then cooled overnight, and the leftover slag was chipped off the lining. A stick containing oil or a flammable element was pushed through a discharge opening in the furnace, lighting the firewood to heat the cupola. (Courtesy of the author's collection; photograph by Mel Horst.)

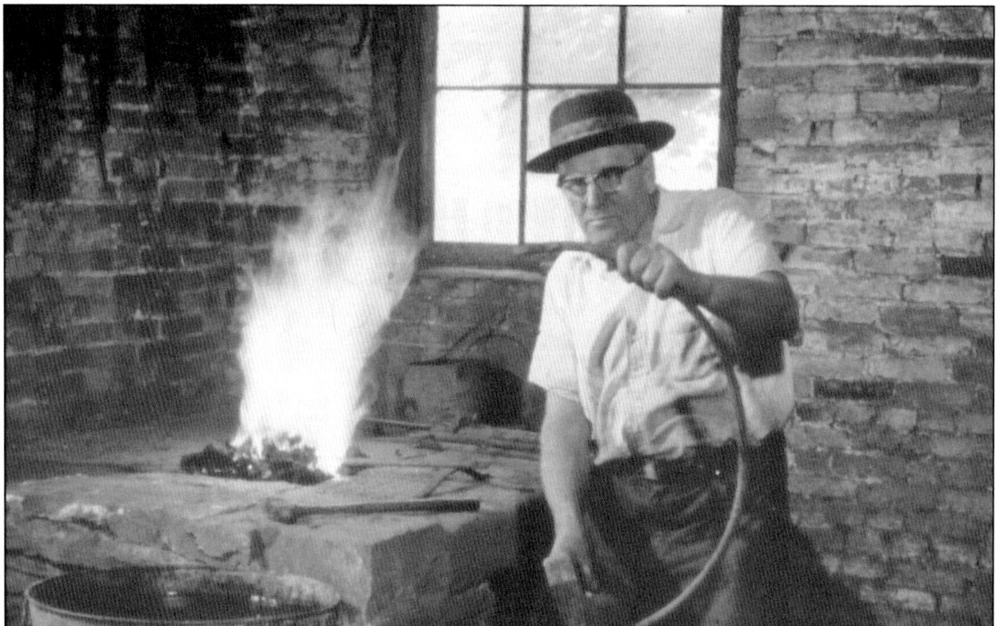

The foundry also had a fully operational blacksmith shop on-site, with very old forming tools hanging on a nearby wall. Orville Schwanger is seen here demonstrating this craft. When this photograph was taken in 1962, the foundry was a fully functional operation and tourist attraction. (Courtesy of the author's collection; photograph by Mel Horst.)

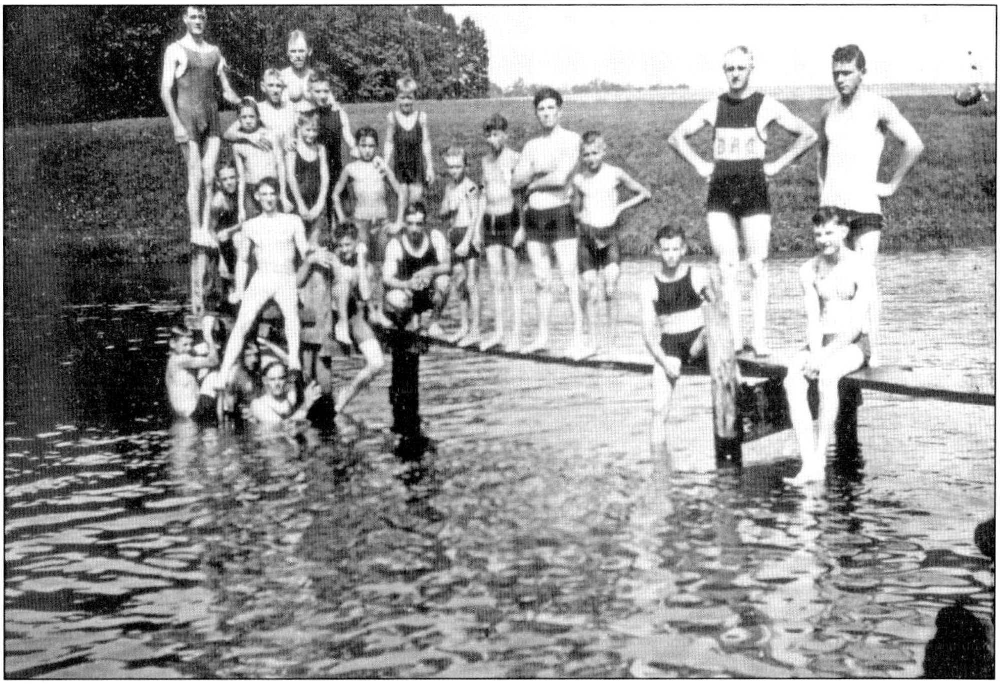

In warm weather, Yerger's Ice Dam was a popular swimming destination utilized by many area residents. The youthful and young at heart would often use this place for a popular swimming hole to cool off during the sweltering summer months. This photograph, taken in 1910, has Lititz residents Vic Stark and Howard Weaver and some friends taking a dip in the cool water. (Courtesy of the Robert "Sketch" Mearig collection.)

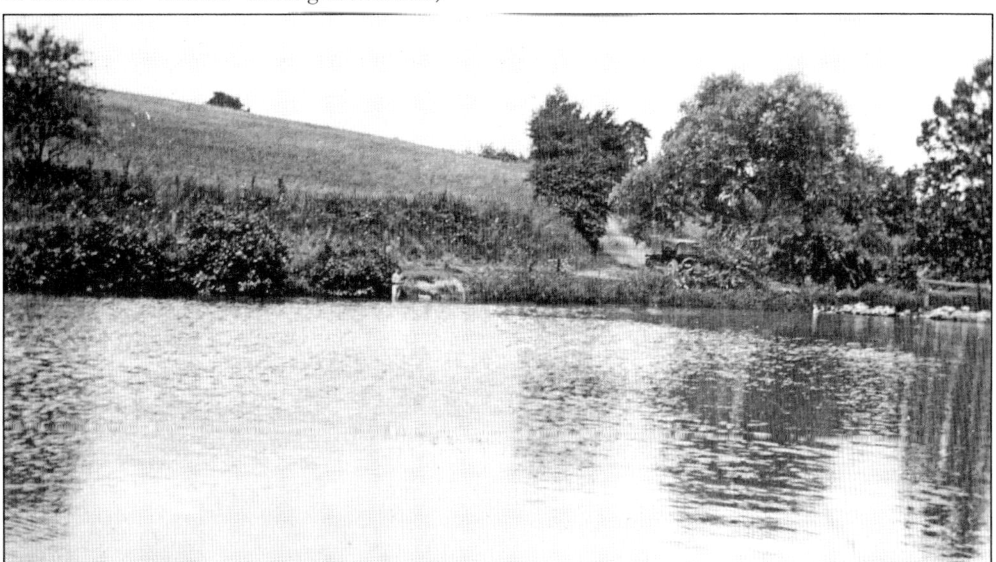

Rudy's Dam is seen here in a photograph taken about 1919. Ice was cut at Rudy's Dam in blocks and stored in a special type of icehouse for use in iceboxes and for summertime use. The public enjoyed ice-skating in the winter, and children and teens used it as a place to cool off to beat the summer heat. (Courtesy of Ronald Reedy.)

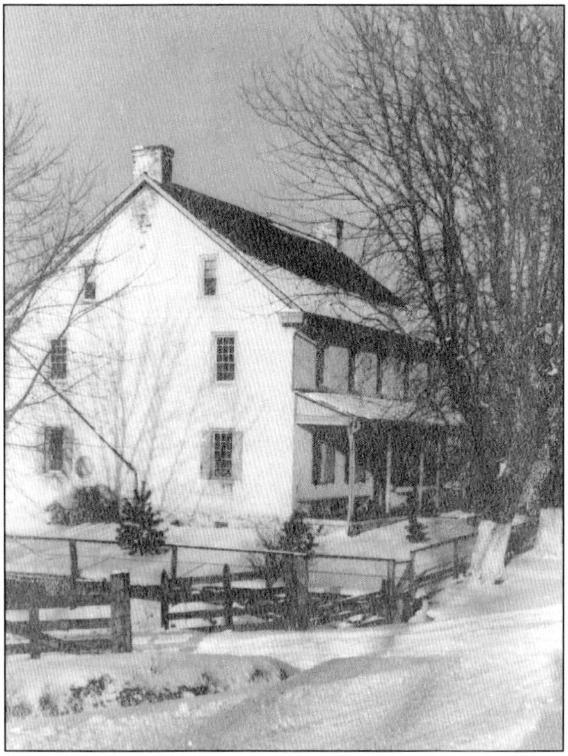

This farmhouse, set behind a wonderful snowfall, was built by John Pfautz in 1813 and is located along Pierson Road near Kissel Hill. The land was originally patented to Michael Pfautz in 1743. When he died, it descended to his son John, subject to an obligation to the widow, Catharine Pfautz. At the time the house was built, Pfautz was one of the largest landowners in Warwick Township. (Courtesy of Wayne Siegrist.)

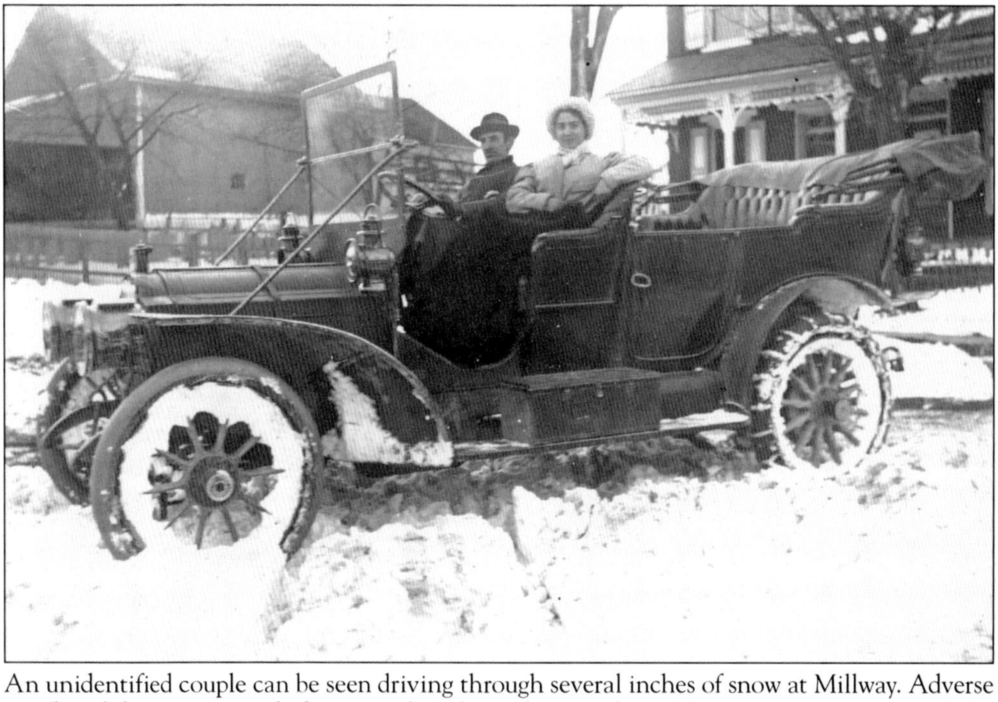

An unidentified couple can be seen driving through several inches of snow at Millway. Adverse weather did not stop people from traveling from place to place. These motorists were no doubt on their way to a family function or in the process of running an errand. The Reitz family home can be seen in the background. (Courtesy of John David Wissler.)

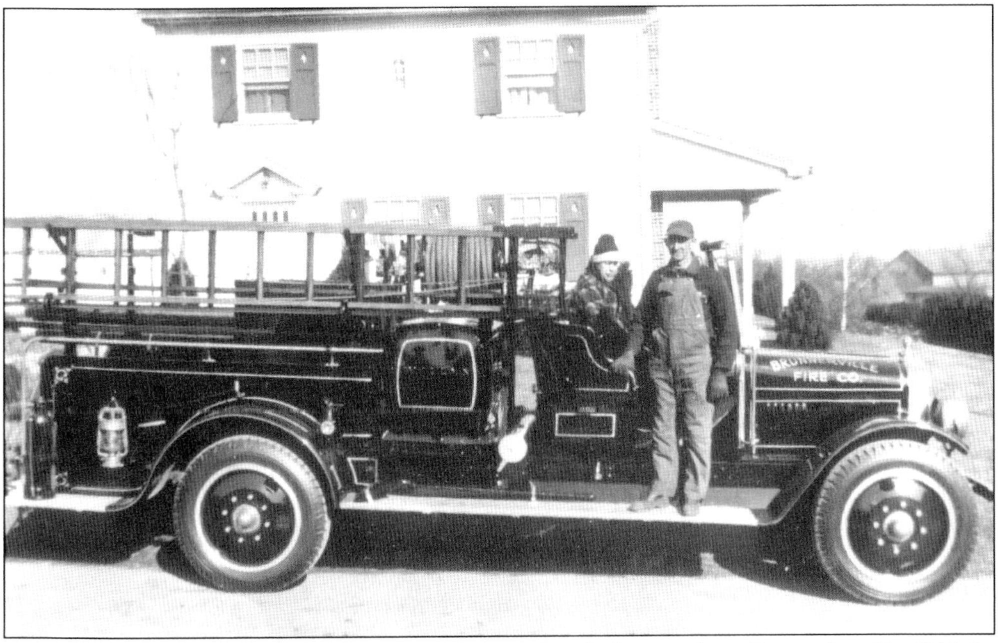

The Brunnerville Fire Company was incorporated and chartered on September 26, 1944. In 1945, Earl Landis, who owned the Brunnerville Foundry during that time, offered a section of the foundry for use as a temporary fire hall. In 1948, the president of the fire company was Morris E. Eckert, the vice president was Clarence Hoffer, and the secretary was Roy Hoffer. That same year, there were 240 paid members. A plot of ground was purchased from Harry Kauffman in 1956, and by 1958, Wayne Grube oversaw the new fire hall's construction, with over 200 men working together to help build this new facility. Over the years, the Brunnerville Fire Company has grown in both membership and in firefighting improvements. Seen here are two of their fire trucks from two different eras. (Both, courtesy of Tom Hackman.)

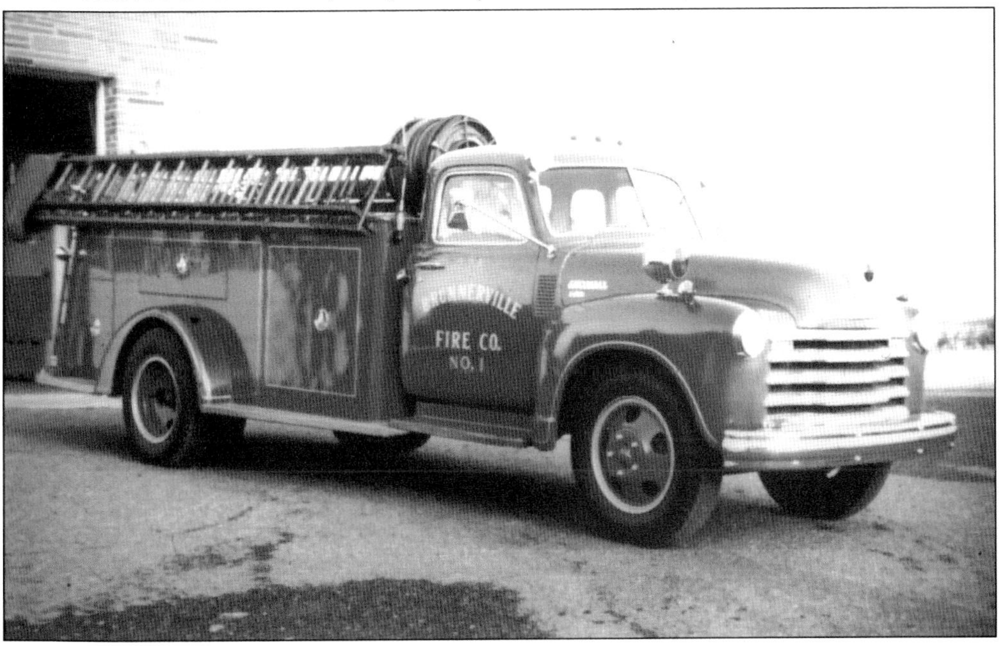